# Environmental Change and Foreign Policy

*Environmental Change and Foreign Policy: Theory and practice* and its companion volume, *Climate Change and Foreign Policy: Case studies from East to West*, examine and explain the role of foreign policy politics, processes and institutions in efforts to protect the environment and natural resources. They seek to highlight international efforts to address human-induced changes to the natural environment, analyze the actors and institutions that constrain and shape actions on environmental issues, show how environmental changes influence foreign policy processes, and critically assess environmental foreign policies.

Focusing on theory and practice, this book:

- Introduces the concepts and theories of environmental foreign policy, providing a theoretical overview as well as addressing the construction of nature, the symbolism of environmental policy, and business and government responses to climate change.
- Explores the practice of environmental foreign policy, describing how both developed and developing countries have approached a variety of environmental issues, including persistent organic pollutants, water, biodiversity, climate change and the trade–environment nexus.

This book will be of great interest to scholars and students of environmental policy and politics, foreign policy, public policy, climate change and international relations.

**Paul G. Harris** is Chair Professor of Environmental Studies at the Hong Kong Institute of Education. From 2000 to 2009 he taught at Lingnan University, Hong Kong, where he was Professor of International and Environmental Studies, Director of the Project on Environmental Change and Foreign Policy, Director of the Environmental Studies Program, and Director of the Centre for Asian Pacific Studies. During the 1990s he taught at universities in Britain and the United States. He is author or editor of a dozen books, most recently *World Ethics and Climate Change* (Edinburgh University Press).

# Routledge Advances in International Relations and Global Politics

# Environmental Change and Foreign Policy

## Theory and practice

**Edited by**
**Paul G. Harris**

Routledge
Taylor & Francis Group

LONDON AND NEW YORK

First published 2009
by Routledge
2 Park Square, Milton Park, Abingdon, Oxon OX14 4RN

Simultaneously published in the USA and Canada
by Routledge
270 Madison Avenue, New York, NY 10016

*Routledge is an imprint of the Taylor & Francis Group, an informa business*

© 2009 Paul G. Harris selection and editorial matter; individual
contributors, their contributions

Typeset in Times New Roman by
Taylor & Francis Books
Printed and bound in Great Britain by
CPI Anthony Rowe, Chippenham, Wiltshire

*British Library Cataloguing in Publication Data*
A catalogue record for this book is available from the British Library

*Library of Congress Cataloging in Publication Data*
Environmental change and foreign policy : theory and practice / edited by
Paul G. Harris.
    p. cm. – (Routledge advances in international relations and global
politics ; 70)
    Includes bibliographical references and index.
    1. Global environmental change. 2. International relations. I. Harris,
Paul G.
    GE149.E58 2009
    363.7'0526–dc22

                                                            2008037555


ISBN 10: 0-415-48343-3 (hbk)
ISBN 10: 0-203-88143-5 (ebk)

ISBN 13: 978-0-415-48343-8 (hbk)
ISBN 13: 978-0-203-88143-9 (ebk)

# Contents

**PART II**
**Practice**                                                                 91

# Figures

# Tables

# Contributors

**Isabella Alcañiz** is an Assistant Professor of Political Science at the University of Houston, Texas.

**Friedrich J. Arndt** is a Research Associate in the project on Transnational Justice and Democracy at the Technical University Darmstadt, Germany.

**John Barkdull** is an Associate Professor of Political Science at Texas Tech University, Lubbock, Texas.

**Thomas L. Brewer** is an Associate Professor in the McDonough School of Business, Georgetown University, Washington, D.C.; and Research Director of Climate Strategies.

**Loren R. Cass** is a Professor of Political Science at the College of the Holy Cross, Worcester, Massachusetts.

**Ricardo A. Gutiérrez** is a Professor in the School of Government, National University of San Martin, Buenos Aires, Argentina.

**Yohei Harashima** is an Associate Professor in the Faculty of International Studies, Takushoku University, Tokyo.

**Paul G. Harris** is Chair Professor of Environmental Studies in the Department of Science and Environmental Studies at the Hong Kong Institute of Education.

**Sara Hughes** is a doctoral candidate at the Bren School of Environmental Sciences and Management, University of California, Santa Barbara.

**Maximilian Mayer** is a Research Fellow and Head of the Energy and Environment in Asia Research Group at the Institute of East Asian Politics, Ruhr-University of Bochum, Germany.

**Mika Merviö** is a Professor of International Politics in the Graduate School of Social Sciences, Kibi International University, Okayama, Japan.

**Aike Müller** is a Project Manager at Adelphi Consult in Berlin and doctoral candidate at the Center for Globalization and Governance at the University of Hamburg, Germany.

**David R. Mutekanga** is a post-doctoral Fellow at the United Nations University, Yokohama, Japan.

**Mihaela Papa** is a doctoral candidate at the Center for International Environment and Resource Policy, Fletcher School of Law and Diplomacy, Tufts University, Medford, Massachusetts.

**Lena Partzsch** is a Research Associate in the Department of Economics, Helmholtz Center for Environmental Research, Leipzig, Germany.

**Charles Thrift** is currently working on a variety of environmental projects with the International Institute for Sustainable Development in Winnipeg, Canada.

**Ken Wilkening** is an Associate Professor and Chair of the International Studies Program at the University of Northern British Columbia, Prince George, Canada.

# Preface

This is the eighth book from the Project on Environmental Change and
Foreign Policy, which I began a decade ago while on the faculty of London
Metropolitan University (formerly London Guildhall University). Other
books from the project include *Climate Change and American Foreign Policy*
(St. Martin's Press/Palgrave Macmillan, 2000), *The Environment, Interna-
tional Relations and U.S. Foreign Policy* (Georgetown University Press,
2001), *International Equity and Global Environmental Politics* (Ashgate,
2001), *International Environmental Cooperation* (University Press of Colorado, 2002), *Global Warming and East Asia* (Routledge, 2003), *Confronting
Environmental Change in East and Southeast Asia* (United Nations University
Press/Earthscan, 2005) and *Europe and Global Climate Change* (Edward
Elgar, 2007). In addition, a companion to this volume – *Climate Change
and Foreign Policy: Case studies from East to West* – is being published
simultaneously by Routledge.

The core objective of the Project on Environmental Change and Foreign
Policy, and of these books, is to better understand the role of foreign policy –
the crossovers and interactions between domestic and international politics
and policies – in efforts to preserve the environment and natural resources.
Underlying this objective is the belief that it is not enough to analyze
domestic or international political actors, institutions and processes by
themselves. We need to understand the interactions among them, something
that explicit thought about foreign policy can help us do. More specifically,
the project has sought to understand foreign policy processes in international
efforts to address human-induced changes to the natural environment; to
analyze the actors and institutions – domestic and international, governmental and nongovernmental – that constrain and shape actions on environmental issues; to show how environmental changes influence foreign
policy processes; and to critically assess environmental foreign policies. Other
objectives of the project are to test the waters of research in this field; to
showcase research from established and new scholars of different backgrounds that has not been forced into traditional empirical, epistemological
or ontological boxes; to give insight to governmental and nongovernmental
practitioners and activists, which might help improve their understanding of

the politics and foreign policy of environmental issues; to disseminate these ideas to government officials and scholars so that they might have some positive effect on policy-making and scholarship; and to enlighten students and laypersons interested in environmental protection, sustainable development, international affairs and foreign policy.

I am grateful to the contributors for adding their work to the project, and to anonymous referees for very helpful comments on the book proposal and individual chapters. I am particularly grateful to K.K. Chan for support during my work on this book, and all the others.

I wish to dedicate this book to the memory of B. Thomas Trout, who was a mentor, boss and teacher at the University of New Hampshire – and a scholar who, decades ago, recognized the importance of studying and understanding the foreign policy aspects of resource exploitation and environmental change.

Paul G. Harris
Hong Kong
August 2008

# Abbreviations

| | |
|---|---|
| AA/VAIP | American Aluminum/Voluntary Aluminum Partnership |
| AAM | American Automotive Manufacturers |
| AAR | Association of American Railroads |
| ABS | Access and Benefit Sharing of Genetic Resources |
| ACC | American Chemistry Council |
| ACP | African, Caribbean and Pacific countries |
| ADB | Asian Development Bank |
| AEPS | Arctic Environmental Protection Strategy |
| AES | Canada's Arctic Environmental Strategy |
| AF&PA | American Forest and Paper Association |
| AISI | American Iron and Steel Institute |
| AMAP | Arctic Monitoring and Assessment Program |
| APEC | Asia-Pacific Economic Cooperation |
| API | American Petroleum Institute |
| APPA | American Public Power Association |
| ASEAN | Association of Southeast Asian Nations |
| ASI | American Semiconductor Industry |
| AU | African Union |
| bn. | billion |
| CAIPAP | Canadian Arctic Indigenous Peoples Against POPs |
| CARC | Canadian Arctic Resources Committee |
| CARU | Uruguay River Administrative Commission (Comisión Administradora del Río Uruguay) |
| CBD | Convention on Biological Diversity |
| CEDHA | Centre for Human Rights and the Environment (Fundación Centro de Derechos Humanos y Ambientales) |
| CELA | Canadian Environmental Law Association |
| CEO | Chief Executive Officer |
| CIS | Commonwealth of Independent States |
| CMP | Canada's Chemicals Management Plan |
| $CO_2$ | carbon dioxide |
| COMESA | Common Market of Eastern and Southern Africa |
| COP | Conference of Parties to the United Nations Framework Convention on Climate Change |

| CRS | Creditor Reporting System (on Aid Activities) |
| CTE | Committee on Trade and Environment |
| DAC | Development Assistance Committee |
| DG | Directorate-General |
| DNA | Designated National Authority |
| DOE | Department of Energy |
| EAC | East African Community |
| ECF | Elementary Chlorine Free |
| EEI | Edison Electric Institute |
| EIA | Environment Impact Assessment |
| ENCE | Spanish National Enterprise of Pulp (Empresa Nacional de Celulosa España) |
| EPA | Environmental Protection Agency |
| EPICI | Electric Power Industry Climate Initiative |
| EPSA | Electric Power Supply Association |
| ES | environmental sustainability |
| ETS | Emission Trading Scheme |
| EU | European Union |
| EUWI | EU Water Initiative |
| FAITC | Foreign Affairs and International Trade Canada |
| FCCC | Framework Convention on Climate Change |
| FTAs | free trade agreements |
| GATT | General Agreement on Tariffs and Trade |
| GCC | Global Climate Coalition |
| GDP | Gross Domestic Product |
| GDPPPP | Gross Domestic Product on the basis of Purchasing Power Parity |
| GEF | Global Environment Facility |
| GHG | greenhouse gases |
| GNI | Gross National Income |
| GTAN | Bilateral High-Level Technical Group (Grupo de Trabajo de Alto Nivel) |
| GWP | Global Water Partnership |
| ICC | Inuit Circumpolar Conference |
| ICJ | International Court of Justice |
| IFC | International Finance Corporation |
| IFCS | Intergovernmental Forum on Chemical Safety |
| INA | Argentine Natural Water Institute (Instituto Nacional de Agua) |
| INAC | Indian and Northern Affairs Canada |
| INC | Intergovernmental Negotiating Committee |
| IPCC | Intergovernmental Panel on Climate Change |
| IPCS | International Program on Chemical Safety |
| IPEN | International POPs Elimination Network |
| IWC | International Whaling Commission |

| | |
|---|---|
| IWRM | Integrated Water Resources Management |
| LPPC | Large Public Power Council |
| LRTAP | Long Range Transboundary Air Pollution Convention |
| MC/IMA | Magnesium Coalition/International Magnesium Association |
| MDGs | Millennium Development Goals |
| MEAs | Multilateral Environmental Agreements |
| MERCOSUR | Common Market of the South (Mercado Común del Sur) |
| METI | Ministry of Economy, Trade and Industry |
| MFA | Ministry of Foreign Affairs |
| MIT | Massachusetts Institute of Technology |
| MOFA | Ministry of Foreign Affairs (Japan) |
| MPs | Members of Parliament |
| NAMA | Non-Agricultural Market Access |
| NATO | North Atlantic Treaty Organization |
| NCP | Northern Contaminants Program |
| NEAP | National Environment Action Plan |
| NEI | Nuclear Energy Institute |
| NEMA | National Environment Management Authority |
| NGO | nongovernmental organization |
| NIEs | Newly Industrializing Economies |
| NIP | National Implementation Plan (under Stockholm Convention on POPs) |
| NMA | National Miners Association |
| NPA | National Planning Authority |
| NRECA | National Rural Electric Cooperative Association |
| NRM | National Resistance Movement (Uganda) |
| NRM-O | NRM Organization (Uganda) |
| ODA | Official/Overseas Development Assistance |
| OECD | Organisation for Economic Co-operation and Development |
| PCA | Portland Cement Association |
| PCBs | polychlorinated biphenyls |
| PEAP | Poverty Eradication Action Plan |
| PISA | Programme for International Student Assessment (of the OECD) |
| POPs | persistent organic pollutants |
| PPMs | processes and production methods |
| RGGI | Regional Greenhouse Gas Initiative |
| S&D | special and differential treatment |
| SEPA | State Environment Protection Administration |
| SMEs | small and medium-sized enterprises |
| $SO_2$ | sulfur dioxide |
| STOs | specific trade obligations |
| STS | Science and Technology Studies |
| TCCC | The Coca-Cola Company |
| TCF | Totally Chlorine Free |

| TRIPS | Trade-Related Aspects of Intellectual Property Rights |
|-------|------------------------------------------------------|
| TVA   | Tennessee Valley Association                         |
| UK    | United Kingdom                                       |
| UN    | United Nations                                       |
| UNCED | United Nations Conference on Environment and Development |
| UNDP  | United Nations Development Program                   |
| UNECE | United Nations Economic Commission for Europe        |
| UNEP  | United Nations Environment Program                   |
| US    | United States                                        |
| USAID | United States Agency for International Development    |
| USSR  | United Soviet Socialistic Republic                   |
| UWA   | Uganda Wildlife Authority                            |
| WCED  | World Commission on Environment and Development       |
| WFD   | EU Water Framework Directive                          |
| WMO   | World Meteorological Organization                    |
| WTO   | World Trade Organization                             |
| WWF   | World Wildlife Fund                                  |

# 1 Environmental foreign policy in theory and practice

## Paul G. Harris

Environmental changes are among the greatest threats to the well-being and possibly the long-term survival of humankind, and they present profound challenges to many other species. It is therefore crucial that scholars and policy-makers do all that they can to understand the human relationship to the environment and the potential means of mitigating our impact on the planet. Much has been done to do this, but it is clear from ongoing global pollution, overuse of natural resources, and the failure of international regimes to adequately address most environmental problems, that the trend is – despite some successes – very much in the wrong direction. Species and habitats are being destroyed, water and air quality deteriorate unabated in most parts of the world, greenhouse gas emissions grow even as signs of climate change become increasingly unmistakable and dangerous – in addition to a huge range of other problems arising from industrialization and modern life. Given our failure to stop, let alone reverse, this trend, it seems reasonable and even imperative to look for new ways of understanding what is happening and why, and to find new ways for people and their governments to respond to environmental problems.

The bulk of literature on environmental policy and politics has tended to focus on various aspects of international cooperation and regimes, on one hand, and the processes of domestic environmental management and sustainable development, on another (see, for example, Lafferty and Meadowcroft 2001; Breitmeier *et al.* 2006). However, less attention has been given to what falls between and across the domestic and the international levels of analysis.[1] There is a "level" of policy that is both internal *and* external to states that also deserves attention. We can call this level of policy practice (which is also a level of policy analysis) *foreign* policy. Foreign policy can play an important, even central, role in determining whether governments and other environmental policy actors actually take steps to address ecological problems effectively. The aim of this book is to define and explore that role.

From a scholarly perspective, foreign policy is a subfield of political science and the study of international relations. It involves the *interplay* between domestic forces, institutions and actors – such as democratic principles, civil society, executive and legislative power structures, government agencies, and diplomatic personnel – and international forces, institutions and actors – such as the processes of globalization (economic, environmental, cultural), international organizations and regimes, and powerful countries, corporations, and nongovernmental organizations. As Gerner (1995: 17) observes:

> Although no subfield in political science is completely self-contained, the study of foreign policy is somewhat unusual in that it deals with both domestic and international arenas, jumping from individual to state to systemic levels of analysis, and attempts to integrate all of these aspects into a coherent whole.

In this chapter, I want to introduce the case studies that follow by starting to answer several questions: What is foreign policy? How can we analyze, understand and explain foreign policy. That is, what is foreign policy analysis? What is *environmental* foreign policy? How can studying environmental foreign policy, and how might environmental foreign policy analysis, help us to better understand how people and especially governments organize themselves to address pollution and ecological decline?

Foreign policy and foreign policy analysis were popular subjects among political scientists in past decades. I want to step back and look at it again. I then want to ask how more concerted, conscious and systematic scholarly attention to foreign policy and foreign policy analysis might aid in finding solutions to environmental problems. I want to point out what is special about the processes of foreign policy for domestic and international environmental action, and to suggest how foreign policy analysis can move us closer to understanding important variables influencing that action. I devote attention to the second question – What is foreign policy analysis? – because foreign policy analysis has been largely closeted for a generation, and because its methodology has not been widely applied to environmental problems. Environmental foreign policy analysis can help to close the gap between the problems we face and our understanding of them.

Subsequent chapters in this book explore conceptions and theories of environmental foreign policy and analyze environmental foreign policy as practiced in a number of important issue areas. Those chapters are summarized below. Together, they help to delineate the field of *environmental* foreign policy analysis and demonstrate its utility in helping to illuminate the human dimensions of environmental change.

## Foreign policy

"Foreign policy" is a concept that means different things to different people, so it can be difficult to define.[2] Generally speaking, foreign policy is *and* is not that which is normally the central focus of many other approaches to understanding international relations: it is what comes between strictly or mostly domestic politics *and* what is strictly or mostly happening at the international and global levels, while being connected to and affected by both. Foreign policy is not *purely* about either international policy (as the term might suggest) or domestic policy, but neither is it separate from either. James Rosenau (1968: 310) defined foreign policy as "governmental under-takings directed toward the external environment." Foreign policy is, in one sense, the "interpenetration of individual states by interests and forces that necessarily restrain or limit the freedom of action of their political leaders and decision makers" (Thompson and Macridis 1976: 2). F.S. Northredge, one of the most prescient observers of foreign policy, wrote of the "paradox of foreign policy":

> that its aims, the product of interaction between pressures internal and external to the state, have a certain perennial quality about them ... and yet the implementation of these aims in the concrete circumstances of the time has to bow to ever-changing realities.
>
> (Northredge 1968: 12)

Indeed, globalization and other forces of modernization, notably transboundary and global environmental changes, mean that more of what was once purely national is now the subject of foreign policy. Thus, Morse (1970: 376) points out that "linkages between domestic and foreign policies constitute the basic characteristic of the breakdown in the distinction between foreign and domestic affairs in the modernized, interdependent international system."

In short, foreign policy – albeit related to the external world (as the term suggests) – cannot be divorced from domestic affairs. It is about the inter-actions between domestic and international affairs. From a policy perspec-tive, foreign policy encompasses the *objectives* that officials of national governments seek to attain; the *values and principles* underlying those objectives; the *methods* by which the objectives are sought; the *processes* by which these objectives, principles and methods are developed and imple-mented; and the *actors and forces* – international and domestic – shaping these attributes (cf. Kegley and Wittkopf 1996: 7). As Rosenau (1968: 314) acknowledged, to the dismay of many foreign policy analysts, foreign policy encompasses "a vast range of phenomena. Circumstances can arise whereby virtually every aspect of local, national, and international politics may be part of the initiatory or responsive stage of the foreign policy process." To be sure, this suggests a high degree of complexity in foreign policy processes and analyses of them. But all is not lost; we can use theory and method to tease out key actors, variables and forces. What we cannot do is ignore the vast range of phenomena to which Rosenau points.

## Foreign policy analysis

How can we analyze and thereby understand and explain (and possibly help officials and stakeholders manipulate) foreign policy? What is foreign policy analysis? It is here where the idea of foreign policy may be useful in under-standing today's efforts to address environmental problems that – like foreign policy itself – are so often about what happens both within and beyond national borders. Foreign policy *analysis*, a discipline that arguably had its heyday more than a generation ago, captures variables that are seldom fully examined by methods of studying environmental issues from mostly national or mostly international perspectives.

How can foreign policy be analyzed? Kenneth Thompson and Roy Macridis describe "ideological" and "analytical" approaches to analyzing foreign policy, advocating the latter (Thompson and Macridis 1976: 2–5). The former approach sees foreign policies as the consequences of "prevailing political, social, and religious beliefs" (ibid.: 2). From a psychological view-point, foreign policy analysis "looks to the motives or ideologies of leaders or governments as essential, if not the sole, determinant of policy" (ibid.: 3). In contrast, the analytical approach proposes that policy "rests on multiple determinants, including the state's historic tradition, geographic location, national interest, and purposes and security needs. To understand foreign policy, the observer must take into account and analyze a host of factors" (ibid.: 3). Thompson and Macridis argue that foreign policy is "susceptible to analysis in terms of a checklist of elements that exist, that can be identified, and that merge and comprise the bases of foreign policy" (ibid.: 5). This checklist of significant factors in the study of foreign policy includes: (1) "relatively permanent" *material elements* (i.e., geography and natural resources), "less permanent" material elements (i.e., industrial and military establishments, changes in industrial and military capacity), quantitative human elements (population) and qualitative human elements (policy-makers and leaders; the roles of ideology and information); (2) foreign policy-making *process* (executive agencies and legislatures) and non-governmental agencies (political parties, interest groups, media, public opi-nion); and (3) *trends and ideas*, such as national purposes of security, power and economic development (ibid.: 6). To these national purposes we can add environmental sustainability and "environmental security" (Pirages and Cousins 2005).

Michael Brecher, Blema Steinberg and Janice Stein propose an approach to foreign policy analysis, the "foreign policy system," which comprises a classification of foreign policy components into three categories – inputs, process and outputs – and which is "constantly absorbing demands and channeling them into a policy machine which transforms these inputs into decisions or outputs" (Brecher *et al.* 1969: 80). The *inputs* include the external (global, bilateral, etc.) and internal (economic capability, political structure, interest groups, etc.) environments, communication (including the media), and the "psychological environment" (ideology, personalities, pressure from elites, etc.). The *process* consists of the formulation of strategic and tactical decisions in traditional foreign policy areas (e.g., military–security, political–diplomatic, economic–developmental, cultural–status) and the implementation of decisions by governmental actors. The *outputs* are the substance of those decisions (ibid.: 80). Brecher, Steinberg, and Stein believe that this sort of foreign policy analysis will achieve "an operationally viable method to explore state behavior in depth and breadth" (ibid.: 93).

Harold Jacobson and William Zimmerman argued that "traditional" explanations of foreign policy can be categorized according to five variables: systemic, environmental, societal, governmental and idiosyncratic/psychological (Jacobson and Zimmerman 1969: 7–9). The *systemic* approach sees foreign policy behavior resulting from the "nature of the international system of which [states] are a part, or because of the role which they [states] have been assigned or have chosen to play within the system" (ibid.: 7). In contrast, the other approaches focus on the characteristics of individual states as being the key variables. The *environmental* approach focuses on a state's geography and raw materials. The *societal* approach sees societal forces and national "personality" as important explanatory variables for analysis. The *governmental* approach examines the characteristics of the ruling regime and the state's system of government. The *idiosyncratic/psychological* approach focuses on personalities. As Jacobson and Zimmerman see it, of these approaches to explaining foreign policy, the systemic approaches are "the most elegant and esthetically attractive. [But] They are also the most difficult to relate to empirical reality" and they "give little indication of the dynamic of state behavior" (ibid.: 9). This is not to say that any one of the other approaches is ideal; each provides valuable insights even while failing to establish a validated theory of foreign policy (ibid.: 10).

Valerie Hudson and Christopher Vore (1995: 212–38) describe three types of foreign policy analysis: comparative foreign policy, foreign policy decision-making and foreign policy context.[3] *Comparative* foreign policy has sought to "tease out cross-nationally applicable generalizations about the foreign policy behavior of states in a systematic and scientific fashion" (ibid.: 212).[4] Rosenau, perhaps the foremost proponent of comparative foreign policy (see Rosenau 1968), in particular, wanted scholars to develop "middle-range theory – theory that mediated between grand principles and the complexity of reality," and he emphasized the integration of information derived from several levels of analysis – from the international system, at one extreme, to the individual decision-maker, at the other (Hudson and Vore 1995: 213; see Rosenau 1966). Rosenau wanted explanations of foreign policy that were "multilevel and multicausal, synthesizing information from a variety of social science knowledge systems" (Hudson and Vore 1995: 213). He took a behavioralist, "scientific" approach to comparative foreign policy (ibid.: 215).

Analysis of foreign policy *decision-making* (ibid.: 213–17; see Snyder *et al.* 1963 and Gold 1978) seeks to illuminate the roles of foreign policy-making in groups, organizations and bureaucracies (the so-called bureaucratic politics approach), and notably the nexus of policy objectives and implementation. This perspective seeks to show how "'rational' foreign policy-making can be upended by the political entities through which decision makers must work," often because there is "slippage" between policy-making and implementation (Hudson and Vore 1995: 217). The study of foreign policy *context* examines the "psycho-milieu of the individuals and groups making a foreign policy decision" (ibid.: 213) notably the "beliefs, attitudes, values, experiences, emotions, and conceptions of nation and self," as well as the "milieu of decision making that includes culture, history, geography, economics, political institutions, ideology, demographics, and innumerable other factors [that] shape society context in which the decision maker operates" (ibid.: 217; see Sprout and Sprout 1965). From this perspective, the characteristics of individual decision-makers, their perceptions and misperceptions, national attributes of countries, opinions of elites and the masses, societal groups, cultural and social factors – as well as the international system in which these actors operate – matter greatly in determining (and understanding) foreign policy (Hudson and Vore 1995: 217–19, 226). Importantly, the boundaries between these approaches – and of course the real-world actors, institutions and forces they illuminate – often overlap.

Much of foreign policy analysis is about ascertaining how domestic politics, agencies and forces shape foreign policies. Northredge (1968: 23) argued that:

> There is virtually nothing existing within the borders of a state, from the politics of the parish pump to the literature the nation reads, which does not have some influence on the postures its government assumes in international affairs. The problem for the observer is one of forming a framework of ideas in terms of which these multitudinous and varied pressures can be handled.

He referred to the "mental hinterland of foreign policy," which includes things like "manners of conducting public affairs in a given country, the political mental [*sic*] habits and inarticulate major premises of a nation colored by tradition and reflected in government policies" (ibid.: 23–4). That this "political style" can profoundly influence foreign policy needs to be considered in foreign policy analysis, even if that means considering a complex set of variables. Thus, Hudson and Vore (1995: 210) point out:

> for scholars involved in foreign policy analysis, "the national interest," a concept that lies at the heart of the realist analysis of IR [international relations], is more productively viewed as the interests of various players – not all of which may coincide, and not all of which are coherently related to anything resembling an objective national interest.

This is why, in large measure, foreign policy analysis "focuses on the people and units that comprise the state" (ibid.: 210).

There is of course only so much we can expect from foreign policy analysis. As Macridis (1958; quoted in Brecher *et al.* 1969: 76) put it, "to attempt generalizations and construction of models that will give us a rigorous scientific understanding and prediction of foreign policy is a hopeless task." Indeed, while systemic theories of International Relations are parsimonious, they can be unsatisfying to many analysts of environmental affairs. To be sure, foreign policy analysis can be data-intensive, time-consuming and often requires expertise in specific countries and regions (Hudson and Vore 1995: 211). However, what some scholars may see as a drawback of foreign policy analysis – its lack of parsimony – may be its strength: it is more realistic.

Hudson and Vore (ibid.: 228) summarize foreign policy analysis as "a bridging field linking international relations theory, comparative politics, and the foreign policy-making community." This latter characteristic is important because it suggests that scholarship can help policy-makers (and other actors) achieve their objectives. The best foreign policy analysis arguably helps bridge the gap between theory and scholarship, on the one hand, and foreign policy practice, on the other (see George 1993 and Zelikow 1994). Berkowitz, Bock and Vincent (1977:11) sum up foreign policy analysis approaches in many respects: "the fundamental issue is *the composition of the 'mix' of foreign and domestic elements within a single policy-making process*, and the effects of this mix on the interaction of political institutions in specific cases." The upshot is that, as William Olson and A.J.R. Groom (1991: 170) put it, foreign policy analysts should recognize that "the distinction between domestic and international politics is confusing, and should be dropped."

## Environmental foreign policy and its analysis

*Environmental* foreign policy can be conceived of as the interplay between domestic forces, institutions and actors involved in environmental decision-making and the implementation of environmental policies, and international forces, institutions and actors, such as environmental changes themselves and their interaction with other forces (e.g., globalization), international organizations and regimes, and influential governments, corporations and non-governmental organizations with a role in shaping human responses to environmental changes.[5] From a policy perspective, environmental foreign policy is about the international *environmental* objectives that officials of national governments seek to attain; the values and principles underlying them; the methods by which the objectives are sought; the processes by which these objectives, values and principles, and methods are developed and implemented; and the domestic and international actors and forces – including but not exclusively environmental ones – shaping environmental policies and actions, both at home and abroad, and which have some international or external character. To be sure, this is a lot to digest, which is one reason why we might have to bite it off in smaller pieces – something that theory can help us do (see Part I and especially Chapter 2).

Foreign policy objectives, actors and processes can be central in determining whether countries cooperate to address environmental problems.

What is particularly important about *foreign* policy for our understanding of *environmental* policy within and among states is that it involves the *crossover and interaction* between domestic politics and processes, on the one hand, and international relations and institutions ("global politics"), on the other. Looking at purely local or international variables seldom explains environmental policies and agreements. Indeed, environmental issues are often distinctive in the manner in which they ignore state borders; problems in one country affect other countries, and problems restricted to one country often require the involvement of other countries (e.g., through financial assistance and technology transfer) if they are to be resolved or remain local. *Many* issues, actors and forces acting domestically and internationally affect and influence countries' national environmental regulations and their environmental foreign policies, and hence they impact international environmental cooperation. Yet, despite obvious (albeit not fully comprehended) connections between local and international policy processes, many studies of environmental policy do not adequately account for the foreign policy aspects of environmental protection efforts, and frequently ignore foreign policy altogether.

Many environmental policy officials are simultaneously pressured to follow international norms and promote national interests and ideals. That is, they are buffeted by domestic *and* international forces. Thinking about foreign policy focuses our attention on interactions among domestic political preferences and positions governments take in negotiations, the balancing of economic growth and popular demands for development with foreign pressures to join environmental regimes, and the rivalries and alliances between foreign policy and domestic policy agencies and the individuals working in them (among many other considerations). A good reason for looking at foreign policy processes more systematically is because doing so can reveal important national and organizational characteristics shaping state environmental behavior, both domestically and internationally.

Foreign policy is, to be sure, about pursuing and promoting national interests. Already complexities arise, however. It is not always clear what a country's national environmental interests are or ought to be, particularly with regard to complex environmental issues, and it is almost always debatable how best to promote them (Webber and Smith 2002: 43–4). This is evidenced by the way that some governments earnestly claim, for example, that their national interests will not allow them to join robust efforts to combat climate change, but when those same governments change, as happened recently in Australia (see Chapter 13), their interests can shift, sometimes markedly, in favor of action. This is an example of how, in the words of Denny Roy, policy-making elites will disagree over national goals and how to achieve them:

> Beyond its most basic formulation, the national interest is not a monolithic, objective concept, but rather a dynamic and unsettled one, subject

to constant debate. [Moreover,] powerful groups and individuals are subject to self-interested behavior, and may support the policy option they calculate will enhance their power and prestige, even if it is not necessarily the best option for the nation as a whole.

(Roy 1998: 137–8)

Thus, defining national interests and ways to achieve them is a problematic and complex undertaking, involving actors and institutions seemingly unimportant to the casual observer, even when issues and associated interests are better understood than they usually are in environmental cases. These difficulties are especially likely with environmental issues, which depend on often uncertain or contested science, helping to explain why countries often fail to respond to environmental changes even when those changes are apparent to prominent environmental scientists, activists and even many government officials, as with the failure of the United States to fully join the global climate change regime (see Harris 2000 and Chalecki 2009).

It would be fatuous to suggest that it is possible to *completely* abstract out the forces of foreign policy, particularly if foreign policy is broadly defined. Foreign policy cannot be separated completely from, for example, domestic politics and institutions, at one end of a spectrum, and global regimes and international power balances, at the other end. To suggest this would be just as absurd as suggesting that almost everything that is important can be explained by the international distribution of power (cf. Waltz 1979) – if so, why are "weak" states often so powerful in international environmental politics, as Malaysia and others were in thwarting American efforts at the 1992 Earth Summit to agree a forest treaty? – or domestic interests (cf. Milner 1997) – why, then, do some states adhere to international environmental norms, as have some Eastern European states, even when, by any reasonable measure, important local interests would not be advantaged, or would even be harmed, by doing so? What is useful, perhaps, is to go beyond thinking in terms of domestic and international levels of analysis to a "two-levels-plus" game (see Putnam 1988; Evans *et al.* 1993). That is, we can consider international political dynamics along with national politics and domestic policy-making processes, but we can also think *explicitly* about the additional "level" of foreign policy processes, features of which almost always fall between, but simultaneously overlap, international and domestic factors.

Foreign policy analysis is well suited to studying responses to environmental changes because, to use the words of Rosenau, it considers the "continuing erosion of the distinction between domestic and foreign issues, between the sociopolitical and economic processes that unfold at home and those that transpire abroad" (Rosenau 1987: 3). Applying foreign policy analysis to environmental policy generally may result in interesting findings simply because it is an approach quite distinct from many others and because environmental issues often share with other foreign policy issues high levels of uncertainty, geographically and often temporally distant impacts, and major disparities in stakeholders' characteristics, capabilities and interests.

## Environmental foreign policy in theory and practice

The chapters that follow adopt a variety of potent approaches to understanding the environmental foreign policies of a variety of states, in the process, illuminating important variables that can help us understand why governments and other actors have attempted to deal with environmental problems – or failed to do so. The book is divided into two parts. Part I focuses on theory of environmental foreign policy. Part II presents a number of case studies of environmental foreign policy in practice.

### *Theory*

In Part I, contributors explore a range of theories of environmental foreign policy. In Chapter 2, John Barkdull and Paul G. Harris identify some areas of theoretical inquiry related to environmental foreign policy. They argue that explanations for the environmental foreign policies of states are necessary for a full understanding of global environmental politics. States make the critical decisions on the entire range of environmental issues, from protecting endangered species to regulating the trade in toxic wastes to addressing global climate change. Yet, significant gaps remain in the scholarly research on how and why states decide their foreign policies on the environment. The vast literature on global environmental politics pertains primarily to international relations rather than to the state-level variables that also determine foreign policy behavior. Barkdull and Harris attempt to begin remedying this gap in theory, in part, by suggesting directions for further research on environmental foreign policy.

Continuing our look at theory, in Chapter 3, Loren R. Cass explores symbolism and "signaling tools" in environmental foreign policy. He points out that environmental foreign policy in practice is frequented with examples of states rhetorically affirming international action to address environmental threats while accepting international commitments that are never implemented. This situation raises troubling questions for the study of environmental foreign policy and compliance with international environmental commitments. One frequent explanation for failure to fulfill commitments is that governments undertake international obligations in good faith but then fail to fulfill them due to domestic political obstacles to implementation. While this is certainly true in many cases, Cass argues that governments frequently utilize environmental foreign policy as a symbolic signaling tool to manage state identities in the eyes of both domestic and international constituencies.

In a similar vein, in Chapter 4, Thomas L. Brewer looks at how theory can help us to better understand both government and business responses to environmental problems. He shows how theories of pluralistic politics and public choice can advance our understanding of environmental foreign policy-making. These theories of political economy link macro-level variables, including government policies, to the micro-level features of corporate behavior. The linkage between the macro and micro levels becomes particularly evident in a cross-national comparative analytic perspective, which Brewer utilizes. The specific focus of his chapter is business–government interactions in US responses to climate change. Because climate change involves externalities and market failures, there is an argument for government intervention on the grounds of economic efficiency. At the same time, however, governments are creating new markets – specifically markets for greenhouse gas emissions credits.

Continuing the theme of exploring ways of explaining and simplifying – that is, theorizing about – complexities in international environmental affairs, in Chapter 5 Maximilian Mayer and Friedrich Arndt explore divergent visualizations of environmental change and their connections to politics. They use visualizations as heuristic devices for theorizing environmental foreign policy. After introducing divergent visualizations of the environment in industrialized and developing countries, they discuss the connections of these perceptions with strategic discourses in public and in foreign policy. They argue that analysis of these discourses, while providing important insights for analysis, does not get to the core of the issue. Drawing on work from the field of Science Studies, their chapter employs the notion of "socionature," which is produced by a complex of political, scientific, technological and cultural practices in which strategic discourses are embedded. Socionature overcomes dualist accounts of nature and reveals central variables for the analysis of environmental foreign policy. Indeed, as Arndt and Mayer argue by way of example, opposing views of greenhouse gas emissions from industrialized and developing countries can be understood as stemming from different underlying socionatures.[6]

## *Practice*

In Part II, the theories presented in Part I, and indeed additional theories, are deployed to analyze and explore the practice of environmental foreign policy. We begin in Chapter 6 with a case study from Africa by David R. Mutekanga. Mutekanga examines the evolution of Uganda's environmental foreign policy on the Convention on Biological Diversity. Uganda is a biodiversity hotspot with a history of poverty, internal conflicts, and military dictatorship. Despite these vulnerabilities, and often because of them, Mutekanga believes that Uganda is in great need of increased tourism and investment from abroad. His chapter describes the role of the major players in Uganda's environmental policies and related foreign policies, including the office of the president, parliament, ministries for environment and foreign affairs, and nongovernmental organizations. Mutekanga argues for transparency in national and local policies, including their regular review, and for a national planning authority able to ensure that Uganda's foreign policy addresses environmental issues. He also recommends enhanced collaboration and synergy between national-level environmental and foreign policies so as to minimize conflict, especially in policy implementation, among ministries and stakeholders.

In Chapter 7, Isabella Alcañiz and Ricardo A. Gutiérrez explore the environmental foreign policy of Argentina. In 2005, neighbors of a small Argentine city bordering on Uruguay began protesting the planned construction of two pulp plants on the Uruguayan side of the shared Uruguay River. Protesters blocked bridges that connect the two countries, claiming pollution from the plants would devastate the local fishing and tourist industry. They demanded that Uruguay halt construction. As the demonstrations grew, the governments of Argentina and Uruguay became involved, eventually taking the dispute to Mercosur, the World Bank and the International Court of Justice. How did a small-scale environmental protest quickly escalate into an international dispute between two historically allied states? The adoption of radical tactics by mostly middle-class protesters coupled with overlapping jurisdictions in water policy quickly internationalized the conflict. Furthermore, the salience of the issue and the lack of an autonomous environmental agency in Argentina pushed the government to adopt the protesters' agenda, resulting in a new environmental foreign policy for Argentina.

In Chapter 8, Mika Merviö studies Finnish environmental foreign policy. Merviö argues that, in their environmental foreign policies, the Finns constantly redefine their roles as a member of Western international organizations (the European Union, the United Nations and the Nordic group of countries); as speakers of a Finno-Ugric, non-Indo-European language; and as a neighbor to Russia. With multiple cultural identities and relatively high awareness of global environmental problems, Merviö believes that the Finns are well placed to understand the need to build supranational institutions to deal with global environmental issues. His chapter shows how Finland's environmental foreign policy is far less "idealistic" or openly nationalistic than that of its Nordic neighbors and, as such, he demonstrates how and why Finland has a more consensual and pragmatist approach to global issues, including environmental ones.

As Ken Wilkening and Charles Thrift argue in Chapter 9, effective lead states are vital to international environmental problem solving. But why do certain states become leaders while others do not? In their case study of another country bordering the Arctic, Wilkening and Thrift look at the historical development of Canada's foreign policy related to international efforts to address global pollution from persistent organic pollutants. They show that a conjunction of actors and factors, especially some related to interests and ideas, explains Canada's foreign policy and particularly its scientific and political leadership. The key actors have been federal ministries, the scientific Northern Contaminants Program, aboriginal groups and environmental organizations. The key factors that bound these actors together are cooperation, consultation, and collaboration. This dynamic of actors and factors propelled Canada to leadership status in international efforts to regulate persistent organic pollutants.

One vector and repository of persistent organic pollutants is water. In Chapter 10, Sara Hughes and Lena Partzsch look at the water-related foreign policies of the United States and the European Union. They draw upon the latest research in sustainable water governance to show that water-related foreign policy programs that have been developed by the United States and the European Union have been useful in meeting many important United Nations' technology- and target-driven Millennium Development Goals. However, Hughes and Partzsch argue that those programs have been less well suited to meeting long-term social and environmental objectives. Their case study locates water foreign policy between well-developed domestic regulations and emerging networks and paradigms at the global level. It shows how and why environmental criteria can be fully integrated into target setting and evaluation criteria for foreign policies related to water.

Turning to environmental foreign policy as practiced in Asia, in Chapter 11, Yohei Harashima undertakes an analytical case study of the relationship between trade and the environment. The aim of his chapter is to identify the positions of Asian developing countries at negotiations of the World Trade Organization's (WTO) Committee on Trade and Environment (CTE). While the WTO/CTE has not produced concrete results concerning its mandate, a definite change can be seen in the negotiating positions of developing countries in Asia, as many of them are now participating proactively in WTO/CTE negotiations. Harashima's case study shows the diversity of views on trade and environment that are held by Asian countries. In some cases, their views oppose each other. He also observes that the negotiating positions of each Asian country in the WTO/CTE are closely related to their trade structures, which are derived largely from progress made in the pursuit of their individual national development strategies. As such, the case study in Chapter 12 demonstrates the importance of looking at international *and* domestic variables when searching for explanations of environment-related foreign policies.

Chapter 12, written by Aike Müller, builds on the foreign aid literature and provides a detailed empirical account of financial flows for environmental purposes. By examining internationally financed water and other environmental projects, Müller shows that environmental aid burdens are not shared equally among donor countries. Nordic countries especially, along with Japan and Switzerland, have shared above-average burdens. This can be explained by varying priorities in donor states and by a set of influential variables, including social expenditure, public debt, military spending and the place of green parties in national parliaments. Müller tests the significance of these variables in a statistical analysis of multilateral environmental aid to the United Nations' Global Environment Facility. The main determinants of the environmental foreign policies she examines are rooted at the domestic level of the donor countries. Müller concludes that domestic factors, as well as state structures, have an especially strong impact on the conduct of environmental foreign policy when money is involved.

We conclude the book with a chapter by Mihaela Papa highlighting many of the theoretical findings from this volume and from additional studies. As Papa shows, despite the fact that the relationship between foreign policy and the environment has been the subject of much debate in academic and policy-making circles, conceptual issues relating to environmental foreign policy have received very little treatment. In response, Chapter 13 provides a comprehensive discussion of the concept of environmental foreign policy, clarifies its meaning and develops a framework for analyzing it. Papa considers the willingness of governments to act on environmental issues in their foreign policies, and explores the opportunities for such action to occur more frequently. Her chapter shows that the challenge of environmental foreign policy is the need for both individual and collective action: It fundamentally questions the responsibilities of states within the contemporary global system.

The upshot is that by thinking more consciously in terms of *foreign policy*, the contributors to this volume illuminate some of the most important actors, ideas and forces shaping the world's responses to pollution and our overuse of natural resources. If taken seriously, their case studies not only can help us understand what is being done to protect the environment, but they can also help policy-makers and stakeholders find new avenues for action to avert further environmental decline and possibly, in the case of climate change, help to avert catastrophe.

## Notes

1 A partial exception is the field of political ecology, although work in this field usually overlooks foreign policy processes and many of the domestic-global interactions encompassed by environmental foreign policy analysis. See, for example, Neumann (2005).
2 For a good summary of the range of interpretations of this term, see Cooper (1972). See also Chapter 13 in this volume. I develop these arguments and apply them to the cases of China, Japan and the United States in Harris (2008).
3 Hudson and Vore (1995) further identify three foundational works for these categories: Rosenau (1966); Snyder *et al.* (1954); and Sprout and Sprout (1956).
4 For a comprehensive discussion of comparative foreign policy analysis, see Andriole *et al.* (1975).
5 See also Chapter 13. In this section I draw on my chapters in Harris (2005, 2007).
6 For a variety of case studies exploring the foreign policy of climate change *per se*, see the companion to this volume: Harris (2009).

## References

Andriole, Stephen J., Wilkenfeld, Jonathan and Hopple, Gerald W. (1975) "A Framework for the Comparative Analysis of Foreign Policy Behavior," *International Studies Quarterly*, 19(2): 160–98.

Berkowitz, Morton, Bock, P.G. and Fuccillo, Vincent J. (1977) *The Politics of American Foreign Policy*, Englewood Cliffs, NJ: Prentice-Hall.

Brecher, Michael, Steinberg, Blema and Stein, Janice (1969) "A Framework for Research on Foreign Policy Behavior," *Journal of Conflict Resolution*, 13(1): 75–94.

Breitmeier, Helmut, Young, Oran R. and Zurn, Michael (2006) *Analyzing International Environmental Regimes*, Cambridge, MA: MIT Press.

Chalecki, Elizabeth L. (2009) "Exceptionalism as Foreign Policy: US Climate Change Policy and an Emerging Norm of Compliance," in Paul G. Harris (ed.) *Climate Change and Foreign Policy*, London: Routledge.

Cooper, Richard N. (1972) "Economic Interdependence and Foreign Policy in the Seventies," *World Politics*, 24(2): 159–81.

Evans, Peter B., Jacobson, Harold K. and Putnam, Robert D. (1993) *Double-Edged Diplomacy*, Berkeley, CA: University of California Press.

George, Alexander L. (1993) *Bridging the Gap: Theory and Practice in Foreign Policy*, Washington, DC: United States Institute of Peace.

Gerner, Deborah J. (1995) "The Evolution of the Study of Foreign Policy," in Laura Neack, Jeanne A.K. Hey, and Patrick J. Haney (eds) *Foreign Policy Analysis*, Englewood Cliffs, NJ: Prentice Hall.

Gold, Hyam (1978) "Foreign Policy Decision-Making and the Environment: The Claims of Snyder, Brecher, and the Sprouts," *International Studies Quarterly*, 22(4): 569–86.

Harris, Paul G. (ed.) (2000) *Climate Change and American Foreign Policy*, New York: St. Martin's Press.

—— (2005) *Confronting Environmental Change in East and Southeast Asia*, London: Earthscan/United University Press.

—— (2007) *Europe and Global Climate Change*, Cheltenham: Edward Elgar.

—— (2008) "Bringing the In-Between Back In: Foreign Policy in Global Environmental Politics," *Politics and Policy*, 36(6).

—— (ed.) (2009) *Climate Change and Foreign Policy: Case Studies from East to West*, London: Routledge.

Hudson, Valerie M. and Vore, Christopher S. (1995) "Foreign Policy Analysis Yesterday, Today, and Tomorrow," *Mershon International Studies Review*, 39: 212–38.

Jacobson, Harold Karan and Zimmerman, William (1969) *The Shaping of Foreign Policy*, New York: Atherton Press.

Kegley, Charles W. and Wittkopf, Eugene R. (1996) *American Foreign Policy*, New York: St. Martin's Press.

Lafferty, William M. and Meadowcroft, James (2001) *Implementing Sustainable Development*, New York: Oxford University Press.

Macridis, Roy C. (1958) "Introductory Remarks," in Roy C. Macridis (ed.) *Foreign Policy in World Politics*, Englewood Cliffs, NJ: Prentice Hall.

Milner, Helen V. (1997) *Interests, Institutions, and Information*, Princeton, NJ: Princeton University Press.

Morse, Edward L. (1970) "The Transformation of Foreign Policies: Modernization, Interdependence, and Externalization," *World Politics*, 22(3): 371–92.

Neumann, Roderick P. (2005) *Making Political Ecology*, New York: Oxford University Press.

Northredge, F.S. (1968) "The Nature of Foreign Policy," in F.S. Northredge (ed.) *The Foreign Policies of the Powers*, New York: Free Press.

Olson, William C. and Groom, A.J.R. (1991) *International Relations Then and Now*, London: HarperCollins Academic.

Pirages, Dennis and Cousins, Ken (eds) (2005) *From Resource Scarcity to Ecological Security*, Cambridge, MA: MIT Press.

Putnam, Robert D. (1988) "Diplomacy and Domestic Politics: The Logic of Two-Level Games," *International Organization*, 19: 345–66.

Neumann, Roderick P. (2005) *Making Political Ecology*, New York: Oxford University Press.

Rosenau, James N. (1966) "Pre-theories and Theories of Foreign Policy," in R. Barry Farrell (ed.) *Approaches in Comparative International Politics*, Evanston, IL: Northwestern University Press.

—— (1968) "Comparative Foreign Policy: Fad, Fantasy, or Field," *International Studies Quarterly*, 12(3): 296–329.

—— (1987) "Introduction: New Directions and Recurrent Questions in the Comparative Study of Foreign Policy," in Charles F. Hermann, Charles W. Kegley, Jr., and James N. Rosenau (eds) *New Directions in the Study of Foreign Policy*, Winchester, MA: Unwin Hyman.

Roy, Denny (1998) "Restructuring Foreign and Defense Policy: The People's Republic of China." in Anthony McGrew and Christopher Brook (eds.) *Asia-Pacific in the New World Order*, London: Routledge.

Snyder, Richard C., Bruck, H.W. and Sapin, Burton (1954) *Decision-Making as an Approach to the Study of International Politics*. Princeton, NJ: Princeton University Press.

—— (1963) *Foreign Policy Decision-Making*. Glencoe, IL: Free Press.

Sprout, Harold, and Sprout, Margaret (1956) *Man-Milieu Relationship Hypotheses in the Context of International Politics*. Princeton, NJ: Princeton University Press.

—— (1965) *The Ecological Perspective on Human Affairs with Special Reference to International Relations*, Princeton, NJ: Princeton University Press.

Thompson, Kenneth W. and Macridis, Roy C. (1976) "The Comparative Study of Foreign Policy," in Roy C. Macridis (ed.) *Foreign Policy in World Politics*, Englewood Cliffs, NJ: Prentice Hall.

Waltz, Kenneth (1979) *Theory of International Politics*, Reading, MA: Addison-Wesley.

Webber, Mark, and Smith, Michael (2002) *Foreign Policy in a Transformed World*, Harlow: Prentice Hall.

Zelikow, Philip (1994) "Foreign Policy Engineering: From Theory to Practice and Back Again," *International Security*, 18(4): 143–71.

# Part I
# Theory

# 2 Theories of environmental foreign policy

## Power, interests, and ideas

### John Barkdull and Paul G. Harris

Explanations for the environmental foreign policies of states are necessary for a full understanding of global environmental politics. States make the critical decisions on the entire range of environmental issues, from protecting endangered species to regulating the trade in toxic wastes to addressing global climate change. Yet, significant gaps remain in the scholarly research on how and why states decide their foreign policies on the environment. The vast literature on global environmental politics pertains primarily to international relations rather than to the state-level variables that determine foreign policy behavior. This chapter identifies some of the areas of inquiry that have not been fully explored and suggests directions for further research on environmental foreign policy.[1]

The study of foreign policy on such issues as security, trade, and foreign aid is extensive. Theoretical approaches are well established. The wider study of foreign policy suggests a typology of research orientations, incorporating two dimensions. The first dimension is the level of analysis (society, state, system). The second dimension is the basic causal variables that motivate behavior (power, interests, ideas). The two dimensions produce a 3 × 3 matrix that helps to organize thinking about foreign policy toward the environment (Table 2.1). Table 2.1 shows the scheme with some examples in each cell. For instance, bureaucratic politics lies at the intersection of state-level theory and interest-based theory. This supposes that bureaucratic struggles take place within the state, and the stakes are the interests of the various agencies to

*Table 2.1* Approaches to the study of environmental foreign policy

| Level of analysis | Basic causal variables | | |
| --- | --- | --- | --- |
| | *Power* | *Interests* | *Ideas* |
| Society | Elite theory | Group theory | Ideology |
| State | Checks and balances | Bureaucratic politics | Policy-maker's "road maps" |
| System | Hegemonic stability | National interest | Cognitive diffusion |

secure and expand domain, resources, mission, and influence. The jostling and bargaining that takes place among the agencies occurs apart from processes occurring in society, such as interest group bargaining. In regard to foreign policy toward the environment, an explanation for policy outcomes would entail identifying the relevant agencies, their interests, the policy preferences they espouse, and the political bargaining that resulted in a particular set of policies. The rest of the matrix will be elaborated below.

Global environmental trends are arguably the most important determinants of humanity's future. With a growing population and demands for higher living standards, the world requires increasing resources to fuel industrial society, and the expansion of human society puts ever-greater pressure on the natural environment. The "limits to growth" could make the dramatic economic growth necessary to meet future demand impossible (Brown 2000). The result could be food shortages, greater social conflict, and much lower quality of life. Because states will make the critical decisions on international cooperation to cope with these challenges, research on foreign policy toward the environment is important to bring humans more into harmony with the environment on which we all depend (see Harris 2000a, 2000b, 2001c, 2002, 2003, 2005, 2007a).

Environmental issues raise a number of significant questions for the study of foreign policy. This review focuses on this question: Why do states adopt particular policies? Other questions include, for instance, what effects do foreign economic, security, and social policies have on the environment? What limits do environmental parameters place on other policy challenges, such as achieving economic growth? What is the relationship between environmental foreign policy and trade, security, immigration, and domestic policy? What is the impact of war and military activities on the environment? How do bilateral and multilateral environmental relations differ?

The general literature on foreign policy suggests ways to investigate environmental foreign policy. Group theory and pluralism highlight the effect of interest group bargaining on policy outcomes. Class analysis and elite theory argue that a small, privileged sector of society wields the decisive influence in the making of foreign policy. Institutional structure and bureaucratic politics indicate the importance of the governmental decision-making process. Psychological approaches and small group analysis focus on the effect of top decision-makers. Game theory and rational choice theory posit the state as a unitary rational actor. Not all of these approaches are well represented in the literature on environmental foreign policy. The following section reviews research on environmental foreign politics in light of the broader work on foreign policy.

## Systemic theories of environmental foreign policy

Systemic theories of foreign policy attempt to abstract from the domestic sources of foreign policy and to locate the causal variables in the structure of international politics. Scholars differ over what counts as systemic or structural. For realists, the distribution of power is the critical structural variable. For liberals, interests and bargaining situations are most significant. Constructivists assert that the structure of cognitive factors matters most.

The upper left cell in the matrix represents power-based systemic theory. From this perspective, states are generally understood to pursue the national interest defined as power (Morgenthau 1985). Explaining foreign policy means showing the efforts that rational, unitary actors have made to survive, enhance their security, and elevate their status relative to other states. Leadership is assumed to speak for the nation, and politics stops at the water's edge. States are rational in that they attempt to pursue policies that will help them achieve their larger strategic goals. Certainly they can and do make mistakes, misperceive, over-reach, and the like. Yet neo-realism suggests that states that fail to pursue power and ensure their own security fall by the wayside of history. Thus, the pressures of international competition ensure that foreign policies converge on one over-riding objective. Moreover, the threat of war forces states to focus on relative gains. Waltz (1979), the leading neo-realist, asserts that "unit-level" theory of foreign policy should be separate from the theory of international politics, and explaining outcomes does not in general require attention to foreign policy beyond the spare assumption that states seek to survive. But Elman (1996) has suggested that a neo-realist theory of foreign policy is possible and necessary.

In addition to the behavioral assumption that states seek to survive, power-based systemic theory also suggests that a state's position in the international pecking order shapes its policy preferences. For instance, a hegemonic power will favor an open international economy. British and US leadership to create open economic orders during the nineteenth and twentieth centuries are cited as evidence. The foreign policies of the hegemon follow, then, from its structural position.

In regard to foreign policy toward the environment, no scholar has forwarded a parallel hypothesis. The reason may be that this perspective posits that environmental issues matter only to the extent they bear on security and relative gains. Because policy-makers must pay attention to immediate conditions, they are not likely to focus on long-term environmental problems. War sweeps away environmental concerns. Thus the environment is insignificant relative to security. Yet, prior emphasis on security does not preclude an argument from structural position to environmental foreign policy. The difficulty lies in specifying the international environmental order a hegemon would prefer. In economics, the advantages a powerful economic actor enjoys in an open international market lead to preferences for free trade and capital mobility. What parallel exists in environmental policy? Perhaps the most plausible answer is that the hegemon would favor an international environmental order that is compatible with, and reinforces, its dominance in economic affairs. The environmental order, then, would rely on market incentives, corporate responsibility, and light regulation that mitigates the side effects of industrial capitalism without disturbing the essential rules of economic exchange. Perhaps a more direct argument from structural position to policy preferences is possible, but no scholar has made it yet. Certainly, studies of US leadership in the creation of international environmental regimes exist (e.g., M'Gonigle and Zacher 1979), but no study explains the preference for such regimes as a consequence of hegemony.

Systemic theory emphasizing interests has resulted in some useful studies. Interest-based theory assumes that rational actors will cooperate to achieve joint gains. Generally, it is assumed that they will seek absolute gains and be relatively unconcerned about relative gains, because in many issue areas the utility of military force is low and the threat of violence is largely absent. Analysts assume that they can identify state interests *a priori* (for instance, all states' interests in achieving enhanced economic growth from comparative advantage). Interests are not understood as the outcome of domestic politics; by assumption, states are rational, unitary actors. Accordingly, this approach tends to adopt game theory and other rational choice models to interpret foreign policy.

Interest-based theory, then, requires specifying various states' interests and the structure of incentives in a given issue area. For example, although states understand that unfettered trade results in optimal global output, they are tempted to cheat, or free ride, on trade agreements to reap short-term gains. The question is how to solve this problem of cheating; state interests in the mutually beneficial outcomes of economic cooperation are assumed. Much literature on international regimes adopts this view: "Foreign policies as well as international institutions are to be reconstructed as outcomes of calculations of advantage made by states" (Hasenclever *et al.* 1997: 23).

Sprinz and Vaahtoranta (1994) adopt the interest-based model to explain environmental foreign policy. They assert that state interests are defined in terms of vulnerability to environmental damages, and costs of abatement. States with high vulnerability and low costs of abatement will be "pushers" that strive for stronger environmental regulations. States with low vulnerability and high abatement costs will be "draggers" who resist stronger regulations. Those with high vulnerability and high costs of abatement will be "intermediates," and states with low vulnerability and low costs of abatement will be "bystanders." The model is tested against two cases: ozone-depleting chemicals, and acid rain. "Overall," the authors conclude, "our theoretical propositions explain much of the positions taken during the negotiations on the Montreal Protocol as well as the Helsinki Protocol" (ibid.: 104). Barkdull (1998) argues in a similar vein that the United States led on policies to reduce marine oil pollution from tankers due to rising vulnerability as imports increased, while the costs of reducing oil pollution would fall largely on foreign owners of oil tanker fleets. Similarly, Fairbrass and Jordan (2001) argue that British preferences for maintaining national autonomy shaped its participation in European Union (EU) biodiversity policy. However, their study also finds that British environmental policy shifted toward EU policy due to increasing integration, which escaped the control of the British state. Eventually, Britain established an environmental agency to coordinate its policies with its European partners (Jordan 2001: 658–60).

In Russia, the concentration of political power in Vladimir Putin's hands means that domestic politics exert relatively little influence on decision-making. Incentives arising from the international system provide more explanatory power. When Russia ratified the Kyoto Protocol, "international incentives in other policy areas and reputational concerns rather than anticipated benefits from Kyoto itself" motivated Putin (Henry and Sundstrom 2007: 57). For Australia, interests were also decisive (Crowley 2007), at least until very recently. Australia feigned compliance with Kyoto while resisting ratification, because ratification would entail commitment to costly abatement measures when future requirements come into play. Australia's heavy reliance on fossil fuels and coal exports puts its national economic interests at odds with the goals of the Kyoto Protocol. Although Australia's political leadership has wanted the appearance of complying with international norms and responding to public opinion in favor of environmental protection, economic interests prevail over norms. Australia, concludes Crowley (ibid.: 136) "has clearly placed national self-interest before multilateral abatement efforts." This may be changing with the advent of a new government at the end of 2007, which promptly ratified the Kyoto Protocol, and with the impact of severe drought and other recent environmental problems on the public's consciousness. However, evidence of significant change will require new policies and actions, not just ratification of the protocol. Given the configuration of interests, this could be a slow process.

The literature on environmental security also represents interest-based systemic theory (Homer-Dixon 1993). One study finds that population pressures can lead to war, especially for countries with low economic development and high population growth (Tir and Diehl 2001). Water conflicts have also received considerable attention. Research shows that military preponderance, democratic regimes, and a single state having control over most of the water resources are related to the likelihood of conflict (Huston 1999). These studies do not attempt to relate their work to theories of foreign policy, but the work has clear implications for the study of environmental foreign policy. Of course, when access to and control over resources are at stake rather than strictly environmental issues (pollution, climate change and the like), the literature is voluminous and covers a wide range of issues from colonialism to resource wars (Tabb 2007). Recently, the question of whether oil drives US policy toward the Middle East and other oil-rich regions has generated immense controversy (Klare 2004; Klare and Voman 2006).

In scholarly and general discourse on environmental policy, authors often adopt an implicit state-as-actor assumption. Critics and supporters of a country's environmental policies will assert that "China" or the "United States" pursued this or that policy as if they were referring to a corporate entity. Often, no attempt is made to account for a given state's policies. For instance, Hunter (2000) offers a critical review of American policy without saying why the United States has adopted environmentally harmful policies. Similarly, Carroll (1986, 1992) and Caldwell (1990) explain environmental foreign policies in terms of perceived national interests. Others (Myers 1987; Mathews 1989; Springer 1988) have called for foreign policies to protect the environment because doing so is in the national interest.

Cognitive approaches have become more prominent in international studies. For Wendt (1999), ideas are the main structural variable, doing most of the work in explanations of international conflict and cooperation. Anarchy, he says, is what states make of it, because the important factor is how inter-subjective understandings define roles and rules. Wendt posits three types of anarchy – Hobbesian, Lockean, and Kantian – defined by states' understandings of self and other. Presumably, one could apply the same reasoning to ecological politics. If states identified themselves as planetary stewards rather than Hobbesian enemies, then the character of international anarchy would change accordingly. Indeed, Michele Betsill (2000) does argue that international norms matter in the making of foreign policy, and Harris (2007b) asserts that international norms regarding climate change have affected US foreign policy on that issue.

American hegemony also suggests that American ideas about how to address environmental concerns will play a major role in the making of global environmental policy. Although no author has made the argument, one could assert that American managerial approaches that leave prevailing economic and political arrangements untouched have shaped international institutions, just as American economic ideas influenced post-war trade and monetary institutions (Ruggie 1998).

Similarly, Finnemore (1996) demonstrates the utility of a sociological approach to international relations. Her research shows that ideas generated in domestic politics can give rise to institutional innovations that are then disseminated via international organizations to other states. Thus, states have almost all created environmental ministries or agencies, regardless of level of development or interest in the environment. They do so because having an environmental ministry has become part of the definition of the modern state. Research on epistemic communities also emphasizes the manner in which ideas spread to influence others' policies and behaviors. Haas's seminal work on the Mediterranean Plan detailed how scientific consensus among experts led states to adopt similar, cooperative environmental policies to protect the sea from further pollution and over-fishing (Haas 1990). Dimitrov (2005) argues that the norm of multilateral environmental management has pushed governments to create a toothless institution, the United Nations Forum on Forests. Hardly any governments wanted a treaty, and they recognized that forest management was not in fact a commons problem, but they had so thoroughly internalized the norm of environmental multilateralism that they felt they could not be seen as inactive in this issue area.

Thus, instead of negotiating a substantive agreement, they created the UNFF to symbolize movement. Consequently, Dimitrov asserts, although the norm guided behavior, it did not result in better environmental protection. Norms are not always beneficial and might result in "hollow institutions" that are the best alternatives to actually doing something.

In general, the message is that systemic cognitive factors affect states' foreign policy choices. Ideas circulate in global channels, affecting problem definition, the range of options states believe are available, and the choices they make. Cognition is not to be understood as a "unit-level" variable properly left out of systemic or structural IR theory. The distribution of ideas is as much systemic as the distribution of material capabilities. (Indeed, ideas define what counts as a relevant material capability.) Ideas both shape state preferences, and constitute the identities of states as empowered international actors. Although some research has developed these insights, much remains to be explored.

Roberts, Parks, and Vasquez (2004) employ a large empirical study of states' propensity to ratify environmental treaties. They find that a state's likelihood of ratifying an environmental treaty depends in part on the state's position in the world economy. In turn, a state's position depends in many cases on the legacy of colonialism. Colonialism results in former colonial countries' "disadvantaged insertion in the world-economy" and the disadvantage reduces states' willingness and ability to carry out environmental commitments (ibid.: 44). That is, the world-system sets and limits the range of choices a state enjoys in regard to environmental policy. The authors believe that relying on world-system theory to account for foreign policy outcomes addresses the issue of explaining states' preferences. The study finds that strong civil society and domestic institutions enhance willingness and ability to carry out environmental commitments, but the strength of civil society and institutions depend on "one's 'insertion' in the world-system. Driving non-ratification, therefore, is a fragile, authoritarian and often corrupt economic structure built on the production and export of a very narrow range of products" (ibid.: 44). The analysis shows the influence of domestic factors on environmental foreign policy, but it accounts for those domestic factors in terms of systemic forces.

## Society-centric theories of environmental foreign policy

Societal theories of foreign policy stress the way in which preferences of domestic actors translate into policies adopted and implemented by various arms of government. "According to the society-centric approach, explanations for foreign … policy are found in the ongoing struggle for influence among domestic social forces or political groups" (Ikenberry *et al.* 1988: 7). Government serves as a neutral arbiter or simply as the arena for conflict, compromise, and bargaining. Group theory, class analysis, and elite theory assert that the dominant determinants of a state's foreign policy are to be found in society, not the state itself. Although the state might enable dominant groups to assert their power, the critical decisions are made independently of the structures of government.

Elite theory and class analysis lie at the intersection of society-centric theory and power-based theory. Elite groups for one, the capitalist class for the other, control the levers of power, from funding candidate campaigns, to owning the media, to selecting the viable candidates for public office. In authoritarian countries, the connection between government and the top sector of society is even more obvious. Elite and class interests change slowly, and so policy change is incremental. Major change occurs when crisis forces the dominant groups to make concessions to mass society in order to restore stability and legitimacy. The primary objective is to ensure the continuation of the existing structure of society, and the accumulation of capital.

In regard to environmental foreign policy, elite groups tend to fall into two camps. Some advocate maximum corporate freedom to ensure unfettered economic growth, while others acknowledge the need for some environmental regulation. The latter endorse a managerial approach to environmental challenges that relies on international organizations, corporate responsibility, and the like while leaving global economic institutions in place. "Sustainable development" is defined in terms congenial to markets and corporate decisions about production. Technological progress is expected to mitigate environmental problems. The market is assumed to be efficient in the use of resources and therefore is the best mechanism for fostering conservation. Limits to growth do not exist (Chaterjee and Finger 1994: 27–9). The leading elements of society both exercise direct influence over policy-makers, and they foster the climate of opinion favorable to their interests by funding think tanks, media outlets, and the like. The result is to narrow the range of "responsible" debate, making more radical proposals appear to be contrary to common sense. To wit, the "ideology of competitiveness" has been so frequently reiterated that it now "has been elevated to the status of natural law" (Rinehart 1996: 87). The notion that countries must maintain their international competitiveness disables them from adopting environmental policies that are contrary to corporate preferences.

Countless critiques of American environmental policy attribute outcomes to the influence of the elite or the capitalist class. One author asserts, "Large multinational firms in particular possess extensive economic and technological power that shapes outcomes in international environmental policy-making" (Falkner 2001: 157). Moreover, the granting of patents on life forms is said to represent a new form of colonialism (Shiva 1997). Free trade is said to result in environmental degradation: "It is important to realize the new free trade agreements were designed and promoted by associations of businesses for whom environmental regulations are no more than costs that interfere with profits and therefore must be minimized" (Goldsmith 1996: 90). Moreover, corporations across the developed world share the same anti-environmental attitudes and influence the US and European governments to limit the scope of environmental regulations (Levy and Newell 2000). A representative statement of the radical view observes:

> Capital's endless pursuit of new outlets for class-based accumulation requires for its continuation the destruction of both pre-existing natural conditions and previous social relations. Class exploitation, imperialism, war, and ecological devastation are not mere unrelated accidents of history but interrelated, intrinsic features of capitalist development.
>
> (Foster 2007)

Clearly, the foreign policies of capitalist states would follow along these lines, including the destruction of natural conditions and ecological devastation.

Interest group politics is a prominent theme in the environmental politics literature. Policy-makers are expected to respond to constituencies if they want to stay in office and have the resources to wage successful campaigns. In exchange for support, they advocate the policies their constituents demand. Environmental groups offer votes, favorable mention in the media, financial support, and moral approbation to policy-makers who adopt pro-environment policies. Their opponents, mainly in the corporate sector, provide policy ideas, money, and approval.

DeSombre's analysis of the domestic sources of US international environmental policy shows the influence of interest groups, in particular that policy-makers internationalize an issue when both the environmentalists and businesses call for it. Yandle (1993: 95) discusses the unlikely pro-NAFTA coalition that included both leading environmental organizations and the business sector. Audley (1993) notes that environmental groups wanted NAFTA only to do no harm, rather than that it enhance environmental values. Mumme (1984) details the coalition of environmentalists and protectionist domestic businesses that wanted stronger environmental regulations on the US–Mexico border. McAlpine and LeDonne (1993), and Shaffer (1995) argue that group influence detracts from environmental protection, while Benedick (1989, 1991) asserts that interest groups helped enact progressive ozone depletion policy. Lerner (1986) argues that a strong foundation in domestic civic organizations is necessary to implementing successful transnational ecosystem management.

Likewise, Weinthal and Parag (2003) employ the case of Israel and the protection of the Mediterranean Sea to show that national environmental ministries require support from civil society to be effective; without support from civil society, compliance with international environmental treaties is more difficult. Asgeirsdottir (2007) finds that strong domestic interest groups both influence state policies on international fisheries management and enable states to bargain more successfully against states with weaker domestic constituencies. Moser (2007) asserts that a bottom-up climate protection movement to address American greenhouse gas emissions is emerging in the United States. Harrison and Sundstrom (2007) employ a comparative

politics framework to explain countries' decisions on Kyoto Protocol ratification; they find that economic and electoral interests, and the level of voter
concern, are significant explanatory factors. Texts on environmental policy
adopt an interest group explanation for US policy, with obvious implications
for foreign policy toward the environment (Smith 1992; Switzer 2001). In
general, the premise is that to explain why a country adopted a particular
policy in international environmental politics requires reference to the interest
groups in that society and their role in the policy process.

The role of widely held ideas in the making of foreign policy entails
study of such phenomena as ideology, belief systems, stereotypes, historical analogies, myths, and public opinion. Of course, policy-makers are
themselves products of their societies and thus share in their broad cognitive currents, but we treat policy-makers' ideas separately below. The issue
here is that social cognitions shape the policy context for elite–mass relations, class relations, and group bargaining. The real action remains in
society, not within the state. Policy-makers might make the "coaching
decisions" but society as a whole sets the rules of the game (Jackson 1993:
111–12). Hunt's (1987) study of ideology and American foreign policy identifies widely held attitudes in American society regarding the country's des-
tiny, racial hierarchy, and attitudes toward revolutionary movements
abroad. A parallel analysis of US foreign policy toward the environment
might focus on the contrasting views of Gifford Pinchot and John Muir, the
former advocating conservation, multiple use, and human benefits from
nature, the latter promoting wilderness preservation (cf. Pinchot 1998;
Muir 1997).

The effect of liberal ideology on US climate change policy is the subject of
Doran's (2000) study. He asserts that "governmentality" limits policy to a
technocratic, managerial approach. More broadly, the commitment of western societies to liberalization and the weakening of state interventions into
the economy limit environmental policies that might hinder market-led economic growth. Missbach argues that the United States is an environmental
laggard because of its ideology of "Fordism" and its commitment to the
American Dream of rising living standards for all. This results in a "waste of
resources and energy" (Missbach 2000: 148). Capitalist countries are committed to premises of growth, technological progress, and consumerism that
are at odds with environmental protection (Crocker and Linden 1998). Barber's analysis of globalization also suggests that the spread of American
consumerism is inimical to protecting the environment (1996: 226–7).
Greenberg (2006) analyzes several trends in American conservative political
beliefs in regard to their attitudes toward consumption. Traditional conservatives
rejected the notion that a society could be built on unbridled consumption,
while today's conservatives largely believe that encouraging consumption is
necessary for economic well-being. In light of the American consumers' large
ecological footprint, this debate within conservative thought has clear
implications for the global environment.

By contrast, European countries have shown greater propensity than the United States to accept environmental burden sharing and foreign aid spending to support sustainable development (Harris 2004). Harris (2007b) has argued that concerns about environmental protection and social justice within European states are now sufficiently entrenched in the minds of publics and officials to extend outward, becoming central to many European states, and especially the EU's, environmental foreign policies. Similarly, Japan accepted the Kyoto Protocol because of "ideas and the power of embedded symbolism" (Tiberghien and Schreurs 2007: 78). National interests, domestic interests, and institutions mattered, but for Japanese decision-makers and the public, the Kyoto Protocol had become a symbol of environmental consciousness, foreign policy prominence, and political leadership. The symbolic significance of the agreement made the difference.

In general, beliefs that are widely held in society shape the societal politics of the environment. Elite and mass, contending groups, public opinion, and the like provide the terrain on which political struggle occurs. Interests are not given *a priori*; they are constructed from the ideas and beliefs that prevail in society.

## State-centric theories of environmental foreign policy

While society-centric theory sees the state as a neutral referee or passive arena for political action, state-centric theory asserts that institutions of government and the people who occupy roles in them also have policy preferences, interests, ideas, and influence. Policy-makers and administrators are actors, leading to emphasis on "the goal-oriented behavior of politicians and civil servants as they respond to internal and external constraints in an effort to manipulate policy outcomes in accordance with their preferences" (Ikenberry *et al.*1988: 10). In addition, state institutions persist and continue to shape policy outcomes long after the events that gave rise to them have faded from memory. Foreign policy outcomes cannot be read off from the structure of the international system or the distribution of influence across groups in society. State actors move independently of both systemic and societal factors to pursue their own preferences and interests.

Explaining foreign policy outcomes requires assessing the distribution of power and influence within the state. In democracies, this can entail exploration of relations between the executive and the legislature. In regard to environmental policy, Paarlberg (1997) argues that Congress thwarted the Clinton administration's effort to restore American leadership in international environmental negotiations. Bryner (2000: 126) likewise attributes US foot-dragging on climate change to the president's weakness relative to Congress. By contrast, Barkdull (1998, 2001) finds that the Nixon administration internationalized marine pollution issues in order to emphasize presidential authority over foreign policy, resulting in treaties governing ocean dumping and pollution from ships.

Bureaucratic politics has long been a rich vein for scholars of foreign policy. Foreign policy is explained in regard to the power struggles among the various agencies and departments of the executive branch. In regard to environmental policy, only a few studies have been published. The concept of "environmental security" leads to investigation of the military's role in environmental politics (Deudney 1990; Deudney and Matthew 1999). Hopgood (1998) finds that policy-makers in the executive branch have been primarily responsible for US environmental foreign policy. Hopgood relies on interviews with key players, internal White House documents, hearings, and other sources to show that environmental interest groups were barely present as the executive branch formulated policy. Meetings between administration officials and interest group representatives occurred mainly to convey the administration's position and solicit support. Barkdull (2001) also found that state officials took the lead in marine pollution, and interest groups were ill prepared to comment on administration initiatives. Vice President Al Gore's presence during the Clinton administration helped shape US environmental foreign policy as well (Gore 1992; Harris 2001b: 195–7). Policy entrepreneurs in government, in short, use the levers of influence to advance their own agendas. Interest groups are often excluded or called upon to help build public support but not to provide input into policy formulation. That is, the real power over policy lies with state actors, and so explaining environmental foreign policy requires attention to which state actors have influence and power within the state itself.

Hovi, Skodvin and Andresen (2003) explain the EU's pursuit of the Kyoto Protocol in terms of institutional path-dependence and the organization's desire to show environmental leadership. The latter motive arose from the notion that EU leadership on environmental issues helped to further the development of a common foreign policy. The former refers to the tendency of institutions to maintain policy orientations from their origins as they develop. It also implies that prior commitments and sunk costs limit current policy options. These factors are most important to explaining the EU's puzzling willingness to forge ahead on climate change policy despite the US exit and Russian reluctance. Harrison (2007) argues that institutions were the critical factor explaining Canada's ratification of the Kyoto Protocol, while the United States rejected the agreement. Canada and the United States faced similar incentives in international markets and both displayed opposition from businesses and an inattentive public. Political leaders in both countries needed a strong normative commitment to protecting the global commons to overcome domestic opposition. During President Clinton's term, this was the case, but Clinton lacked the decisive institutional setting to enable movement toward ratification. Canada's parliamentary system provided the institutional support while the capacity to block action in Congress thwarted climate change policy in the United States.

Interest-based state-centric theory raises two questions: what are the interests of the state?, and what is the role of interests within the state? For instance, the state might want to maximize tax revenue, legitimacy, autonomy, or regime stability. These interests exist apart from social factors. In regard to environmental policy, the researcher would posit a link between such interests and particular policy outcomes. For example, the state might seek greater regulatory control over the energy sector in order to strengthen its influence relative to powerful energy companies. Indeed, the Clinton administration sought support from other industries, including insurance and alternative energy, to increase its influence relative to the oil majors. Had it succeeded, it could have bolstered its power to regulate the fossil fuel sector (Harris 2001b: 172–8). Looking within the state, bureaucracies have interests in budgets, domain, staffing, jurisdiction, and mission (Allison and Zelikow 1999: 255). Presumably, these interests could lead agencies to pursue those environmental policies that enhance their resources and roles. Barnett (2001) asserts that the concept of environmental security has been used this way, to increase the position of agencies that had lost their Cold War missions. Poor bureaucratic organization can also be a hindrance to implementing policy, as Schwartz (1992) argues in regard to Great Lakes environmental protection.

Environmental ideas should affect politics and policy-making within the state as well. Goldstein and Keohane (1993) posit that world views, principled beliefs, and causal frameworks serve as policy road maps. This enables actors to produce policies despite lack of clear direction or prior experience with the particular issue. (Unfortunately, the edited volume that develops this insight lacks a chapter on environmental policy.) Others have suggested that science shapes environmental foreign policy. Because environmental policy depends more than most issues on scientific knowledge, the "national basis of decision making" leads to the predominance of countries with strong scientific establishments (Skolnikoff 1995: 259–60). Scientific uncertainty is said to explain lack of consensus on climate change policy (Skolnikoff 1990) and to subsequent failure of US leadership on the issue (Paarlberg 1999: 247–8). Although policy-makers turn to scientists for dispassionate, objective analysis, research shows that scientists bring their non-scientific values and preferences into their interpretations of evidence (Spiller and Rieser 1986). In addition, "knowledge brokers" use the findings of scientific research to support their policy positions (Litfin 1993: 80–1; Litfin 1998).

Small group decision-making and individual psychology also focus on cognitive factors within the state. Hypotheses on perception and misperception, group think, parochialism in the agencies, and the like are tested to account for a wide range of foreign policy outcomes (Jervis 1976; Janus 1972; Hart *et al.* 1997). Yet, research that investigates how such factors affect environmental foreign policy is scarce (see Harris 2001b: 190–9). A rare exception is Below's (2008) analysis of presidential decisions in the cases of ozone depletion and climate change, where she finds that poliheuristic theory – combining rational and cognitive decision-making processes – can be shown to explain environmental foreign policy:

Most presidents' decision-making processes could be explained using cognitive heuristics (relying on individual beliefs, values and/or personality) in the initial stages and rational decision-making in the second. While each president comes to the table with their own affinity for environmental protection or industry and big business, each weighs the domestic political challenges inherent in each policy choice and reduces the options in hopes of minimizing or avoiding political loss. After doing so, the presidents narrow the "short list" of options using more calculative processes.

(Below 2008: 13)

Other work helps us understand how societal groups shape policy-makers' values and scientific understanding of environmental challenges. Harris (2001a: 31) notes that nongovernmental organizations have used conferences and other activities to increase public awareness of environmental problems, and NGOs in the United States have played an important role in Congressional deliberations (Boas 2001). Tangentially, the research on global civil society and transnational activism could also suggest ways in which state actor perceptions are formed.

## Conclusion

We have offered a 3 × 3 matrix (Table 2.1) as a way to organize thinking about theories of environmental foreign policy, and to help identify gaps in existing knowledge. Research on security and economic foreign policy indicates some of the unexplored areas for the study of environmental foreign policy. For example, system theory postulates that a hegemonic power will prefer an open economic system, but no parallel argument has been offered in regard to environmental policy preferences. More research on the effects of bureaucratic actors would add to our understanding as well. Recently, a number of studies have appeared on the role of ideas and of institutions in shaping state responses to environmental challenges. Several authors have engaged in the debate over the role of norms and ideas, with some asserting that cognitive factors are decisive, while others argue that national interests, domestic bargains, and institutions make the critical differences.

One of the difficulties for the typology proposed here is that state responses to environmental challenges are often directed at changes to the ecosystem rather than toward a specific actor. We are accustomed to thinking of foreign policy in terms of actors' relationships to one another, not to external conditions unconnected to identifiable actors. Rather than negotiate agreements or engage in signaling, states must develop adaptive capacities: "As a general statement, however, global environmental change, by requiring states to prepare for and adapt to its consequences, increases the demand for the administrative, organizational, technological, and financial capacity of the state – a demand which some states will find easier to meet than others" (Bierman and Dingwerth 2004: 3). Moreover, the global character of today's environmental problems creates new forms of interdependence: "nation states are bound to suffer environmental harm that has been caused by the community of nations as such" (ibid.: 6). States do not have the option to end the interdependence, as they might an unsatisfactory trade treaty.

In addition, indirect consequences of environmental change can generate security risks, such as domestic turmoil, with no obvious "enemy" to combat. Accordingly, states respond with national measures aimed at persuading others to follow suit, or with international cooperation. Establishing a stronger regulatory framework to manage a coastal zone, for example, might inspire other states to do the same, resulting in cleaner seas. To achieve such outcomes depends on policy and institutional diffusion, which is not the usual meaning of "foreign policy."[2] Participation in international organizations, international regimes, and other cooperative arrangements appears more straightforwardly part of foreign policy, but in the literature, the result is an indistinct line between foreign policy studies, the study of international organization, and general international relations. Thus, research on foreign policy toward the environment is often difficult to identify or classify. Because of the attributes of the subject matter, scholars do not necessarily think of their work as part of the body of foreign policy studies, even though it is about state adaptations to the complexities of environmental change that is "external" to the territorially defined sovereign state.

The larger question is in regard to the state itself – its coherence and viability as the fundamental unit of international politics. If global environmental politics blurs the scholarly lines, in part, this is because the traditional boundaries of world politics are becoming increasingly indistinct. The lack of an "enemy" or "other" to act upon is one side of the coin, while uncertainty about who is doing the acting is the other. Indeed, for EU countries, "independent national environmental policy no longer exists" (Trittin 2004: 24). Thus, research on the nation state and environmental policy is pulled toward such problems as explaining the diffusion of ideas and institutions, describing the rise of new centers of policy-making and influence, and assessing the effects of global environmental institutions on state behavior (Bierman and Dingwerth 2004: 12–16). The focus on these puzzles, rather than traditional questions of foreign policy, reflects the declining relevance of territorial sovereign states in global environmental governance. Indeed, Karkkainen (2004) argues that, while states remain important, the appropriate focus for research on global environmental politics is "collaborative problem-solving" that involves a variety of international actors. Instead of assuming that sovereign states make the crucial decisions:

[S]overeign states themselves have come to recognize that some environmental problems lie beyond the limits of ordinary state competence, too complex to be resolved through straightforward exercises of state sovereignty or inter-sovereign agreements. Consequently, states are joining nonstate actors in ambitious experiments seeking to address problems of this character through multi-party collaborative governance arrangements that pool, recombine, and coordinate the deployment of varied resources and competencies of multiple actors ... They [problem-solving colla-borations] operate through broad, open-ended, and often informal yet surprisingly durable commitments by diverse sets of actors to address complex problems jointly by means of ongoing multi-party collaboration, pragmatic problem-solving deliberation, and concerted action.

(ibid.: 74–5)

While some scholars question the centrality of the state by noting such multi-actor processes, others posit that "empire" better captures the current global order than either sovereignty or polycentric collaboration: "Territorial assumptions about sovereignty are not very useful in a world of imperial power" (Dalby 2004: 1). Dalby outlines the many connections between imperialism and exploitation of peripheral areas. For example, the extraction of many natural resources causes immense ecological damage. Gaining access to mineral deposits, oil fields and the like often requires displacing indigenous peoples and destroying the ecological basis for their social exis-tence. Ensuring that mining and oil companies have access to resources and secure property rights is a major purpose of intervention in the developing world. Foreign policy, that is, supports the ecologically destructive activities of major multinational corporations around the world.

Nonetheless, political identity and a large part of the policy process occur within the nation state, even in Europe, the most integrated region in the world: "We still have an individual and collective national identity – only a few of us are already global citizens with a global identity" (Trittin 2004: 27). It would go much too far to claim that states do not make foreign policy toward the environment, or that their policies do not matter. Perhaps the state system is passing from the scene. But the process is slow and incre-mental, and foreign policy will remain an essential part of the study of international relations for some time to come. Thus, the typology offered here does suggest some possible lines of inquiry that would add to our understanding of global environmental politics.

## Notes

1 Some of the ideas in this chapter first appeared in Barkdull and Harris (2002).
2 For an analysis of the diffusion of environmental technology, and an argument that the nation-state remains the locus of policy, see Janicke and Jacob (2004).

## References

Allison, Graham and Zelikow, Philip (1999) *Essence of Decision: Explaining the Cuban Missile Crisis*, 2nd edn, New York: Longman.
Asgeirsdottir, Aslaug (2007) "Oceans of Trouble: Domestic Influence on Interna-tional Fisheries Cooperation in the North Atlantic and Barents Sea," *Global Environmental Politics*, 7(1): 120–44.

Audley, John (1993) "Why Environmentalists Are Angry about the North American Free Trade Agreement," in Durwood Zaelke, Paul Orbuch, and Robert F. Housman (eds) *Trade and the Environment: Law, Economics, and Policy*, Washington, DC: Island Press.

Barber, Benjamin (1996) *Jihad Versus McWorld: How Globalism and Tribalism are Reshaping the World*, New York: Ballantine Books.

Barkdull, John (1998) "Nixon and the Marine Environment," *Presidential Studies Quarterly*, 28(3): 587–605.

—— (2001) "US Foreign Policy and the Ocean Environment: A Case of Executive Branch Dominance," in Paul G. Harris (ed.) *The Environment, International Relations, and US Foreign Policy*, Washington, DC: Georgetown University Press.

Barkdull, John and Harris, Paul G. (2002) "Environmental Change and Foreign Policy: A Survey of Theory," *Global Environmental Politics*, 2(2): 63–91.

Barnett, Jon (2001) "Environmental Security and US Foreign Policy: A Critical Examination," in Paul G. Harris (ed.) *The Environment, International Relations, and US Foreign Policy*, Washington, DC: Georgetown University Press.

Below, Amy (2008) "US Presidential Decisions on Ozone Depletion and Climate Change: A Foreign Policy Analysis," *Foreign Policy Analysis*, 4(1): 1–20.

Benedick, Richard Elliot (1989) "US Environmental Policy: Relevance to Europe," *International Environmental Affairs*, 1(2): 91–102.

—— (1991) *Ozone Diplomacy: New Directions in Safeguarding the Planet*, Cambridge, MA: Harvard University Press.

Betsill, Michele (2000) "The United States and the Evolution of International Climate Change Norms," in Paul G. Harris (ed.) *Climate Change and American Foreign Policy*, New York: St. Martin's Press.

Bierman, Frank and Dingwerth, Klaus (2004) "Global Environmental Change and the Nation State," *Global Environmental Politics*, 4(1): 1–22.

Boas, Morten (2001) "Multilateral Development Banks, Environmental Impact Assessments, and Nongovernmental Organizations in US Foreign Policy," in Paul G. Harris (ed.) *The Environment, International Relations, and US Foreign Policy*, Washington, DC: Georgetown University Press.

Brown, Lester R. (2000) "Challenges of the New Century," in Linda Starke (ed.) *State of the World 2000*, New York and London: W. W. Norton & Company.

Bryner, Gary (2000) "Congress and the Politics of Climate Change," in Paul G. Harris (ed.) *Climate Change and American Foreign Policy*, New York: St. Martin's Press.

Caldwell, Lynton K. (1990) "International Environmental Politics: America's Response to Global Imperatives," in Norman J. Vig and Michael E. Kraft (eds) *Environmental Policy in the 1990s*, Washington, DC: CQ Press.

Carroll, John E. (1986) "Water Resources Management as an Issue in Environmental Diplomacy," *Natural Resources Journal*, 26(2): 207–20.

—— (1992) "Environment, Free Trade, and US–Canada Relations," in Jonathan Lemco (ed.) *The Canada–United States Relationship: The Politics of Energy and Environmental Coordination*, Westport, CT: Praeger.

Chaterjee, Pratap and Finger, Matthias (1994) *The Earth Brokers*, London: Routledge.

Crocker, David A. and Linden, Toby (1998) *The Ethics of Consumption: The Good Life, Justice, and Global Stewardship*, New York: Rowman and Littlefield.

Crowley, Kate (2007) "Is Australia Faking It? The Kyoto Protocol and the Greenhouse Policy Challenge," *Global Environmental Politics*, 7(4): 118–39.

Dalby, Simon (2004) "Ecological Politics, Violence, and the Theme of Empire," *Global Environmental Politics*, 4(2): 1–11.

DeSombre, Elizabeth (2000) *Domestic Sources of International Environmental Policy: Industry, Environmentalists, and US Power*, Cambridge, MA: MIT Press.

Deudney, Daniel (1990) "The Case Against Linking Environmental Degradation and National Security," *Millennium: Journal of International Studies*, 19: 461–76.

Deudney, Daniel and Matthew, Richard A. (eds) (1999) *Contested Ground: Security and Conflict in the New Environmental Politics*, Albany, NY: State University of New York Press.

Dimitrov, Radoslav S. (2005) "Hostage to Norms: States, Institutions and Global Forest Politics," *Global Environmental Politics*, 5(4): 1–24.

Doran, Peter (2000) "Upholding the 'Island of High Modernity': The Changing Climate of American Foreign Policy," in Paul G. Harris (ed.) *Climate Change and American Foreign Policy*, New York: St. Martin's Press.

Elman, Colin (1996) "Horses for Courses: Why Not Neorealist Theories of Foreign Policy?" *Security Studies*, 6(1): 7–53.

Emmanuel, Jorge (1990) "Environmental Destruction Caused by US Military Bases and the Serious Implications for the Philippines," *World Bulletin*, 6(2, 3, and 4): 18–62.

Fairbrass, Jenny and Jordan, Andrew (2001) "European Union Environmental Policy and the UK Government: A Passive Observer or a Strategic Manager?" *Environmental Politics*, 10(2): 1–21.

Falkner, Robert (2001) "Business Conflict and US International Environmental Policy: Ozone, Climate, and Biodiversity," in Paul G. Harris (ed.) *The Environment, International Relations, and US Foreign Policy*, Washington, DC: Georgetown University Press.

Finnemore, Martha (1996) *National Interests in International Society*, Ithaca, NY: Cornell University Press.

Foster, John Bellamy (2000) "Capitalism's Environmental Crisis: Is Technology the Answer?" *Monthly Review*, 52(7): 1–13.

—— (2007) "The Ecology of Destruction," *Monthly Review*, 58(8). Online. Available at: http://www.monthlyreview.org/0207jbf.htm.

Gedicks, Al (1993) *The New Resource Wars: Native and Environmental Struggles Against Multinational Corporations*, Boston: South End Press.

Goldsmith, Edward (1996) "Global Trade and the Environment," in Jerry Mander and Edward Goldsmith (eds) *The Case Against the Global Economy*, San Francisco: Sierra Club Books.

Goldstein, Judith and Keohane, Robert O. (1993) "Ideas and Foreign Policy: An Analytical Framework," in Judith Goldstein and Robert O. Keohane (eds) *Ideas and Foreign Policy: Beliefs, Institutions, and Political Change*, Ithaca, NY: Cornell University Press.

Gore, Al (1992) *Earth in the Balance: Ecology and the Human Spirit*, New York: Houghton Mifflin.

Greenberg, Nadivah (2006) "Shop Right: American Conservatisms, Consumption, and the Environment," *Global Environmental Politics*, 6(2): 85–111.

Haas, Peter M. (1990) *Saving the Mediterranean: The Politics of International Environmental Cooperation*, New York: Columbia University Press.

Harris, Paul G. (ed.) (2000a) *Climate Change and American Foreign Policy*, New York: St. Martin's Press.

—— (2000b) "International Norms of Responsibility and US Climate Change Policy," in Paul G. Harris (ed.) *Climate Change and American Foreign Policy*, New York: St. Martin's Press.

—— (2001a) "International Environmental Affairs and US Foreign Policy," in Paul G. Harris (ed.) *The Environment, International Relations, and US Foreign Policy*, Washington, DC: Georgetown University Press.

—— (2001b) *International Equity and Global Environmental Politics: Power and Principles in US Foreign Policy*, Aldershot: Ashgate.

—— (ed.) (2001c) *The Environment, International Relations, and US Foreign Policy*, Washington, DC: Georgetown University Press.

—— (2002) *International Environmental Cooperation: Politics and Diplomacy in Pacific Asia*, Boulder, CO: University Press of Colorado.

—— (2003) *Global Warming and East Asia: The Domestic and International Politics of Climate Change*, London: Routledge.

—— (2004) "International Development Assistance and Burden Sharing," in Norman J. Vig and Michael Faure (eds) *Green Giants: Environmental Policy of the United States and the European Union*, Cambridge, MA: MIT Press.

—— (ed.) (2005) *Confronting Environmental Change in East and Southeast Asia: Eco-Politics, Foreign Policy, and Sustainable Development*, London: Earthscan/United Nations University Press.

—— (2007a) *Europe and Global Climate Change: Politics, Foreign Policy, and Regional Cooperation*, Cheltenham: Edward Elgar.

—— (2007b) "Sharing the Burdens of Global Climate Change: International Equity and Justice in European Policy," in Paul G. Harris (ed.) *Europe and Global Climate Change: Politics, Foreign Policy, and Regional Cooperation*, Cheltenham: Edward Elgar.

Harrison, Kathryn (2007) "The Road Not Taken: Climate Change Policy in Canada and the United States," *Global Environmental Politics*, 7(4): 92–117.

Harrison, Kathryn and Sundstrom, Lisa McIntosh (2007) "The Comparative Politics of Climate Change," *Global Environmental Politics*, 7(4): 1–18.

Harrison, Neil E. (2000) "From the Inside Out: Domestic Influences on Global Environmental Policy," in Paul G. Harris (ed.) *Climate Change and American Foreign Policy*, New York: St. Martin's Press.

Hart, Paul, Stern, Eric K. and Sundelius, Bengt (eds) (1997) *Beyond Groupthink: Political Group Dynamics and Foreign Policy-Making*, Ann Arbor, MI: University of Michigan Press.

Hasenclever, Andreas, Mayer, Peter and Rittberger, Volker (1997) *Theories of International Regimes*, Cambridge: Cambridge University Press.

Henry, Laura A. and Sundstrom, Lisa McIntosh (2007) "Russia and the Kyoto Protocol," *Global Environmental Politics*, 7(4): 47–69.

Hollis, Martin and Smith, Steve (1991) *Explaining and Understanding International Relations*, New York: Oxford University Press.

Homer-Dixon, Thomas (1993) *Environmental Scarcity and Global Security*, Headline Series No. 300, New York: Foreign Policy Association.

Hopgood, Stephen (1998) *American Foreign Environmental Policy and the Power of the State*, New York: Oxford University Press.

Hovi, Jon, Skodvin, Tora and Andresen, Steinar (2003) "The Persistence of the Kyoto Protocol: Why Other Annex I Countries Move on Without the United States," *Global Environmental Politics*, 3(4): 1–23.

Hunt, Michael (1987) *Ideology and US Foreign Policy*, New Haven, CT: Yale University Press.

Hunter, David (2000) "Global Environmental Protection in the Twenty-First Century," in Martha Honey and Tom Barry (eds) *Global Focus: US Foreign Policy at the Turn of the Millennium*, New York: Palgrave.

Huston, Raymon (1999) "Can Water Start a Fire? An Analysis of International Water Conflicts," doctoral dissertation, Texas Tech University.

Ikenberry, G. John, Lake, David A. and Mastanduno, Michael (eds) (1988) *The State and American Foreign Economic Policy*, Ithaca, NY: Cornell University Press.

Jackson, Robert H. (1993) "The Weight of Ideas in Decolonization: Normative Change in International Relations," in Judith Goldstein and Robert O. Keohane (eds) *Ideas and Foreign Policy: Beliefs, Institutions, and Political Change*, Ithaca, NY: Cornell University Press.

Janicke, Martin and Jacob, Klaus (2004) "Lead Markets for Environmental Innovations," *Global Environmental Politics*, 4(1): 29–46.

Janus, Irving L. (1972) *Victims of Groupthink: A Psychological Study of Foreign Policy*, Boston: Houghton Mifflin.

Jervis, Robert (1976) *Perception and Misperception in International Politics*, Princeton, NJ: Princeton University Press.

Jordan, Andrew (2001) "National Environmental Ministries: Managers or Ciphers of European Union Environmental Policy?" *Public Administration*, 79(3): 643–63.

Kameyama, Yasuko (2003) "Climate Change as Japanese Foreign Policy: From Reactive to Proactive," in Paul G. Harris (ed.) *Global Warming and East Asia*, London: Routledge.

Karkkainen, Bradley C. (2004) "Post-Sovereign Environmental Governance," *Global Environmental Politics*, 4(1): 72–96.

Klare, Michael T. (2004) *Blood and Oil: The Dangers and Consequences of America's Growing Petroleum Dependency*, New York: Metropolitan Books.

Klare, Michael and Volman, Daniel (2006) "America, China and the Scramble for Africa's Oil," *Review of African Political Economy*, 33(108): 297–309.

Lake, David A. (1988) "The State and American Trade Strategy in the Pre-Hegemonic Era," in John Ikenberry, David A. Lake and Michael Mastanduno (eds) *The State and American Foreign Economic Policy*, Ithaca, NY: Cornell University Press.

Lerner, Sally (1986) "Environmental Constituency-Building: Local Initiatives and Volunteer Stewardship," *Alternatives*, 13(3): 55–60.

Levy, David L. and Newell, Peter (2000) "Oceans Apart? Business Responses to Global Environmental Issues in Europe and the United States," *Environment*, 42 (9): 8–20.

Litfin, Karen T. (1993) *Ozone Discourses: Science and Politics in Global Environmental Cooperation*, New York: Columbia University Press.

—— (ed.) (1998) *The Greening of Sovereignty in World Politics*, Cambridge, MA: MIT Press.

M'Gonigle, R. Michael and Zacher, Mark W. (1979) *Pollution, Politics, and International Law: Tankers at Sea*, Berkeley, CA: University of California Press.

Mathews, Jessica Tuchman (1989) "Redefining Security," *Foreign Affairs*, Spring: 162–77.

McAlpine, Jan C. and LeDonne, Pat (1993) "The United States Government, Public Participation, and Trade and Environment," in Durwood Zaelke, Paul Orbuch, and Robert F. Housman (eds) *Trade and the Environment: Law, Economics, and Policy*, Washington, DC: Island Press.

Missbach, Andreas (2000) "Regulation Theory and Climate Change Policy," in Paul G. Harris (ed.) *Climate Change and American Foreign Policy*, New York: St. Martin's Press.

Morgenthau, Hans J. (1985) *Politics Among Nations*, revised by Kenneth W. Thompson, New York: McGraw-Hill.

Moser, Susanne C. (2007) "In the Long Shadows of Inaction: The Quiet Building of a Climate Protection Movement in the United States," *Global Environmental Politics*, 7(2): 124–44.

Muir, John (1997) *John Muir: Nature Writings*, ed. William Cronon, New York: Library of America.

Mumme, Stephen P. (1984) "The Cananea Copper Controversy: Lessons for Environmental Diplomacy," *Inter-American Economic Affairs*, 38(1): 3–22.

Muñoz, Heraldo (1997) "Free Trade and Environmental Policies: Chile, Mexico, and Venezuela," in Gordon J. MacDonald, Daniel L. Nielson, and Marc A. Stern (eds) *Latin American Environmental Policy in International Perspective*, Boulder, CO: Westview Press.

Myers, Norman (1987) *Not Far Afield: US Interests and the Global Environment*, New York: World Resources Institute.

Ohta, Hiroshi (2005) "Japan and Global Climate Change: The Intersection of Domestic Politics and Diplomacy," in Paul G. Harris (ed.) *Confronting Environmental Change in East and Southeast Asia*, London: Earthscan.

Paarlberg, Robert (1997) "Earth in Abeyance: Explaining Weak Leadership in US International Environmental Policy," in Robert J. Lieber (ed.) *Eagle Adrift: American Foreign Policy at the End of the Century*, New York: Longman.

—— (1999) "Lapsed Leadership: US International Environmental Policy Since Rio," in Norman J. Vig and Regina S. Axelrod (eds) *The Global Environment: Institutions, Law, and Policy*, Washington, DC: CQ Press.

Pinchot, Gifford (1998) *Breaking New Ground*, Washington, DC: Island Press.

Princen, Thomas and Finger, Matthias (eds) (1994) *Environmental NGOs in World Politics*, London: Routledge.

Putnam, Robert D. (1988) "Diplomacy and Domestic Politics: The Logic of Two-Level Games," *International Organization*, 42(3): 427–60.

Rinehart, James (1996) "The Ideology of Competitiveness: Pitting Worker Against Worker," in Kevin Danaher (ed.) *Corporations are Gonna Get Your Mama*, Monroe, ME: Common Courage Press.

Roberts, J. Timmons, Parks, Bradley C. and Vasquez, Alexis A. (2004) "Who Ratifies Environmental Treaties and Why? Institutionalism, Structuralism and Participation by 192 Nations in 22 Treaties," *Global Environmental Politics*, 4(3): 22–63.

Ruggie, John Gerard (1998) *Constructing the World Polity*, London: Routledge.

Schwartz, Alan M. (1992) "Great Lakes, Great Rhetoric," in Jonathan Lemco (ed.) *Tensions at the Border: Energy and Environmental Concerns in Canada and the United States*, New York: Praeger.

Shaffer, Martin B. (1995) "An Aerial Photograph of Presidential Leadership: President Carter's National Energy Plan Revisited," *Presidential Studies Quarterly*, 35(2): 287–99.

Shiva, Vandana (1997) *Biopiracy: The Plunder of Nature and Knowledge*, Boston: South End Press.

Skolnikoff, Eugene B. (1990) "The Policy Gridlock on Global Warming," *Foreign Policy*, 79: 77–93.

—— (1995) "Science and Technology: The Sources of Change," in Nazli Choucri (ed.) *Global Accord*, Cambridge, MA: The MIT Press.

Smith, Zachary A. (1992) *The Environmental Policy Paradox*, Englewood Cliffs, NJ: Prentice Hall.

Soden, Dennis L. (ed.) (1999) *The Environmental Presidency*, Albany, NY: State University Press of New York.

Spiller, Judith and Rieser, Allison (1986) "Scientific Fact and Value in US Ocean Dumping Policy," *Policy Studies Review*, 6(2): 389–98.

Springer, Allen L. (1988) "United States Environmental Policy and International Law: Stockholm Principle 21 Revisited," in John E. Carroll (ed.) *International Environmental Diplomacy*, Cambridge: Cambridge University Press.

Sprinz, Detlef and Vaahtoranta, Tapani (1994) "The Interest-Based Explanation of International Environmental Policy," *International Organization*, 48(1): 77–105.

Switzer, Jacqueline Vaughn (2001) *Environmental Politics: Domestic and Global Dimensions*, 3rd edn, New York: Bedford/St. Martin's.

Tabb, William K. (2007), "Resource Wars," *Monthly Review*, 58(7). Online. Available at: http://www.monthlyreview.org/0107tabb.htm.

Tiberghien, Yves and Schreurs, Miranda A. (2007) "High Noon in Japan: Embedded Symbolism and Post-2001 Kyoto Protocol Politics," *Global Environmental Politics*, 7(4): 70–91.

Tir, Jaroslav and Diehl, Paul F. (2001) "Demographic Pressure and Interstate Conflict," in Paul F. Diehl and Nils Peter Gleditsch (eds) *Environmental Conflict*, Boulder, CO: Westview Press.

Trittin, Jürgen (2004) "The Role of the Nation State in International Environmental Policy," *Global Environmental Politics*, 4(1): 23–8.

Viotti, Paul R. and Kauppi, Mark V. (1999) *International Relations Theory: Realism, Pluralism, Globalism, and Beyond*, Boston: Allyn and Bacon.

Waltz, Kenneth N. (1979) *Theory of International Politics*, Reading, MA: Addison-Wesley.

—— (1996) "International Politics is Not Foreign Policy," *Security Studies*, 6(1): 54–7.

Wapner, Paul (1996) *Environmental Activism and World Civic Politics*, Albany, NY: SUNY Press.

—— (1995) "Politics Beyond the State: Environmental Activism and World Civic Politics," *World Politics*, 47(3): 311–40.

Weinthal, Erika and Parag, Yael (2003) "Two Steps Forward, One Step Backward: Societal Capacity and Israel's Implementation of the Barcelona Convention and the Mediterranean Action Plan," *Global Environmental Politics*, 3(1): 51–71.

Wendt, Alexander (1999) *Social Theory of International Politics*, Cambridge: Cambridge University Press.

Yandle, Bruce (1993) "Bootleggers and Baptists: Environmentalists and Protectionists–Old Reasons for New Coalitions," in Terry L. Anderson (ed.) *NAFTA and the Environment*, San Francisco, CA: Pacific Research Institute for Public Policy.

# 3 The symbolism of environmental policy

## Foreign policy commitments as signaling tools

*Loren R. Cass*

Environmental foreign policy is fraught with examples of states rhetorically affirming international action to address environmental threats and accepting international commitments that are never met in practice. This situation raises troubling questions for the study of environmental foreign policy and compliance with international environmental commitments. This is particularly true in the case of developed states, which typically possess the resources to comply with international agreements if there is sufficient political will. The foreign policy establishments of states value national reputations for fulfilling international obligations. Most states are thus reluctant to take on commitments that cannot be met. Given this general tendency to fulfill international obligations, why have developed states been willing to undertake environmental commitments without fulfilling them?

One frequent explanation for failure to fulfill commitments is that governments undertake international obligations in good faith but then fail to fulfill them due to domestic political obstacles to implementation (Levy *et al.* 1993: 404–8; VanDeveer 2005). While this is certainly true in many cases, this chapter argues that governments frequently utilize environmental foreign policy as a symbolic tool to manage international identities in the eyes of both domestic and international constituencies. "Social identities are sets of meanings that an actor attributes to itself while taking the perspective of others, as a social object" (Wendt 1994: 385). States have a social identity that encompasses a self-understanding of the role and purpose of the state (Reus-Smit 1999, 22). This identity operates at two interconnected levels. Domestically, a state's identity emerges from the history, values, and political culture of the state. However, state identities are also projected into the international system and are shaped in reference to other actors and institutions in that system, which in turn feeds back into the domestic identity of the state (Wendt 1999: 224). National identities are maintained and evolve in response to government action and rhetoric, which then stimulates feedback from other actors both domestically and internationally, which continues to shape the national identity.

The concept of "legitimacy" is closely linked to the identity of the state as an actor at both the domestic and international levels. For a government to rule effectively domestically it must either be perceived as legitimate by a substantial majority of the population or be capable of imposing its will through force to maintain control. The voluntary compliance with the law associated with the perception of legitimacy is much cheaper for governments than the constant threat and use of force. Governments thus value the domestic perception of legitimacy.

Legitimacy is also linked to the identity of the state at the international level. Ian Clark provides the most definitive discussion of the concept of legitimacy in international relations (2005). A full elaboration of the theoretical understanding of legitimacy is beyond the scope of this chapter, but a brief description of the relationship between international norms and legitimacy is necessary. As Clark notes, "Legitimacy possesses no independent normative context of its own" (ibid.: 207). A consensus on the appropriate norms to govern behavior in the international system provides the framework for states to be accepted as legitimate within the system. At the international level, the perception of legitimacy, or what some authors refer to as a state's status or reputation, by other states is critical to the effective pursuit of foreign policy objectives (Johnston 2001: 501–2). Cooperation and compromise are much easier to achieve when states view one another as legitimate members of the international community that share a common set of values and norms. It is thus essential for governments to maintain identities as legitimate actors to secure their interests. Legitimacy is inherently a social concept. It is the acceptance of the state's identity, interests, and actions as appropriate by those affected by the state's actions (Reus-Smit 2007: 158–9). As Reus-Smit notes, "Actors establish their legitimacy, and the legitimacy of their actions, through the rhetorical construction of self-images and the public justification of priorities and practices, and other actors contest or endorse these representations through similar rhetorical processes" (ibid.: 163).

Legitimacy in the current international system is tied to a state's acceptance of a range of international norms associated with liberal democratic states (Clark 2005). States that do not affirm these norms are viewed with greater suspicion and find it more difficult to convince others of the rectitude of their foreign policy positions and will have greater difficulty achieving their national interests. Governments therefore have an incentive to affirm liberal international norms to cultivate an identity as a legitimate international actor even though the government may have no intention of fulfilling the behavioral changes associated with the norm. This is a form of symbolic politics, which will be discussed in greater detail below.

The character of environmental politics makes it particularly conducive to symbolic politics. Liberalism's focus on the rights of the individual and restraint of government power has increasingly been supplemented by the inclusion of environmental protection as a state obligation. Affirmation of sustainable development as a core economic and environmental objective of the state has increasingly become associated with acceptance as a legitimate state within the international community; thus, states face pressure to affirm norms related to sustainability.

Environmental policy is also ripe for symbolic politics because enforcement mechanisms in environmental agreements have been lax, and the second tier diplomatic status of most environmental issues has meant that states are unlikely to face substantial political or economic costs or military consequences from failure to fulfill international environmental commitments. States can thus more easily take on environmental commitments without fearing the consequences of failure to meet those commitments. These issues will be taken up in greater detail below, but the important point is that the nature of environmental policy creates incentives for states to pursue symbolic environmental politics. The focus of this chapter is on how symbolic politics has affected the pursuit of environmental foreign policy and how this in turn has impacted the capacity for states to successfully address the environmental problems facing the international community.

This chapter falls within the "Ideas" column of the Barkdull and Harris matrix, but it does not fit neatly into a single level of analysis. The role of international state identities and related norms operate at the systemic level and fundamentally shape the definition of environmental foreign policy interests and their strategic pursuit. However, governments seek to establish state identities in the eyes of both domestic and international actors. State identities are shaped by societal values and norms and the tension between international norms and domestic norms can be problematic for environmental foreign policy. The evolution of state identities and the relationship between identities, norms, and foreign policy cannot be understood without reference to all three levels of analysis. It is often useful to analyze one level in isolation in studying a particular aspect of global environmental politics; however, the relationships among these ideational variables and environmental foreign policy is much more complicated and requires evaluating the influence of forces operating across multiple levels.

The chapter is organized into four sections. The first section explores the nature of symbolic politics and the forms that it may take in environmental foreign policy. The second section evaluates the reasons that environmental politics lend themselves to symbolic politics, and the third section briefly explores some examples of the use of symbolic politics to illustrate the arguments put forth in the first two sections of the chapter. Finally, the role of symbolic politics raises important questions related to environmental regime effectiveness. What is the effect of symbolic politics on efforts to address transnational environmental problems? Does the repeated rhetorical affirmation of a norm eventually produce compliance or does it provide a mechanism for sustained evasion of concrete actions while avoiding the challenge to legitimacy that would result from outright rejection of the relevant norms? These issues will be taken up in the conclusion.

## Identity, legitimacy, and environmental politics

The manner in which a state defines and pursues its national interests is dependent in part upon how the state constructs its social identities at the domestic and international levels. Emphasizing the social identities of states in the definition of national interests is not intended to minimize the critical importance of material forces and strategic choices shaping state interests and strategies (Finnemore and Sikkink 1998: 888–9). Rather, it is to recognize that social identities define the nature of actors and their understanding of their interests. The identity of a state is tied to issues of domestic and international legitimacy. Governments simultaneously seek to maintain identities as the legitimate authority over the territorial state and its people while cultivating identities as legitimate members of the international system (Jepperson *et al.* 1996: 59). The identities that the government seeks to cultivate may differ at each level, which makes it difficult for the state to manage its identity effectively. Reus-Smit captures the difficult balancing act that governments face in trying to manage national identities,

> rulers and governments have always faced the challenge of 'dual socialisation', the difficult task of balancing the normative imperatives of international society with personal predilections or domestic political demands as they go about defining national interests and pursuing their national and international policy agendas.
>
> (2002: 10)

The concept of "dual socialization" captures the simultaneous effects of domestic and international interactions on national identities.[1] Chapter 5 in this volume by Mayer and Arndt expands on this relationship.

In cultivating an identity as a legitimate domestic and international actor, governments will emphasize the most politically salient norms in their political communication. Actors typically justify their interests and strategies with reference to established norms and values. As Reus-Smit notes, "the reasons that carry the greatest weight in practical discourse are those that appeal to deep-rooted, collectively shared ideas that define what constitutes a legitimate social agent" (1999: 28). Increasingly, recognition as a legitimate state in the international system has been tied to acceptance of a range of international norms linked to liberal ideals. In particular, Sikkink argues that "those [norms] involving bodily integrity and prevention of bodily harm for vulnerable or 'innocent' groups, especially when there is a short causal chain between cause and effect" would be most effectively transmitted across states and cultures (1998: 520).

Framing norms in these terms is vital to achieving norm prominence, and affirming norms that are consistent with these values is an essential element of maintaining an identity as a legitimate, liberal, democratic state in today's international system. As Sikkink notes, "Human rights norms have a special status because they prescribe rules for appropriate behavior and they help define identities of liberal states" (ibid.: 520). Support for human rights norms has thus achieved a special standing as an indicator of legitimacy for states. Governments that deny the sanctity of human rights law face ostracism and widespread condemnation that de-legitimizes the state at both the domestic and international levels. States may seek to challenge the dominant international norms and proffer alternative norms such as a stricter interpretation of the norm requiring non-interference in the internal affairs of states; however, as long as the dominant norms are broadly viewed as legitimate, the challenging state will be viewed with suspicion, and its status as a legitimate international actor will be weakened.

Arguably, support for norms related to international environmental issues has achieved prominence internationally similar to that accorded to human rights. The 1972 Stockholm Conference, the 1972 publication of the Club of Rome's *Limits to Growth*, the 1987 publication of *Our Common Future*, the 1992 and 2002 Earth Summits, among numerous other events and publications have produced a growing focus on "sustainable development" as the dominant paradigm for the pursuit of economic development consistent with the needs of future generations. Support for sustainable development has become one of the touchstones of maintaining a state's identity as a legitimate member of the society of liberal states. Debates abound regarding what it means in practice, but reference to sustainable development is essential to provide legitimacy to a proposed environmental policy and often to economic policy as well (Bernstein 2002).

The emphasis on sustainable development and the needs of developing countries makes it easier to frame global environmental problems as doing great damage to vulnerable populations around the world. Environmental NGOs have also sought to extend the emphasis to the natural world with a focus on vulnerable emblems of environmental degradation such as whales, polar bears, elephants, rain forests, coral reefs, etc. To cultivate an identity as a legitimate member of the international system, a government must typically affirm the need to address these problems. The need to accept action does not necessarily mean that governments will fulfill the domestic policy changes implied by those commitments. Environmental policies permit states to take these positions with the knowledge that international enforcement remains weak. As a characteristically secondary issue area in international relations, states can pursue environmental policies in opposition to dominant international actors without fear of significant retribution. Human rights and environmental politics thus provide opportunities for states to pursue policies to establish their identities as legitimate international actors without significant political costs. It also means that states can take on commitments or affirm international norms that they may not be able to fulfill without fear of significant retribution if they fail to live up to their commitments. This is a form of symbolic politics that will be discussed below.

## Symbolic environmental politics

In seeking to cultivate a particular national identity, states typically appeal to norms consistent with that identity. Symbolic politics can play an important role in demonstrating support for international norms and for managing a state's identity in the eyes of both its international partners and its domestic public. The concept of symbolic politics can be traced to Edelman (Edelman 1964). Symbolic politics can be defined

> as a political process, in which certain goals and measures are announced and enforced, which already at the very early stage of publication either represent sheer rhetoric and thus only target a signaling effect or are designed in such a way that these goals and measures should or could not be realized and implemented in the same way as they are announced.
>
> (Matten 2003: 216)

Blühdorn argues that there are two primary forms of symbolic politics that can be distinguished based upon the intent of the actors (2007: 254–7). The first form relates to the political use of symbols to communicate with other policy-makers and the broader public. This "progressive" form of symbolic politics helps actors to mobilize segments of society, to reduce the complexity of the issue being addressed, and to generate broader support for the policies advocated by the actor (ibid.: 254–6). "[S]ymbolic politics in this under-standing always entails the strategic construction of realities and manipulation of mass audiences" (ibid.: 256). At the international level, this strategy may be used to help establish an international identity with the intent of altering domestic policy and/or influencing international negotiations to convince the target audience of the need to change. In this sense, symbolic politics is a communication strategy that is indispensable to shaping the public and/or international debate on a given issue. Critically, the intent is to create momentum toward meeting commitments that are initially merely symbolic in nature.

The alternative form of symbolic politics is more insidious. In this form, symbolic politics represents the substitution of symbolic acts for real action. In other words, symbolic actions are undertaken not in an attempt to generate momentum toward action to address a problem but rather to deceive that audience and lead it to believe that actions are being undertaken to address a concern when in fact the symbolic actions will not have the stated or implied effect. This is the original form of symbolic politics that Edelman explored (1964). The two forms of symbolic politics have very different effects. The first form should provide increased support for action consistent with the symbolic position and ideally the symbolism will be replaced with concrete action. The second form is more likely to generate cynicism. Over time it could produce a backlash against the symbolism or it could subvert meaningful action over a long period of time.

Under what conditions will political actors pursue symbolic politics? Newig hypothesizes that four conditions tend to promote the use of symbolic measures (2007: 282–5). First, when there is high political pressures, decision-makers feel compelled to do something to address the problem. This creates a political incentive to utilize symbolic politics if there is not an obvious, uncontroversial policy response. Second, if the short-term costs of addressing the problem are high relative to the short-term benefits or if there are not any viable policy options available, decision-makers are likely to resort to symbolic politics. Third, higher levels of conflict within society will tend to promote symbolic legislation. Finally, greater complexity in an issue and asymmetrical availability of information tend to promote symbolic legislation (ibid.: 282–5).

Environmental policy is a particularly ripe field for the pursuit of symbolic politics because some combination of these conditions is frequently present. Many environmental problems generate strong public demands for action, but they also frequently involve substantial short-term costs to address them with often only long-term benefits. Costs are often concentrated on a small number of actors while the benefits are more diffuse. Most environmental issues are complex, involving substantial scientific and policy-related uncertainties. This complexity makes monitoring and compliance evaluation difficult. Thus, environmental issues by their very nature create incentives for the use of symbolic politics. In addition, the link between international environmental policy and the identities of states as legitimate members of the society of liberal democratic states creates an added incentive to utilize symbolic politics. The incentive to use environmental commitments to manage the state's identity along with the combination of the nature of environmental policy discussed above, the second tier status of environmental policy as a diplomatic issue, and the relative weakness of enforcement mechanisms make environmental foreign policy particularly conducive to symbolic politics.

In terms of environmental policy, there should be a small number of international environmental problems that create the greatest potential for symbolic action to shape state identities. Problems that are characterized by effects on a global scale should generate more attention than bilateral or regional problems and could thus be utilized effectively to alter a national identity. However, bilateral or regional problems may also generate symbolic politics if the target audience is regional or possibly domestic. Issues which are perceived to have the greatest effect on human health, particularly for vulnerable populations, should be ripe for symbolic politics. Problems related to species or ecosystems with high popular attachment should also be likely to be used for symbolic purposes. Based upon these criteria, a range of environmental problems would likely generate symbolic politics. Climate change, as a global threat with massive potential consequences for vulnerable populations around the world and substantial scientific and policy uncertainties, as well as potentially high costs to address the problem, should be a frequent candidate for symbolic politics. Biodiversity protection would also be a likely candidate for symbolic politics due to the popular image of many threatened species and ecosystems. To a lesser extent, acid rain, ozone depletion, water pollution, and hazardous waste disposal could also be open to their use in symbolic politics, though the effects are typically on a smaller scale, often with primarily bilateral or regional consequences, so they may be less useful for altering state identities. These issues should provide the cases to evaluate the effects of symbolic politics on environmental foreign policy.

## International norms and symbolic politics

The process of norm emergence entails competition among norm entrepreneurs advocating rival positions. During this process, states may assume competing positions in the normative debates. However, once a norm reaches a "tipping point" and a norm cascade begins, it becomes much more difficult for states to contest the legitimacy of the norm (Finnemore and Sikkink 1998: 901–3). There is a continuum of support for an emergent norm. At one end would be outright rejection. Rejection of a norm after it has achieved prominence is costly internationally in terms of the perception of legitimacy and would likely pose domestic legitimacy costs as well. Outright rejection of prominent international norms should be rare unless there are compelling domestic political reasons to justify the international costs of norm rejection. Along the continuum of norm support, the next stage would be governments that face compelling reasons for rejecting an international norm but for whom the international costs of rejection would be too high to accept. This is a perfect case for symbolic politics. The government may affirm the international norm – even in the face of substantial domestic opposition – but it does not intend to fulfill the policy changes consistent with the norm. This is an example of the more insidious form of symbolic politics. The government is seeking to avoid the condemnation associated with norm rejection while also avoiding the costs of fulfilling the practical consequences of norm acceptance. This situation presents an opportunity for at least short-term cultivation of an identity as a legitimate international actor. The question is whether this is sustainable over the longer term. Does the failure to fulfill the commitments associated with the norm eventually produce a backlash – either domestically or internationally – against the state's failure to uphold the commitments? The involvement of the Soviet Union and the East European states in the Long Range Transboundary Air Pollution Convention (LRTAP) as well as Japanese participation in the global whaling regime would appear to fit in this category.

The next stage along the continuum would be governments that support the international norm and would like to fulfill the international commitments but are unable to do so due to domestic political obstacles to implementation. This situation is also ripe for the use of symbolic politics, though the intent is to utilize symbolic politics to advance an agenda consistent with the international norm. The strategy is intended to build political support for future action and avoid international condemnation, though present domestic fulfillment of the commitments is not politically possible. European Union climate policy would appear to fit in this category.

The final point along the continuum would be full support for the international norm and implementation of the associated policy changes. There is no need for symbolic politics in this situation because the state's behavior is consistent with the international norm. The focus of symbolic politics is thus in the situations in which there is conflict between the domestic and international pressures for norm affirmation and the realities of domestic politics. The brief case studies in the next sections provide some insight into the nature of the symbolic politics in each situation.

### Insidious symbolic politics

States faced with the weakening of domestic or international legitimacy will seek opportunities to pursue policies to bolster their legitimacy. Symbolic politics may provide an opportunity to achieve this in the short term. States may rhetorically affirm emergent norms to curry favor at either the international or domestic levels. To the extent that the associated policy changes lack transparency or are sufficiently complex to make oversight difficult, the state may be able to rhetorically affirm the emergent norm without pursuing unwanted policy changes. There would appear to be a number of cases that would fit this profile.

The Long Range Transboundary Air Pollution Convention provides excellent examples of the use of symbolic politics to manage national identities. The origins of LRTAP were in the détente period of the Cold War when the Soviet Union pursued issues and forums to improve relations with the West. Following the 1975 Helsinki Conference, the Soviets sought to identify additional areas for cooperation that did not involve human rights or arms control. Both issues fit well with the dominant liberal norms of the West, and Soviet participation in these areas would bolster its legitimacy. However, the Soviet leadership was unwilling to pursue additional policies in either area (Levy 1993: 81).

Given the 1972 Stockholm Convention and the growing international interest in environmental policy, acid rain provided an opportunity for the Soviet leadership to align itself with the growing emphasis on environmental protection and avoid more difficult normative debates related to human rights. The Soviets were determined not to alter domestic policy, but their symbolic support for international action launched a process that over the subsequent thirty years has proved to be quite successful, though Russia's performance has not kept pace with the progress made by most of the rest of Europe. The Soviets hoped to cultivate a more legitimate international identity while in practice failing to fulfill the domestic responsibilities for change.

One of the norms that emerged in the LRTAP negotiations was that states should accept a commitment to reduce sulfur dioxide emissions by 30 per cent. The Soviets initially rejected this norm, but they reversed their position in 1984. The reason for the change was not a profound shift in Soviet thinking on acid rain; rather, it was a way to boost Soviet legitimacy and embarrass the United States which had rejected the norm (Sokolov and Jäger 2001: 143–4). Support for the 1988 nitrogen oxide protocol demonstrated similar logic as Russian experts declared that compliance was practically impossible (ibid.: 144).

The states of Eastern Europe also sought to use LRTAP immediately following the end of the Cold War to demonstrate their commitment to western norms and establish their worthiness for acceptance into the European Union. In evaluating Eastern European support for LRTAP, Munton *et al.* concluded that the Eastern states sought to demonstrate that "they [were] worthy partners for political and economic integration in Europe, and they calculated that supporting the LRTAP process [was] a good way to demonstrate this worthiness. There [was], however, little evidence of a deeper commitment than the symbolic" (1999: 193–4). The authors note that these states went on to sign the 1994 sulfur protocol "without any sense of what implementation measures would be required or how much such measures would cost" (ibid.: 194). The acceptance of LRTAP was intended to bolster an identity that was consistent with the dominant West European norms related to environmental protection, even though the governments did not have immediate plans to fulfill their commitments. Recession, restructuring, and EU membership have led to improvements in environmental performance, but it is difficult to determine the effects of earlier symbolic politics on subsequent performance.

Japanese participation in the international whaling regime is also emblematic of symbolic politics on two levels. First, Japanese opposition to the international whaling moratorium is largely directed at domestic audiences. Whaling is of limited economic significance for Japan today. However, Japanese politicians have highlighted their rejection of the moratorium as an effort to preserve part of Japan's cultural heritage and to prevent the western world from imposing its values on Japan (Hirata 2005). The active opposition to the International Whaling Commission (IWC) can thus create political benefits for Japanese politicians. However, Japan has not left the IWC. Instead, it has maintained its membership and justified its whaling as "scientific whaling," despite the fact that the several hundred whales that are harvested annually are processed and the meat sold in the marketplace. The IWC has severely limited Japanese whaling, but Japan has maintained its position within the IWC rather than leave it and face the overwhelming international condemnation and challenges to its international legitimacy that would accompany such a move. Japan has no intention of abiding by the preservationist norms of today's IWC. The IWC moratorium was agreed in 1982, and yet Japan has not ceased its whaling. In fact, Japan has been aggressively expanding its whale harvest in recent years. Does Japan's symbolic endorsement of the IWC and its associated norms matter? Can the whaling regime be effective in its efforts when key members undermine its legitimacy by violating the norms associated with the regime without substantial consequences?

### Positive symbolic politics

Even for governments that are supportive of an emerging international norm, the domestic political context may make it difficult for the state to fulfill the behavioral changes associated with the norm. Symbolic politics in this case can also be used effectively to build political support for future action, undermine opponents of policy changes, and create pressure on other states to support the emergent norm. The European Union has been particularly active in seeking to define its values in universal terms, extend them to the international system, and then pressure states to affirm its preferred norms.

Scholars of European foreign policy have increasingly focused on the role of the European Union as a "normative power," defined as an international actor capable of framing international opinion in a given issue area and convincing others of the rectitude of its understanding of the problem and its responses to the problem. It is the ability of an actor to shape conceptions of what is normal in international affairs (Manners 2002: 239). Normative powers are able to influence the values of other actors – not through military force or economic pressures – but rather through the appeal of the norms themselves (Diez 2005).

The European Union has been constructed in part by emphasizing a common set of norms that can bridge the differences across the member states. Manners has argued that this normative foundation predisposes the EU to pursue a normative foreign policy (2002: 252). The attempts to extend its norms to the international system further legitimate its identity as an actor in that system. In creating an identity for the EU in the international system, it has been useful to establish its identity as distinct from that of the "other" (Diez 2005). The European Union has often sought to highlight its differences with the United States across a range of issues and then emphasize that the European sponsored norms are not only different from norms favored by the US but also superior to them. The efforts to convince the United States of the errors of its ways and to stimulate domestic value changes further legitimates the European Union's position both internally and within the international system.

The EU has sought to construct an identity as a force for peace, respect for international law, and protection of human rights (Diez 2005: 634; Pace 2007). It has staked out its moral authority in opposition to perceived laggards. For example, the EU has been at the forefront of efforts to abolish the death penalty in contrast to other perceived laggards such as the United

States and China (Manners 2002). This is not a symbolic policy because the EU has fulfilled the behavioral changes associated with the norm by outlawing the death penalty, but it is consistent with the liberal international norms that the EU seeks to promote globally. The EU has been a prime supporter of the International Criminal Court and ratification of the Kyoto Protocol (Scheipers and Sicurelli 2007). In all of these cases, the EU has staked out its position as distinct from and superior to that of the United States and/or China, Russia, Turkey, etc. In doing so, it has also established the bar for other states to be considered legitimate actors in the international system. In establishing these "vanguard" positions, the European Union has placed implicit pressure upon other states that seek to be identified as legitimate liberal democratic states in the international system to affirm these positions.

The European Union's promotion of sustainable development has helped shape the EU's identity as a legitimate political actor at the forefront of international efforts to address global environmental problems (Manners 2002). It has shaped the EU's identity as distinct from and superior to the United States in environmental politics (Baker 2007). Climate change has provided a rich area for the EU to utilize symbolic politics to bolster its legitimacy across the EU and in the international system. The member states of the EU have been willing to give the Commission the mandate to negoti-ate on behalf of the member states. This mandate has permitted the Com-mission to stake out bold positions on behalf of the EU that have been supported by the European public, environmental NGOs, international institutions, and many other states. The Commission thus has an incentive to move aggressively in climate policy to bolster its legitimacy – even if many of the positions are symbolic in nature.

European leaders would undoubtedly object to the characterization of European climate policy positions as symbolic. However, it is clear that many of the EU positions have been undertaken in the knowledge that they would not be met in practice. This is not to argue that the EU is aggressively seeking to misrepresent its interests or that it is not committed to addressing climate change. Rather, the EU's policy is an example of the first form of symbolic politics. The EU is seeking to push policy in the direction of addressing climate change, and it has staked out leading positions to press other states to move beyond the status quo. However, the specific commitments are often more symbolic than real when they are announced.

There are many examples of the symbolic nature of European climate policy. One of the early norms to emerge in the climate negotiations was that all states should accept a carbon dioxide emission reduction commitment. One of the first manifestations of this norm was the United Nations Fra-mework Convention on Climate Change's objective for states to return domestic carbon dioxide emissions to 1990 levels by 2000. The EU enthusiasm for this norm belied the fact that only the United Kingdom and Germany were likely to achieve this objective – for reasons largely unrelated to climate policy.[2] However, the leadership position staked out by the EU provided a strong counterpoint to the US in the negotiations and generated support for actions to address climate change (Cass 2006: 149).

The European Union's position on the emission reduction commitment to be included in the Kyoto Protocol was also largely symbolic. The EU proposed a 15 per cent cut in emissions despite the difficult internal negotiations on how this commitment should be allocated across the member states. The internal burden sharing agreement could only agree on how to allocate a 10 per cent reduction, but the EU maintained its commitment to the 15 per cent proposal. Again, the aggressive – largely symbolic – position placed pressure on other states to increase their commitments. However, when the EU agreed to a 9 per cent emission reduction commitment at Kyoto, it led to a mad scramble by member states to reduce their individual contributions toward the common EU commitment (ibid.: 194–6). In the end, many of the individual states are still facing difficulty in meeting their commitments as they have struggled to agree on meaningful policies to meet the emission reductions at the EU level. The EU's role in advancing the climate negotiations is well documented. Does it matter that some of the EU's positions represent symbolic politics? In part, the answer depends on how the EU's policies evolve. It is too early to judge the EU's performance, but presumably substantial progress toward meeting the EU's stated positions will be necessary to avoid charges of hypocrisy and a loss of legitimacy at both the internal and international levels.

## Conclusion

The focus on symbolic politics highlights the importance of the "Ideas" column in the Barkdull and Harris matrix. The brief case studies illustrate the ways in which ideational variables have shaped environmental foreign policy across all three levels of analysis – system, state, and society. The focus on symbolic politics also poses important questions related to regime effectiveness and the conduct of environmental foreign policy. The two forms of symbolic politics have the potential to have very different impacts on environmental foreign policy. If states can effectively avoid adverse political consequences by engaging in the symbolic support for international norms without fulfilling their obligations, there is a risk that environmental commitments will go unmet and regime effectiveness will suffer. The brief case studies suggest that this is indeed a problem. However, if the long-term affirmation of the appropriateness of the international norms creates sufficient tension with the lack of observed behavioral change, then perhaps there is the potential to force policy changes over time. This also creates questions surrounding enforcement mechanisms and oversight of state behavior.

Currently, enforcement mechanisms remain weak in the area of environmental politics. The situation has been created by precisely those states that were unwilling to block international agreements but also feared that they would be unable or perhaps were unwilling from the beginning to fulfill their treaty commitments. The stripping away of enforcement mechanisms at the Marrakech meeting to finalize the Kyoto Protocol is indicative of this situation. In light of weak enforcement mechanisms, can international institutional or nongovernmental oversight provide shaming mechanisms to force states to move beyond symbolic commitments? The high profile climate negotiations will provide a test of the effectiveness of attempts at shaming. The United States, Canada, and Australia, among others, face considerable international and domestic pressure to meet their climate commitments. Are there ways to improve oversight and expand public awareness of state failure to act? These are some of the questions that need to be addressed related to how to transform symbolic politics into concrete action.

The more positive form of symbolic politics also raises important questions. Do symbolic commitments intended to rally public support for a cause, to create pressure for other states to support the cause, and to create momentum for action work in practice? Certainly, it is conceivable that these efforts can transform what may initially reflect symbolic politics into concrete action, but it is also possible that this approach can generate a backlash of cynicism that could undermine support for the desired action. The European Union's climate policy has indeed led to an expansion in the number and complexity of EU measures to address climate change. On the other hand, the Canadian government's consistent advocacy of action has produced little beyond additional symbolic politics. The case studies are suggestive, but there has been little empirical study of the long-term effects of symbolic politics on state behavior.

## Notes

1 Domestic values and identities are also a source of conflict within the state. Various groups seek to increase the political salience and public acceptance of their preferred values, norms, and associated policy positions. This chapter touches upon these domestic conflicts and their relevance to environmental foreign policy, but the focus is on government attempts to utilize symbolic politics to manage the state's identity at the international and domestic levels. This is not meant to minimize the importance of domestic political conflict but rather to highlight the conditions under which governments will seek to utilize symbolic politics to manage the identity of the state.

2 German reunification and the closure of the most inefficient and polluting power plants and factories in the former East provided dramatic emission reductions for Germany as a whole despite the fact that West German emissions had not fallen significantly. British emissions declined rapidly as a result of the shift from coal to natural gas for electricity generation, which reflected broader political and economic changes in Britain rather than an attempt to reduce carbon dioxide emissions.

## References

Baker, Susan (2007) "Sustainable Development as Symbolic Commitment: Declaratory Politics and the Seductive Appeal of Ecological Modernisation in the European Union." *Environmental Politics,* 16(2): 297–317.

Bernstein, Steven (2002) "International Institutions and the Framing of Domestic Policies: The Kyoto Protocol and Canada's Response to Climate Change," *Policy Sciences,* 35(2): 203–36.

Blühdorn, Ingolfur (2007) "Sustaining the Unsustainable: Symbolic Politics and the Politics of Simulation." *Environmental Politics,* 16(2): 251–75.

Cass, Loren R. (2006) *The Failures of American and European Climate Policy: International Norms, Domestic Politics, and Unachievable Commitments,* Albany, NY: State University of New York Press.

Clark, Ian (2005) *Legitimacy in International Society,* New York: Oxford University Press.

Diez, Thomas (2005) "Constructing the Self and Changing Others: Reconsidering 'Normative Power Europe'," *Millennium: Journal of International Studies,* 33(3): 616–36.

Edelman, Murray J. (1964) *The Symbolic Uses of Politics,* Urbana, IL: University of Illinois Press.

Finnemore, Martha and Sikkink, Kathryn (1998) "International Norm Dynamics and Political Change," *International Organization,* 52(4): 887–917.

Hirata, Keiko (2005) "Why Japan Supports Whaling," *Journal of International Wildlife Law and Policy,* 8(2–3): 129–49.

Jepperson, Ronald L. *et al.* (1996) "Norms, Identity, and Culture in National Security," in Peter J. Katzenstein (ed.) *The Culture of National Security: Norms and Identity in World Politics,* New York: Columbia University Press, pp. 33–75.

Johnston, Alastair Iain (2001) "Treating International Institutions as Social Environments," *International Studies Quarterly,* 45(4): 487–515.

Levy, Marc A. (1993) "European Acid Rain: The Power of Tote-Board Diplomacy," in Peter M. Haas, Robert O. Keohane, and Marc A. Levy (eds) *Institutions for the Earth: Sources of Effective International Environmental Protection,* Cambridge, MA: MIT Press, pp. 75–132.

Levy, Marc A. *et al.* (1993) "Improving the Effectiveness of International Environmental Institutions," in Peter M. Haas, Robert O. Keohane, and Marc A. Levy (eds) *Institutions for the Earth: Sources of Effective International Environmental Protection,* Cambridge, MA: MIT Press, pp. 397–426.

Manners, Ian (2002) "Normative Power Europe: A Contradiction in Terms?" *Journal of Common Market Studies,* 40(2): 235–58.

Matten, Dirk (2003) "Symbolic Politics in Environmental Regulation: Corporate Strategic Responses," *Business Strategy and the Environment,* 12: 215–26.

Munton, Don *et al.* (1999) "Acid Rain in Europe and North America," in Oran R. Young (ed.) *The Effectiveness of International Environmental Regimes: Causal Connections and Behavioral Mechanisms,* Cambridge, MA: MIT Press, pp. 155–248.

Newig, Jens (2007) "Symbolic Environmental Legislation and Societal Self-Deception," *Environmental Politics,* 16(2): 276–96.

Pace, Michelle (2007) "The Construction of EU Normative Power," *JCMS: Journal of Common Market Studies,* 45(5): 1041–64.

Reus-Smit, Christian (1999) *The Moral Purpose of the State: Culture, Social Identity, and Institutional Rationality in International Relations,* Princeton, NJ: Princeton University Press.

—— (2002) "Lost at Sea: Australia in the the Turbulence of World Politics," Australian National University Working Paper 2002/4, Canberra: ANU.

—— (2007) "International Crises of Legitimacy," *International Politics,* 44: 157–74.

Scheipers, Sibylle and Sicurelli, Daniela (2007) "Normative Power Europe: A Credible Utopia?" *JCMS: Journal of Common Market Studies,* 45(2): 435–57.

Sikkink, Kathryn (1998) "Transnational Politics, International Relations Theory, and Human Rights," *PS: Political Science and Politics,* 31(3): 517–24.

Sokolov, Vassily and Jäger, Jill (2001) "Turning Points: The Management of Global Environmental Risks in the Former Soviet Union," *Learning to Manage Global Environmental Risks,* vol. 1, *A Comparative History of Social Responses to Climate Change, Ozone Depletion, and Acid Rain,* Cambridge, MA: MIT Press, pp. 139–66.

VanDeveer, Stacy D. (2005) "Effectiveness, Capacity Development and International Environmental Cooperation," in Peter Dauvergne (ed.) *Handbook of Global Environmental Politics,* Northampton, MA: Edward Elgar, pp. 95–110.

Wendt, Alexander (1994) "Collective Identity Formation and the International State," *American Political Science Review,* 88(2): 384–96.

—— (1999) *Social Theory of International Politics,* New York: Cambridge University Press.

# 4 Pluralistic politics and public choice

## Theories of business and government responses to climate change

*Thomas L. Brewer*

Two political-economy theories – the "pluralistic politics" theory and the "public choice" theory – can advance the theoretical literature of environmental policy-making by revealing how the political economy of governmental institutions and policy processes affects the strategic agendas and choices of businesses, as well as their political activities. The theories focus on key features of businesses' strategic behavior – namely, it is driven by *economic interests*, and it is developed and implemented in the context of *political institutions*. Both theories contribute to an understanding of businesses' strategic behavior by linking the micro and macro levels of analysis.

This chapter reports quantitative data and cases about businesses' responses to climate change issues to illustrate propositions derived from the theories. In the context of the principal concerns of this book, therefore, I examine domestic institutional determinants of responses to the environmental problem of climate change. My specific focus is business–government interactions. I thus aim to contribute to our understanding of environmental foreign policy by focusing on the role of business and government actions and their interactions, within an analytic framework that combines micro-level and macro-level concerns. See Chapter 2 by Barkdull and Harris in this volume for a broader theoretical approach.

I do not present definitive "tests" of the theories in the most rigorous sense of that term; rather, I present the theories as complementary theoretical perspectives which offer useful conceptualizations, insights and propositions about how businesses deal with the issues associated with global warming. The analysis uses both data and cases to indicate how the theories can be applied. I thus seek to advance both the conceptual literature about environmental foreign policy-making in general and the empirical-case literature on US responses to climate change issues in particular.

## Overview of the theories

I use the term "pluralistic politics theory" to refer to a body of literature, particularly about the US political system, but also more generally about economically pluralistic and democratic countries. Issues regarding the *political-institutional context* of businesses' behavior are central to the *pluralistic politics theory*. A diverse economic system is assumed to create multiple interests along industry lines and regional lines. Numerous organized interest groups, representing conflicting interests in the political system, share power with governmental institutions in coalitions on particular issues. Government policies consist of compromises; policies are outcomes of a bargaining, consensus-building process, including many governmental, industry and other organizations with diverse interests. A business or industry rarely gets all of what it seeks on a particular issue, because it must compromise with other political actors representing conflicting interests.[1]

Environmental foreign policy, therefore, can be seen from this theoretical perspective as a compromise response to the diverse economic interests that are represented in a decentralized policy-making process. However, the interests and influence in the environmental foreign policy process are distinctive, as are the compromise outcomes. Such issue-specific patterns are taken into account in the pluralistic politics theory. In fact, a theme of that theoretical perspective is that business–government interactions and the influence of individual businesses and industry associations vary across issues. In order to determine the effects of government policy on business – or the effects of firms on government policy – in the context of the pluralistic politics theory, one must take into account the distribution of power across issues in a decentralized political system. The pluralistic politics theory assumes that interest groups are organized and politically active *across* institutional lines; such groups join coalitions involving executive and legislative actors, along with interest group organizations representing segments of industry and the public. The pluralistic politics theory further assumes that there are countervailing coalitions opposing one another on issues.

Much of the pluralistic politics literature has focused on the US. In addition to Harris (1998; 2000), see especially Bauer, Pool and Dexter (1972), Deardorf and Stern (1998), Destler (1995), and Destler and Balint (1999) on US trade policy-making. In a study of the effects of government "industrial" policies on firms' strategies and competitive positions, Murtha and Lenway (1994) include "pluralist private enterprise" as one type of "public/private political economic interest intermediation system," and they mention the UK, India, Canada and Italy, as well as the US, as examples. For early development of the intellectual underpinnings of the theory, see especially Bentley (1967), Dahl (1972), Schattschneider (1935), and Truman (1971).

The other theoretical perspective of the chapter – *public choice theory* – is closely associated with the names of a few scholars, particularly Buchanan and Tullock (1962), Downs (1957), and Olson (1965). The theory has been refined and applied by numerous scholars to diverse issues (Shepsley and Bonchek 1997; Weingast 1980). Applications to trade policy, for instance, include studies by Grossman and Helpman (1994) and Thornbecke (2000). Spar (2001: 221) has noted that the theory "rings true in many cases, especially those concerning the formation of trade policy in democratic states."

Other studies have applied the theory to environmental issues, for instance, Bohm and Russel (1985) and Dijkstra (1999). For applications to other issues and extensions of the theory, see Becker (1983), Brown (1974), and DeClercq (1996).

Businesses' economic interests and political activities are among the central concerns of public choice theory, and they are contrasted with the economic interests of consumers (i.e., the public) in several respects. The assumptions of the theory concerning economic interests can be highlighted as follows: The distributions of economic interests are asymmetric for producers and consumers; while they are highly concentrated for producers, they are widely dispersed for the public. Therefore, whereas producers have strong economic incentives to be politically active to protect their interests in profits and jobs, the public has only small, marginal interests in the form of incremental price differences and thus little incentive to be politically active.

There is consequently an asymmetry in the benefits of political activity. The greater marginal economic incentives of producers induce them to undertake individual and/or collective political action to achieve their objectives. There is also an asymmetry in the feasibility and costs of political activity, according to the public choice theory. It is easier and cheaper for producers than the public to organize for political action because there are relatively small numbers of producers. As a result, government policy tends to favor the narrow economic interests of producers over the wider interests of the public.

In the context of the public choice theory, then, an analyst begins with businesses' economic interests, and then determines how the asymmetry of economic interests affects its political activities and government policies – which in turn affect its interests. The public choice theory thus tends to emphasize enduring structural features of the political economy and the role of the economic interests of businesses.[2] In some public choice analyses, ideological, institutional and macro-economic considerations are also included (Thornbecke 2000: 85). The inclusion of such additional factors, of course, expands the analytic scope of the public choice theory beyond its core. However, it also distracts from the central insight of the theory – namely, *the existence and consequences of asymmetries in the interests and political activities of firms and the public*. Table 4.1 contains a comparative summary of the two theories.

## Data and case studies

The theories can be used to explain firms' responses to climate change issues and their interactions with government.[3] In particular, they can account for: variations in those responses among units within multinational corporations, variations among firms according to their home countries, variations within industries, and variations among industries. These data and case studies thus represent applications of both theories as explanations for numerous types of key variations in business responses to climate change issues.

*Table 4.1* Summary comparisons of theories

| Points of comparison | Theories | |
|---|---|---|
| | *Public choice* | *Pluralistic politics* |
| Firms' strategic interests | Economic interests, as reflected in shareholder stock value | Diverse economic and non-economic interests, as reflected in conflicting group preferences inside and outside the firm |
| Firms' strategic decision-making process | Analytic process of determining present value equivalents of expected future revenue and expense streams | Political process of building consensus among groups with conflicting preferences |
| Firms' role in government policy-making process | Revealing policy preferences to government officials | Building consensus with diverse political actors, which differ across issues and over time |
| Government policy outcomes in relation to firms' preferences | Consistent with firms' stated preferences and economic interests | Compromise outcomes of consensus-building |

### Conflicts in multinational corporations

Large multinational firms with affiliates in many countries are particularly prone to experience centrifugal tendencies as they try to adjust to foreign market and non-market conditions. This is a central theme of much of the international strategy literature based on the "global integration-local responsiveness" framework (Bartlett and Ghoshal 1989; Prahalad and Doz 1987; Tallman and Yip 2001; also see Boddewyn and Brewer 1994). In this framework, there are inherent tensions between the economic pressures on firms to globalize their operations in order to take advantage of economies of scale, on the one hand, and the political pressures exerted on firms by governments to be responsive to local political, cultural and economic conditions. Some firms conform more closely to the public choice theory of centralized control, while others conform more closely to the pluralistic politics theory of decentralized, conflicting groups, on the other.

### Hierarchical, globally integrated corporations

Corporations with centralized, hierarchical structures and strategies driven by concerns for global integration tend to adopt relatively monolithic approaches to global warming issues (as is consistent with the public choice theory). For instance, ExxonMobil prohibited officials of its European affiliates from attending climate change conferences for many years because their mere attendance would have undermined the parent corporation's position that global warming was not a problem.

### Decentralized, locally responsive corporations

Corporations with decentralized structures and strategies driven by responsiveness to localization pressures tend to adopt relatively varied approaches (which is consistent with the pluralistic politics theory). Cases that illustrate this tendency include a split between Volvo of Sweden and its US parent Ford. A high-level executive of Volvo announced that it still supported the Kyoto Protocol in mid-2001, while its parent Ford opposed it (*Wall Street Journal* 2001: B1). Shell Oil offers further evidence of centripetal tendencies within a multinational corporation and local responsiveness on climate change issues; it is often regarded as more like a confederation than a tightly controlled and centralized firm. A split within Shell between the US affiliate and its parent corporation, Royal Dutch Shell of the UK and the Netherlands, led Shell of the US to lag behind its parent of the UK and Netherlands in withdrawing from the Global Climate Coalition (GCC), which opposed the Kyoto Protocol.

Such cross-national conflicts among the units of multinational corporations are consistent with the pluralistic politics theory; in both instances, local affiliates were responsive to local political conditions – widespread support for the Kyoto Protocol in Sweden, the Netherlands and the UK, and at the same time opposition in the US. In yet another case, among auto firms, there were cross-national conflicts in DaimlerChrysler (before Daimler sold Chrysler); a mixture of ambivalence and contradictory opinions emanating from Daimler and Chrysler officials could be attributed in part to the not yet fully integrated intra-firm differences in corporate cultures and *home countries* of the two "merging" firms at that time (Hamilton 2003).

### Home-country, intra-industry differences

Differences in corporations' responses within industries are related to the parent corporations' home-country political-institutional setting (as in the pluralistic politics theory). Among the four "super-major" oil corporations, the two European-based corporations – BP in the UK, and Shell in the UK and Netherlands – have been more involved than their US rivals ExxonMobil and ChevronTexaco in the climate change programs of environmental NGOs. Similarly, US-based firms in commercial banking, investment banking, insurance, the automotive industry and others have tended to be laggards on climate change issues compared with their foreign rivals in Europe, Japan and, in some instances, Canada.

### Industry associations and intra-industry differences

Intra-industry differences are sometimes reflected in the positions of industry associations on government policy issues. For instance, there are some energy industry associations that support mitigation measures: the American Council for an Energy Efficient Economy and the US Council for Energy Alternatives. Also within the US, some electric utilities publicly endorsed *mandatory* $CO_2$ emissions limits for their industry, while others opposed them, before the Edison Electric Institute did so for the industry as a whole. The evidence on industry-specific associations thus reflects important differences within industries, as well as countervailing power among them – and it is thus consistent with the pluralistic politics theory.

At the same time, some issue-specific organizations have been opposed to mandatory mitigation efforts. For several years, the Global Climate Coalition (GCC) was a major lobbying organization against the Kyoto Protocol, and it disputed the consensus view of scientists, including the Inter-Governmental Panel on Climate Change. In the late 1990s in the US, a small number of large producers represented in the Global Climate Coalition virtually dominated the "debate" over climate change issues, particularly in regard to the issue of US ratification of the Kyoto Protocol, and then beginning in January 2001, an even smaller group of producers had access to the White House in the early months of the Bush administration when it announced its opposition to the Kyoto Protocol and also its opposition to domestic limits on carbon dioxide emissions. In short, an intense lobbying effort by a small and highly motivated group of producers enabled it to achieve the kind of government policies it wanted – a process and result consistent with the public choice theory.

However, within key industries some corporations joined the GCC earlier and left later than their rivals, and some did not join at all. Within the auto industry, Ford left the GCC during 2000; then DaimlerChrysler left a month later; and General Motors subsequently left. On the other hand, Japanese and other non-US auto corporations never joined. Within the oil industry, Shell and BP left before Texaco, which was the first US-based corporation to leave (DiPaola and Arris 2001: 255–6, 263–4). The US affiliate of Shell remained a member for a matter of months after the parent corporation Royal/Dutch Shell of the UK and the Netherlands withdrew. ExxonMobil was a key participant throughout. There is evidence again, therefore, of a pattern in the intra-industry differences, namely, non-US corporations were less likely to join and faster to leave if they did join – a home-country pattern consistent with the pluralistic politics theory. Thus, in the intra-corporation differences noted in the previous subsection as well as this subsection, we have seen evidence of home-country effects on corporations' strategic behavior. International explanations of differences are evident in both intra-corporation and intra-industry differences.

## Inter-industry differences

Both theories predict differences across industries in corporations' responses to global warming issues, though for different reasons. The public choice theory emphasizes the importance of expected revenue and expense streams to corporations as they calculate their economic interests and determine their strategic objectives on issues that confront them. In the case of global warming, the industries that are particularly dependent on fossil fuel prices in either their revenue or expense streams are likely to oppose regulatory action to mitigate global warming, as are industries where other types of greenhouse gas emissions are particularly intensive. Thus, corporations in the coal, auto and oil sectors would be expected to be among the opponents, while industries (e.g. semiconductors) where greenhouse gas emissions are not so problematic would be expected to be more supportive of mitigation efforts, as would the casualty insurance industry which suffers losses from more frequent and serious severe weather events. Industry differences are also consistent with a pluralistic politics theory, but such a theory further emphasizes differences across corporations within industries because of differences in the political pressures that they encounter from within and without the corporation.

## Differences among industries in strategic responses

The two theoretical perspectives offer two different views of why there are differences among industries in their strategic responses to climate change issues. The public choice theory suggests that differences across industries in corporations' strategic responses result from differences in how revenue and expense streams in the industry are affected by global warming or its mitigation. The pluralistic politics theory suggests that differences across industries in corporations' strategic responses result from differences in the political pressures they encounter.

The industry-specific data in Table 4.2 provide evidence of differences across industries in their responses to the US government's voluntary "Climate VISION" program, which was announced in February 2003. The program formally and directly involves participation by industry associations (US Department of Energy 2003). The data document variability across industries in how they approach issues about greenhouse gas emissions. There are two notable patterns in the data in this respect. First, there are differences in the types of greenhouse gases of interest; whereas most industries focus on carbon dioxide, some such as the aluminum, magnesium and semiconductor industries narrow their concern to other types of greenhouse gases (PFCs, HFCs, SF6). Second, the data indicate which industries are willing to state targets to reduce *absolute* emissions levels, or only reduce *relative* levels that relate emissions to an indicator of business activity and *typically entail actual increases* in the absolute levels of emissions. The

Table 4.2 Variations across industries in voluntary targets under "US Climate VISION Program"

| Industry/organization | Members: number of firms | Members: per cent of industry | Type of emissions or other focus[a] | Reduction target | Base year | Target year |
|---|---|---|---|---|---|---|
| Oil & Gas API | na | Over 60% of US refining capacity | Aggregate energy efficiency of US refinery operations | 10% | 2002 | 2012 |
| Coal NMA | na | 70% of US primary electricity fuels | Coalmine methane, carbon sequestration | 10% increase in efficiency in systems in NMA-DOE Allied Partnership | 2002 | 2012 – date of "projected" reductions of GHG by 1 mmt annually |
| Electricity EPICI[b] | na | 100% of US electricity production | "Carbon Impact" | 3–5% | 2002 | 2012 |
| Cement PCA | na | More than 95% of US cement production | Carbon dioxide emissions | 10% per ton of cement | 1990 | 2020 |
| Steel AISI | 33 | Nearly ¾ of US steel production capacity | Sector-wide average energy efficiency | 10% | 1998 | 2012 |
| Aluminum AA/VAIP | na | na | PFC emissions | "further reductions" | 2002 | 2005 |
| Magnesium MC/IMA | na | 100% of US primary magnesium production, 80% of US casting and recycling | SF6 | Eliminate | – | 2010 |

Table 4.2 (continued)

| Industry/organization | Members: number of firms | Members: per cent of industry | Type of emissions or other focus[a] | Reduction target | Base year | Target year |
|---|---|---|---|---|---|---|
| Semiconductors ASI | 22 | Over 70% of sector emissions of HFC, PFC, SF6 | HFC, PFC and SF6 emissions | 10% | 1995 | 2010 |
| Chemicals ACC | na | 90% of US chemical industry production | Overall GHG intensity | 18% | 1990 | 2012 |
| Motor vehicles AAM | na | Over 90% of US vehicle sales | GHG emissions from manufacturing facilities | 10% | 2002 | 2012 |
| Railroads AAR | na | na | GHG intensity of Class 1 railroads | 18% | 2002 | 2012 |
| Forestry AF&PA | na | na | GHG intensity | 12% | 2000 | 2012 |

Notes:
a Several associations have additional, less specific goals, such as developing management programs to facilitate GHG reductions or participating in US EPA or US DOE partnership programs.
b The EPICI consists of seven organizations – EEI, NRECA, APPA, LPPC, EPSA, NEI, TVA – whose commitments vary but are typically general and/or involve increases in use of their particular type of electricity generating capacity, including both nuclear (NEI and TVA) and renewables (APPA, LPPC).

aluminum, magnesium and semiconductor industries are in the former group, while the "energy efficiency" targets of the oil and coal industries and the "GHG intensity" targets of the railroads put them in the second group. Further, the motor vehicle industry association is careful to note that its target specifically concerns emissions from "manufacturing facilities," and by implication not emissions from its products, i.e. motor vehicles.

The data in Table 4.2 indicate differences across industries that are consistent with both the emphases of the public choice and pluralistic politics theories on industry group behavior. However, these data do not enable us to distinguish between the roles of economic interests as in the public choice theory or the political processes as in the pluralistic politics theory. We thus turn to evidence on the activities of industry associations for further information about inter-industry differences in corporations' behavior.

### Industry associations

The two theories also offer conflicting perspectives on the behavior of industry associations. The public choice theory suggests that industry associations representing producers in political processes tend to prevail and obtain government policies they prefer. The pluralistic politics theory suggests that industry associations tend to form countervailing coalitions representing conflicting interests on any given issue.

The positions and activities of a variety of industry associations are pertinent to these propositions, as reflected in the following five cases. First, in July 2000, the US Chamber of Commerce and 25 other industry groups petitioned the US Environmental Protection Agency (EPA) to oppose a proposal under consideration for the EPA to limit carbon dioxide as a greenhouse gas. This industry petition was a response to an earlier petition in October 1999 by environmental organizations that the EPA should apply the Clean Air Act to greenhouse gas emissions (DiPaola and Arris 2001: 290). Subsequently in the summer of 2001, in a different political context, another industry association, the Small Business Survival Committee, lobbied the US government to resist European pressures to adopt controls on greenhouse gas emissions. The EPA, at the direction of the White House, accordingly excluded carbon dioxide emissions by decisions in 2001 and 2003 – a set of facts consistent with the public choice theory.

Second, the American Petroleum Institute (API) has been a consistent opponent of mitigation measures. For instance, the API (2001) challenged the analysis by the US National Academy of Sciences (NAS) (2001) of the Third Assessment Report of the Intergovernmental Panel on Climate Change (IPCC) (2001), because both concluded that there is a scientific consensus on the existence of a global warming problem and that it results in substantial part from human activities. The US administration adopted the critical position of the API, despite the fact that the NAS report was an official response by a scientific panel to a request by the administration to evaluate the IPCC work. In short, the administration accepted the position of an industry association rather than the position of a panel of independent government-appointed scientists – an outcome consistent with the public choice theory.

The third case, involving a comparative international perspective on the positions and activities of major business organizations, is more in line with a pluralistic politics interpretation of industry associations. The International Chamber of Commerce (ICC) and the World Business Council for Sustainable Development (WBCSD) have adopted different positions on climate change issues. The ICC, whose positions on issues are often heavily influenced (even determined) by US preferences, has been opposed to the Kyoto Protocol; the WBCSD, which has more of a European orientation, has been supportive.

Fourth, within the United States Council for International Business (USCIB), which represents several hundred large multinational corporations, there have been conflicts between US-based and European-based corporations, with many of the latter being less supportive of the Council's hostility to the Kyoto Protocol. International differences which are consistent with the pluralist theory, therefore, are evident within industry associations as well as among them.

Finally, the formation of the US Climate Action Partnership (US CAP) reflected the pluralistic nature of US business. With a membership of more than 25 firms, the US CAP membership includes many major corporations such as Alcoa and GE. Yet, within many individual industries, there are leaders on climate change issues who have joined but there are also major firms within those same industries that are climate change laggards and have not joined. For instance, within the insurance industry, AIG belongs but Allstate does not, within the oil industry, ConocoPhillips belongs but Exxon Mobil does not, and among soft drink firms, Pepsi is a member but Coca-Cola is not.

## Implications

The principal implication of the analysis is that environmental foreign policy – certainly in the case of climate change – needs to take into account the economic interests of business and the interactions of business and government within national institutional settings. Two theoretical perspectives – pluralistic politics and public choice – offer insights into the patterns of those business interests, how they influence business strategy and business political activity, and how business interacts with government. There are both some underlying similarities in those patterns in environmental policy-making and policy-making in other issue areas, but there are also distinctive patterns associated with specific issues. Since the theoretical perspectives, as presented in this chapter, are both theories of political economy, the key implications naturally involve both business and government behavior, and their interactions, in environmental foreign policy-making.

For climate change – the environmental foreign policy issue of specific interest in this chapter – there are three key implications that can be derived from the analysis: The first concerns *varying attributes of issues*, in particular, the occurrence of market failures and the role of government intervention in addressing them; the second concerns linkages between the *micro and macro levels of analysis*; the third concerns the importance of *cross-national differences* in the political-economy and institutional context of environmental decision-making, including for multinational corporations as well as for governments.

## Attributes of issues

The issues related to climate change are similar to other environmental issues confronting corporations in at least one important respect that affects the political-economy context and thus the nature of the issues corporations face. As with other environmental issues, because climate change issues inherently involve externalities and market failures, there is an argument for government intervention on the grounds of economic efficiency. The government intervention can consist of taxes and/or subsidies and/or other regulations. These three types of government policies therefore pose recurrent issues for corporations.

An additional feature of the policies that are being developed to address climate change, however, is that governments are creating new markets – specifically markets for greenhouse gas emission credits. This market-based approach is furthest advanced in Europe, in the form of the EU Emissions Trading Scheme (ETS). However, in the US a cap-and-trade system known as the Regional Greenhouse Gas Initiative (RGGI) of ten northeastern states began operation in 2008; and another regional cap-and-trade organization including several western US states and Canadian provinces was also being formed. There are also voluntary market mechanisms, such as the Chicago Climate Exchange, in operation in the US. As a result of these developments, the institutional context of the strategic issues corporations encounter is becoming more internationally complex, as well as more highly developed.

## Micro and macro levels of analysis

Together, the two political-economy theories link macro level features of the political-economic environment of corporations to the micro level of corporations' behavior. The theories offer complementary explanations of corporations' strategic behavior. The public choice theory focuses on corporations' core economic interests and the structural features of their economic and political circumstances that tend to be enduring. The assumption of the public choice theory that corporations' strategic behavior is driven by their economic interests and thus the present value equivalent of their future revenues and expenses is an appropriate starting point for understanding corporations' responses to climate change issues.

Further, a key insight of the public choice theory is that it focuses on a core feature of climate change issues – namely, the asymmetry of the distribution of costs and benefits of inaction or of mitigation measures concerning climate change. There are small numbers of large producers with an incentive (and the financial means and political access) to be active in efforts to prevent mitigation measures. And they were successful, at least in the US, for many years. Major industry associations were able to block government mitigation efforts.

However, over time there has been increased conflict within industries and increased political activity by countervailing industry and environmental organizations. In that respect, it can be said that the political economy of business action on climate change issues in the US has shifted from a period of correspondence with the public choice theory to a period of increased correspondence with the pluralistic politics theory. Yet, the outcome and implications of changes of the positions of individual corporations and concomitant shifts in the coalitions remain to be seen.

## Cross-national differences

The linkage between the macro and micro levels becomes particularly evident in a cross-national comparative analytic perspective. The macro level political-institutional context of European and Japanese corporations – where there is widespread public and government support for climate change mitigation measures – tends to lead corporations to respond strategically at the micro level in ways that are congruent with the political pressures in their national environments. At the same time, US-based corporations are generally less supportive of mitigation measures, reflecting the relatively less concerned and activist political circumstances on climate change issues in that country – though this tendency for US-based firms to be laggards was diminishing by 2008 as a few major US corporations such as WalMart began to take action on climate change. Theorizing about corporations' behavior on environmental issues, therefore, should not ignore the effects of cross-national differences in political-institutional contexts on inter-corporation differences in parent corporations' behavior.

The cross-national differences, furthermore, are not only evident in comparisons among parent corporations with different home countries; they are also evident in cross-national conflicts between parent corporations and their foreign affiliates or between internationally merged corporations. Because a distinctive feature of multinational corporations is that they have physical assets in at least two countries, with a parent corporation in one country, and foreign subsidiaries in other countries, they are inevitably subject to the different and often conflicting pressures of different national political economies and institutional contexts. Their strategic issues and responses are often directly shaped by these cross-national differences.

Theories about the issues and decisions of corporations concerning environmental issues must be explicit about the nature of multinational corporations. They face intra-corporation conflicts that stem from their presence in multiple political-economies, and thus explanations of how corporations respond to the issue need to take into account cross-national differences in values and attitudes on the underlying issues – in this case, the protection of the environment, health, safety and wealth distribution issues posed by climate change.

## Conclusion

Two developments at the international climate conference COP-13/MOP-3 in Bali, Indonesia, in December 2007 make the explicit and systematic inclusion of the emphases of this chapter – namely economic interests, business strategy and business-government interactions – essential elements in explanations of policy-making on climate change issues. First, *sectoral* approaches were placed on the agenda for negotiating a new post-2012 multilateral climate regime. This means that the post-2012 international climate regime may include agreements about the greenhouse gas emissions, production processes and other operational aspects of specific industries such as steel, electric power, automobiles, aviation, maritime shipping, and others. Understanding the political economy of policy-making on these agreements will require the kinds of conceptual and empirical concerns reflected in this chapter.

A second relevant development at the Bali climate change conference was an informal meeting of *trade* ministers – the first held in the context of a climate conference and thus a symbol of the increasingly widespread recognition that climate change issues and trade issues intersect in many ways. Thus, the analysis of the political economy of trade policy-making overlaps with the political economy of climate policy-making – a subject that would take us beyond the limits of this chapter but which is under active consideration in other on-going research projects (e.g. Brewer 2007). Future studies of US and other countries' responses to climate change issues will therefore need to broaden and deepen the analysis of the political economy of those issues. That need became even more apparent in early 2009 with the inauguration of the new US administration and the increased intensity of negotiations for a post-2012 international climate regime.

## Notes

1 There are consistencies and parallels between the pluralistic politics theory and the stakeholder theory of business strategy (Donaldson 1999; Donaldson and Preston 1995; Freeman 1984; Janwahar and McLaughlin 2001; Jones and Wicks 1999). Both theories assume that firms' strategies are based on the diverse interests and preferences of many groups. The stakeholder theory builds on the work of Cyert and March (1963) and Simon (1957). The theory accordingly views "the corporation as a coalition of a number of interests including shareholders, managers,

and other employees;" corporations in the stakeholder theory are thus presumed to "pursue a wide range of goals. This diversity of goals is a reflection of the variety of different interest groups that make up the firm" (Grant 1991: 16). By extension, one can add the array of governmental and nongovernmental organizations that represent those group interests outside the formal organizational structure of the firm.

2 There are consistencies between the public choice and the shareholder wealth-maximization theories: both focus on the economically rational motivations of corporations' executives. They assume that economically rational alternatives for the firm are ascertainable on the basis of market forces that include the preferences of consumers and competitive conditions in the industry. In this context, a financial approach to shareholder value-maximizing choices addresses issues about the time periods and risks in strategic decision-making by focusing on present value calculations. Thus, in the context of the shareholder value maximization theory, "the purpose of strategy is to increase the long-term profitability of the corporation ... By maximizing the present value of the firm, management maximizes the wealth of the owners of the firm" (Grant 1991: 17).

3 The chapter builds on and extends the previous work on US climate change policy-making in Harris (1998; 2000) in two respects: first, by comparing the "pluralistic politics" theory, which is central to that work, and the "public choice" theory; and second, by focusing specifically on the responses of business and their interactions with government. Several of the chapters in Harris (2000) discuss the domestic politics of US policy-making and thus provide useful complementary reading for the present chapter; see especially Bryner (2000), Harrison (2000) and Park (2000). The latter provides an historical narrative of the evolution of US government climate change policy, including brief references to the role of multinational corporations.

# References

American Petroleum Institute (2001) *Comparison of Findings: National Academy of Sciences Report and the Intergovernmental Panel on Climate Change Report*, Washington, DC: American Petroleum Institute.

Bartlett, Chris A. and Ghoshal, Sumantra (1989) *Managing Across Borders: The Transnational Solution*, Boston: Harvard Business School Press.

Bauer, Richard A., Pool, Ithiel and Dexter, Lewis A. (1972) *American Business and Public Policy: The Politics of Foreign Trade*, Chicago, IL: Aldine-Atherton.

Becker, Gary S. (1983) "A Theory of Competition among Pressure Groups for Political Influence," *Quarterly Journal of Economics*, 98: 371–400.

Bentley, Albert (1967) *The Process of Government*, Cambridge, MA: Harvard University Press.

Boddewyn, Jean and Brewer, Thomas L. (1994) "International-Business Political Behavior: New Theoretical Directions," *Academy of Management Review*, 19: 119–43.

Bohm, Paul and Russel, Chris S. (1985) "Comparative Analysis of Alternative Policy Instruments," in A.V. Kneese and J.L. Sweeney (eds) *Handbook of Natural Resources and Economics*, Amsterdam: North-Holland, pp. 395–460.

Brewer, Thomas L. (2007) "US Climate Change Policies and International Trade Policies: Intersections and Implications for International Negotiations." Available at: www.usclimatechange.com.

Brown, Allen (1974) *The Economic Theory of Representative Government*, Chicago, IL: Aldine.

Bryner, Gary (2000) "Congress and the Politics of Climate Change," in Paul G. Harris (ed.) *Climate Change and American Foreign Policy*, New York: St. Martin's Press, pp. 111–30.

Buchanan, James M. and Tullock, Gordon (1962) *The Calculus of Consent*, Ann Arbor, MI: University of Michigan Press.

Cyert, Richard M. and March, James G. (1963) *A Behavioral Theory of the Firm*, Englewood Cliffs, NJ: Prentice Hall.

Dahl, Robert A. (1972) *Pluralist Democracy in the United States*, Chicago, IL: Rand McNally.

Deardorf, Alan V. and Stern, Robert M. (eds) (1998) *Constituent Interests and US Trade Policies*, Ann Arbor, MI: University of Michigan Press.

DeClercq, Marc (1996) "The Political Economy of Green Taxes," *Environmental and Resource Economics*, 8: 273–91.

Destler, I.M. (1995) *American Trade Politics*, 3rd edn. Washington, DC: Institute for International Economics.

Destler, I.M. and Balint, Peter J. (1999) *The New Politics of American Trade: Trade, Labor, and the Environment*, Washington, DC: Institute for International Economics.

Dijkstra, B. R. (1999) *The Political Economy of Environmental Policy: A Public Choice Approach to Market Instruments*, Cheltenham: Edward Elgar.

DiPaola, M. and Arris, L. (eds) (2001) *Global Warming Yearbook: 2001*, Arlington, MA: Cutter Information.

Donaldson, Thomas (1999) "Making Stakeholder Theory Whole," *Academy of Management Review*, 24: 237–41.

Donaldson, Thomas and Preston, Lee E. (1995) "The Stakeholder Theory of the Corporation: Concepts, Evidence, and Implications," *Academy of Management Review*, 20: 65–91.

Downs, Anthony (1957) *An Economic Theory of Democracy*, New York: Harper and Row.

Freeman, Ronald E. (1984) *Strategic Management: A Stakeholder Approach*, Boston, MA: HarperCollins.

Grant, Robert M. (1991) *Contemporary Strategy Analysis: Concepts, Techniques, Applications*, Oxford: Basil Blackwell.

Grossman, G.M. and Helpman, E. (1994) "Protection for Sale," *American Economic Review*, 84: 833–50.

Hamilton, Kirsty (2002) Unpublished notes on DaimlerChrysler.

Harris, Paul G. (1998) *Understanding America's Climate Change Policy: Realpolitik, Pluralism, and Ethical Norms*, Oxford: Oxford Centre for the Environment, Ethics and Society.

—— (ed.) (2000) *Climate Change and American Foreign Policy*, New York: St. Martin's Press.

Harrison, Neil E. (2000) "From the Inside Out: Domestic Influences on Global Environmental Policy," in Paul G. Harris (ed.) *Climate Change and American Foreign Policy*, New York: St. Martin's Press, pp. 89–109.

Janwahar, I.M. and McLaughlin, G.L. (2001) "Toward a Descriptive Stakeholder Theory: An Organizational Life Cycle Approach," *Academy of Management Review*, 26: 397–414.

Jones, Thomas M. and Wicks, Andrew C. (1999) "Convergent Stakeholder Theory," *Academy of Management Review*, 24: 206–21.

Murtha, Thomas P., and Lenway, Stephanie A. (1994) "Country Capabilities and the Strategic State: How National Political Institutions Affect Multinational Corporations' Strategies," *Strategic Management Journal*, 15: 113–29.

Olson, Mancur (1965) *The Logic of Collective Action*, Cambridge, MA: Harvard University Press.

Park, Jacob (2000) "Governing Climate Change Policy: From Scientific Obscurity to Foreign Policy Prominence," in Paul G. Harris (ed.) *Climate Change and American Foreign Policy*, New York: St. Martin's Press, pp. 73–87.

Prahalad, C. K. and Doz, Yves L. (1987) *The Multinational Mission: Balancing Local Demands and Global Vision*, New York: Free Press.

Schattschneider, E.E. (1935) *Politics, Pressures and the Tariff*, New York: Prentice-Hall.

Shepsley, K.A. and Bonchek, M. S. (1997) *Analyzing Politics: Rationality, Behavior and Institutions*, New York: W.W. Norton.

Simon, Herbert A. (1957) *Administrative Behavior*, New York: Macmillan.

Spar, Deborah (2001) "National Policies and Domestic Politics," in A.M. Rugman and T.L. Brewer (eds) *The Oxford Handbook of International Business*, Oxford: Oxford University Press, pp. 206–31.

Tallman, Stephen B. and Yip, George S. (2001) "Strategy and the Multinational Enterprise," in Alan M. Rugman and Thomas L. Brewer (eds) *The Oxford Handbook of International Business*, Oxford: Oxford University Press, pp. 317–48.

Thornbecke, Willem (2000) "A Public Choice Perspective on the Globalizing of America," in Thomas L. Brewer and G. Boyd (eds) *Globalizing America: The USA in World Integration*, Cheltenham: Elgar, pp. 83–97.

Truman, David B. (1971) *The Governmental Process*, New York: Knopf.

US, Department of Energy (2003) Press release. Online. Available at: www.energy. gov/HQPress/releases/03 (accessed 12 February 2003).

US, National Academy of Sciences (2001) *Climate Change Science: An Analysis of Some Key Questions*, Washington, DC: National Academy Press.

*Wall Street Journal* (2001) "Global-warming Treaty Opens Corporate Rifts, and Activisits Jump in," August 27: B1.

Weingast, B. R. (1980) "Congress, Regulation, and the Decline of Nuclear Power," *Public Policy*, 28: 231–55.

# 5    The politics of socionatures

## Images of environmental foreign policy

*Maximilian Mayer and*
*Friedrich J. Arndt*

Ever since climate change became a major focus of public debate and international affairs, media news, literature and policy documents in industrialized countries have almost inevitably contained scientific graphs and images. We have become accustomed to a range of related visual representations: among them – mostly taken from the third and fourth reports of the Intergovernmental Panel on Climate Change (IPCC) – the "hockey stick" showing the sharp rise of mean temperatures since the middle of the twentieth century; images from the climate simulation models; and also photographs that point to the imminent threats of global warming such as shrinking glaciers or threatened polar bears. For the most part, people do not appear in such pictures.

At first sight, humankind seemingly agrees on these graphs and images as viable representations of global warming. However, when one considers non-western media sources such as Chinese or Indian sources, one is puzzled by the fact that it is difficult to find those IPCC graphs at all. Instead, pictures showing people, mostly suffering or hard-working, serve to visualize climate change. The Chinese magazine *Beijing Review* (Lan 2007), for example, published a photograph under the headline "Curbing Global Warming," showing farmers in a field. Here, nature is neither wilderness nor reduced to objective graphs strictly separate from human beings, but a concrete category in the everyday life of ordinary citizens. The Indian government used a child's painting as the cover picture for its report "India: Addressing Energy Security and Climate Change" (Government of India 2007) of a hand holding a drop of water, backed by a friendly sun shining on urban housing, a wind generator and solar cells. Again, the topic is embedded in a concrete form of daily life, yet, unlike the picture in the *Beijing Review*, it seems change-oriented. This implies an interesting divergence of visualization choices, which it is worth considering at length.

## Analyzing socionatures through images

To grasp complex issues that are invisible at first, we often use images to render the invisible nevertheless seen, and thus visually comprehensible.

Especially in today's essentially visual culture, images serve as an inevitable means of signification. Furthermore, images are more easily comprehensible than language and act as powerful argumentative devices (Pörksen 1997). "The image has become a powerful aspect of culture, not just through its cultural omnipresence but also through its ability to contribute to, respond to and in some cases ignite, political change" (Fuery and Fuery 2003: 95).

Global climate change is invisible, becoming intelligible only through the combination and interpretation of multiple statistical datasets. Due to its complexity, visualization choices are important when representing climate change in the bigger picture, which, in a more general sense, also holds true for the natural sciences (Mersch 2006). Since various framings of "nature" exist in parallel (Macnaughten and Urry 1998), divergent visual representations present different framings of climate change and evoke differing connotations.

Scholars have already pointed out the fundamental problems of communicating creeping environmental risks in general and global warming in particular via images (Adam 1998; Weart 2005; Doyle 2007). Yet, despite their central role, visualizations in climate policy have not received appropriate attention in the scholarly debate. How can the emergence of differing visual representations of global warming be explained? How does the analysis of images enrich our understanding of environmental foreign policy?

To answer these questions, we examine the connection between divergent visualizations and global climate discourses and politics. We frame this issue in theoretical terms of a continuous *co-production of socionatures*, drawing on insights from the field of Science and Technology Studies (STS). Methodologically, we apply a two-level epistemology to sketch a one-level ontology (see Figure 5.1). On the first level, we analyze states' differing positions in terms of strategic discourses, of which visualizations of climate change are an integral part. The pre-reflexive function of images allows us to use them on a second level as a heuristic device to understand what renders the discourses meaningful for all actors involved. That is not to say, though, that

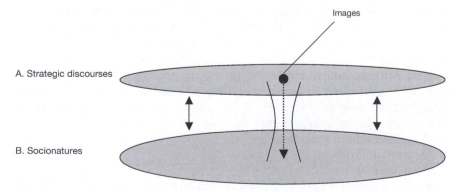

*Figure 5.1* Images as heuristic devices

this epistemologically deeper level of socionatures has a privileged ontological status – quite the contrary: the co-production of socionatures refers to the specific everyday formation of natural and societal order in which social (discursive) practices and material (technological, economic, natural) factors play an active role. The isolation of the socionatural level is an analytical move; ontologically, level A and B are not separate. Specific socionatures serve as somewhat idealized sets that are not found in pure form empirically.

Our aim is not to provide a final and comprehensive account of empirical material, but to use the visualization puzzle as a heuristic tool to develop a complementary theoretical approach. In the next section, we consider the place of visualizations in policy discourses and their strategic role. Subsequently, we untangle the "embeddedness" of climate discourses within the complex of nature–society relations by means of visualizations, before drawing final conclusions.

## Visualizations, discourses, and policy

In the wake of the Stern Report and Al Gore's movie, global warming has become mainstreamed in global discourses and now sits high on the international agenda. As the issue is part of almost daily media coverage in industrial and developing societies alike (Boykoff and Roberts 2007),[1] there exist various competing narratives that frame the issue in various ways, claiming authoritative meaning in public debates (Hulme 2008). Regarding the choice of visual representations, one of the most striking differences is to be found between the scientific-based images that prevail in developed countries and the sort of pictures that appear in the developing countries' media, as indicated in the introduction to this chapter.

The fact that there are differing visualizations points to the divergent imaginations of climate and the Earth. Indian and Chinese images, for example, often show a profane perspective that deals with the unequal dwelling conditions of humans. Far from that view, the image of the blue planet that gave birth to the metaphor of "Spaceship Earth" constructs the world as beautiful and fragile, yet manageable, rendering human lives both equal and invisible.[2] From this perspective, it becomes clear that the positions of the "southern camp" and the "northern camp"[3] in global climate negotiations are closely intertwined with competing environmental discourses. The mainstream western media and politicians perceive climate change as a common global challenge demanding collective action. Discourses in developing nations contrarily emphasize the "differentiation" of responsibilities. How do the chosen images fit into this?

### *The homogenization of climate*

The IPCC, founded in 1988 by the World Meteorological Organization (WMO) and the United Nations Environment Program (UNEP), has become the most authoritative source of scientific knowledge and advice on national and international climate policy. The basic scientific consensus is the conviction that climate change poses a serious threat to all mankind and can only be tackled effectively on a global scale. The IPCC (2007a: 3) views global warming as the "net effect of human activities since 1750." Its core documents present historic GHG emissions and future scenarios of GHG emissions only at the most advanced level of globally aggregated data.[4] Thereby, the historic emissions of developed nations are omitted and the different conditions of emission ("subsistence" or "luxury") are not taken into account. As a result, in either case, though depicted as lower than in affluent nations, developing countries' amount of GHG emissions looms decisively larger than otherwise visualized. Consequently, the *summary* proceeds by stating that until 2030 up to three-quarters of GHG emission will originate in non-Annex I regions. It further points to "global per capita growth" and the "global population growth" as "drivers of increasing energy related $CO_2$-emissions" (IPCC 2007c: 3f) – making no difference between Laotian farmers and Swedish businessmen.

The visualization choice reflects this homogenous treatment of GHG, referring to all human beings as a single entity. As the image of the blue planet on the cover of the first part of the last IPCC (2007a) report visualizes the Earth as a single system, the famous "hockey stick" graph showing the sharp rise of global mean temperature has become an icon of climate change. Adding to the deserted illustrations of nature, these homogenizing images shift attention away from specific life conditions of human beings towards a more systemic view. The internationally acknowledged need for sound scientific knowledge about climate change is thus a double-edged sword for developing countries. It systematically weakens their position by equalizing all GHG emissions, emphasizing collective responsibility and action, whereas several industrialized countries have employed the argument of the global challenge to refuse their own emission reductions.

The IPCC is not to blame for these consequences as they originate in the ideal of objective natural sciences, free from political questions (see below). However, questions of equity and responsibility – especially with regard to developing countries' needs of climate adaptation – have largely been relegated to the fringe of scientific discourses (Najam *et al.* 2003; Adger *et al.* 2006).[5] When scientists consider the "most pressing" equity issues, "northern concerns," namely "the issue of allocating emission mitigation targets" dominate, whereas "southern concerns," namely "the discrepancy between responsibility for, and the distribution of, climate impact burdens" are widely ignored (Müller 2002: 9). According to Kameyama (2004), southern proposals for future climate regimes tend to focus on equity issues, which are seldom to be found in proposals by authors with a northern background. Indeed, the predominant "northern concern" – reflecting a neoliberal twist in global managerialism – is economic efficiency in mitigation, which increasingly becomes the decisive criterion (Oels 2005; Hulme 2008).

*Visual counter-strategies*

Officials from India, Brazil or China sometimes utter harsh protest or distrust of the IPCC's procedures, although their own scientists also participate in this scientific endeavor. In China, the official news agency *Xinhua* and *Renmin Ribao*, the mouthpiece of the Communist Party, established special websites featuring climate change several years ago, but the topic was rarely mentioned in the broader public until very recently. As noted above, in official and commercial Chinese websites, magazines, and government reports, IPCC graphs are hard to find. *China Daily*, China's leading english newspaper, did not replicate them even when it reported at great length on its front page about the newly published first part of the fourth report in February 2007. Instead, the effects of local weather for people or, less often, animals and the environment visually represent global warming. Images such as the one from the *Beijing Review* (Lan 2007) unequivocally show the huge difference between "luxury" and "subsistence" emissions (*China Daily* 2007), implying that China's contribution to climate protection is at the expense of the latter.

In Indian discourse on climate, this is even more outspoken. In a special issue on the Bali conference, the famous Indian environmental journal *Down to Earth* does take into consideration western discourse and visualization of climate change and reproduces the "hockey stick," unlike the Chinese media. However, this classical IPCC graph is surrounded by several articles deconstructing its homogeneous imagination of global warming by using alternative graphs, texts, and images in order to make inequalities visible and to raise questions of responsibility and fairness (*Down to Earth* 2007; see also Narain 2007). In outright agreement with this view, India's Minister of Finance Chidambaram stated during the United Nations high level event on climate change: "The earth's atmosphere is a common resource for all of humankind. The problem lies not in accessing this resource, but in its excessive usage" (Permanent Mission of India to the United Nations 2007: 2). To put it another way, the Indian government implies that the amount of GHG cannot be seen as a homogenous sum, regardless of the individual sources. Rather, the heart of the problem lies in the specific and more or less proper social circumstances of the production of GHG.

Directly linked to the discrimination between "luxury" and "survival" emission is the discourse of "ecological colonialism." Raising this issue, Agarwal and Narain (1991) point to the social character of GHG emissions. They basically question the legitimacy of the homogenization of all emissions in terms of equity due to the uneven development conditions. Put forward by these prominent Indian environmentalists, this view still influences many developing nations' policy within FCCC. For example, Pan Yue (2006), Vice-Minister of the Ministry of Environmental Protection (formerly SEPA), without hesitation, recently linked "the issue of global warming developed nations are most concerned with" to colonialism.

## Socionatures in constant co-production

The initial puzzle of this chapter has been the unusual choices of visualization of climate in Chinese and Indian publications. Now we want to reverse the alienation effect and direct it at the dominant visual representations we are accustomed to. The reason why we do not question these visualizations lies in the fact that our everyday experience is constituted by a modernist nature–society relationship, which renders, we suppose, the former intelligible. Instead of explaining competing images and environmental discourses in terms of national interests or the importance of ideas, we treat climate change as a socially constructed phenomenon (Pettenger 2007) in order to explore the correspondence between natural and social orders.

Following discussions in STS, we call these orders "socionatures." The notion of a continuously co-produced socionature accounts for the fact that knowledge production, emerging technologies, political action, and everyday practice are intertwined. According to this view, climate discourses are embedded in a wider set of practices, representations, and narratives concerning the relationship between humans, ideas, and material objects (Latour 1993).[6] Socionatures, as we understand them here, are constantly co-produced through a "nexus of science, technology, culture, and power" (Jasanoff 2004b: 1). Of course, this concept goes much further than we can elaborate here (see Latour 2004b).[7]

### *The modernist co-production of climate change*

Among the central, interconnected aspects of the modernist socionature that play an important part in the co-production of climate, are: (1) the "great divide;" (2) science as policy advocacy; and (3) technological devices:

(1) According to its website, the IPCC is dedicated "to provide the decision-makers and others interested in climate change with an objective source of information about climate change" (IPCC 2007e). The IPCC's self-image thus appeals to the common modern metaphysics that postulates a strict borderline between nature and society/culture. From a constructivist point of view, this overarching narrative of modernity led to the construction of such separated spheres of nature and society in the first place. Nevertheless, the global expansion of European modernism has led to the virtually unquestioned status of this foundation in the practice of science and politics (Latour 1993; 2004b). Accordingly, the "great divide" that separates natural from social sciences within the work of IPCC is maintained with great effort and success.

Against this background, climate change without doubt belongs to the realm of natural order and is thus dealt with by natural sciences; the main driving forces of climate change are first and foremost defined in terms of physics and chemistry. In accordance with these "hard" sciences, which alone are in a position to speak for the objective nature and to determine the global (Glover 2006: 235), the IPCC conceives GHG, once diffused in the atmosphere, as an indivisible whole.

Thus, whenever measures are examined and discussed, the starting point is the global, i.e. the Earth's climate as a single system and the related focus is to find planetary solutions via mitigation. Among the concepts for a political order corresponding to the necessity of the global is *Earth System Analysis* (Schellnhuber and Wenzel 1998). Similarly, technical proposals for "carbon management" emphasize bioengineering or geo-engineering on a planetary scale (Schneider 2001). Obviously, the modernist political order is a mixture of global biopolitics and the "gardener state."

(2) Although it has recently been increasingly contested,[8] the "great divide" is still explicitly taken for granted in the context of the IPCC. However, notwithstanding adherence to the modernist narrative, when advising the politicians, natural sciences and climatology in particular have to frame the natural order to fit it to the necessity of political decisions (Demeritt 2001).

As scientific policy advice in general (Kropp *et al.* 2007: 21), the IPCC's main task is to predict the future and prepare for it (Jasanoff and Wynne 1998). The complex and open-ended research has to be presented as an unambiguous and self-contained field. The scientific and the political code merge to generate a form of practical knowledge that combines the focus on clear action with the legitimacy of scientific objectivity,[9] thereby presenting the field as manageable. This is the precondition to allow natural science to partake in the international climate negotiations, which are marked by "managerialism" (Adger *et al.* 2003: 192).

When looking at the IPCC graphs, it becomes apparent that the natural and the political order are mutually constitutive – co-produced through the politico-scientific procedures of the IPCC. A comment by a climatologist reveals the political implications of image choices:

> The full IPCC document includes extensive consideration of abrupt climate changes and variability, but the enduring images given to policy makers represent a world that is less variable and hence more favourable to humans and ecosystems than is likely to occur ... Based on a palaeoclimatic perspective, the future could prove more challenging climatically than indicated by IPCC (2001), and especially the Summary for Policymakers.
>
> (Alley 2003: 1843–4)

Smooth graphs contain the very option of manageability. Despite differing "story lines" all simulations of future temperatures within the IPCC reports display a gradual warming trend. The communicated reality draws a process that can be predicted and controlled, fitting neatly in with the managerial and neoliberal turn of international climate discourses.

(3) Additionally, technological devices and standardization procedures have a great impact on the constructions of the climate. While computer modeling

technology – the most important research tool in climate science – made possible and necessary the imagination of a single global climate as long ago as the 1970s (Miller 2004), the notion of "system" used by the IPCC helped to reassemble and harmonize the multiple strands of research by means of methodological standardization, validation benchmarking and the formulation of collaborative research agendas (Jasanoff and Wynne 1998: 59f.).

Because the combination of measured and theory-based data and the scope of hundreds of thousands of lines of programming code cannot be overseen by any single scientist, the crucial question of which data and which theories become part of the model and how they will interact, cannot be seen in detail once the model programming is complete (see Gramelsberger 2006). On the level of visual representations, the "blue planet icon" and the simulation models used in climate science merge into an objective and simulatable imagination of the Earth.

As Latour (2004a) has argued, when dealing with large invisible entities, which only come into existence by means of data collecting and aggregating, it is important to examine the practice and the centers of the collection process. This is also the case with climate, which is both invisible and based on vast data collection. In particular, its temperature dimension is the result of a construction process in the first place. It emerges by means of collecting and aggregating single local (weather) data dots, and then using statistical processing to construct a global, regional or national mean, the mean's variability and its trend (Rayner 2001; von Storch 1999).

Politically the most important graphs in the IPCC reports, although composites of vast data sources, suggest to the spectator the existence of an entity called "mean global temperature." The visualized output of simulation models thereby not only facilitates the perception of such constructs as part of the natural order, ontologizing the mean global temperature. On the political level, it also has effectively bound all actors involved in climate policy to this construct, since they focus on the 2-degree limit for the future rise of mean temperature in order to determine "dangerous climate change" (see Liverman 2009) The dominance of global climate models obviously comes at the expense of, for example, local climate variability, which is nearly impossible to simulate yet is actually affecting people's daily lives, as a Chinese climatologist claims.[10]

## The developmental co-productions of climate change

When searching for alternative socionatural conditions in the global South, it is apparent that socionatures are not strictly separate spheres representing a cultural clash, but are closely interrelated. While traditional local practices persist, and societal path dependency may have created "multiple modernities," the modernist project with its nature–society divide still lies at the core of processes of colonialism as it did in the past as well as in the processes of development and globalization today. "Unique" alternative practices and views therefore are rarely found.[11] Hence, even if a comprehensive analysis of alternative socionatural settings requires additional categories, for the purpose of this chapter, we will concentrate on the first two aspects mentioned above.

(1) There may be a specific developing nature–society relationship in China (Weller 2006), however, it is by no means characterized by a philosophy-based Chinese "holism," fusing humans and nature inseparably, as some European thinkers have claimed. Both historically (Roetz 2008) and more recently the "great divide" is a feature of socionature. This is best exemplified by the Maoist campaigns to conquer nature. Yet, unlike the modernist socionature described above, the "great divide" in China has not been translated into the dominance of "hard sciences" as the only legitimate speaker for nature. On the contrary (Shapiro 2001), scientists often were silenced in the pursuit of environmental policy. Even if these Mao era practices have changed considerably, allowing science a greater influence on policy (Heggelund 2004), climatology, chemistry and physics still play only a marginal role in the context of climate policy while economics takes the lead.[12]

Generalizing from the Chinese case and taking into account the comparably small role of the natural sciences in developing societies, the question arises of which other actors and practices prevail in the construction of climate change. When reexamining pictures of hard-working people visualizing climate change in the Chinese press or the painting of a human hand, carefully carrying houses, water, and wind turbines, in official Indian documents, the ways in which humans relate to (and depend on) non-human actors such as plants, soils, animals, etc. are centralized. Rather than focusing on beautiful, endangered species or vanishing landscapes, those images of humans in relation to nature suggest that human activity is primarily embedded in the environment. The view of nature inseparably connecting humans and non-humans relates better to the immediate daily labor and experience of hundreds of millions of farmers in the global periphery.

The contrast with a climate that is essentially detached from humans and mediated through the means of science and technology as a global, homogenized whole seems not so much due to the economic cleavage of "developed/underdeveloped," but rather to an urban/rural fault. Climate seen from the South is essentially local, a part of daily labor ensuring subsistence (Smith 2007).

Climate change is "constituted as a reality at the intersection of its physical and social history" (Byrne and Glover 2005: 6). The weakness of natural sciences as well as the local focus fits in with the political rationale of non-Annex I developing countries to concentrate on equity, impacts, and adaptation strategies instead of primarily focusing on global actions on mitigation. From their perspective, collective action is not primarily about mitigation but about financial and technological assistance from developed countries to adapt to climate change and promote sustainable development.

Thus, from the formulation of the FCCC to the latest conference in Poznań, the group of G77, led by the Indian and Chinese governments, has firmly refused to accept emission caps (Kobayashi 2003).[13] The prevailing visualizations correspondingly put into perspective the different national or per-capita responsibilities instead of graphs simply based either on trends in *physical global overall* GHG emissions or on mean temperature.

(2) Second, science advocacy plays a crucial role in Chinese politics, e.g. in the promotion of agricultural biotechnology and population policy. According to Greenhalgh (2008), a missile scientist convinced the top leaders through his mechanical approach to population control – which eventually became China's one-child policy – by using telling images and graphs. However, in the case of climate change, scientific policy advice is constrained by the historical experience of colonialism and the current distribution of the climate scientists in favor of the developed countries.

In China's case, lagging behind in advanced climate expertise – before 2000, Beijing even took a "no voice" stance regarding emission trading mechanisms due to lack of knowledge (Yu 2004: 73) – in combination with the weak position climatologists occupy in China – makes the IPCC the most powerful scientific source of pressure on the government.[14] Yet, as the Chinese people can well recall the experience of colonialism, and capitalism for a long time was officially perceived as an alien enemy, what renders knowledge on and visualizations of climate change suspect is their origin, as coming from abroad.

Due to their dependence on "outside" scientific knowledge in framing the natural order, the Indian and Chinese governments deal with climate change foremost in terms of autonomous political action and national sovereignty (Ramajani 2008; Zhang 2003) rather than as an "objective" global challenge that has to be tackled with economic efficiency. This explains why, when industrialized countries' governments point to objective science, many official and private actors from developing countries feel uneasy, and talk of "ecological colonialism." Even though a few of their "own" scientists contribute to the IPCC reports and their official delegates give their blessing to these reports, developing countries do not place too much trust in the body's findings (Lahsen 2007).

## Conclusion

The emergence of differing visualizations of climate change and their role in foreign policy discourses can be explained by reference to causal variables such as interests and ideas at the level of state and society (see Chapter 2 of this volume), for example, by approaches that focus on national interests, energy policy, epistemic communities or bureaucratic processes.[15] In a complementary way, we show in this chapter how these visualizations can be employed to enrich our understanding of foreign climate policy at the intersection of nature, society, science and technology. We do so by exploring divergent visualizations that represent climate change in order to understand their connections to socionatures arising from political-scientific practices. Images can be used as means to access a second analytical sphere in which the relevant actors and practices important to foreign policy analysis are rearranged and which shows why these discourses make sense to all the actors involved in the first place. Here, scientific practices, the use of technology and material factors play a much greater role. Analytically this can be an important enhancement in foreign environmental policy analysis as these aspects play a pivotal role in climate politics.

It is thus necessary to go beyond the concepts of "national interest," and even "perception gaps" related to climate change. Rather, the actors' strategic discourses match the powerful – because quotidian – underlying socionatures of which they are part. Analysis of the constant co-production of socionatures helps to fully appreciate the repercussions of science and technology – otherwise political analysis can hardly avoid the trap of either almost ignoring the latter at all (as the political-economy, institutional and realist approaches do, but see Litfin 2000) or of overly politicizing it as a purely ideological tool of northern power politics (as Marxist approaches do, but see Castree 2002).

This chapter does not provide a ready-to-use theoretical approach to foreign environmental policy analysis. But it opens up a complementary view that changes the context, the relevant actors, and the processes that determine foreign environmental policy. Methodologically, it invites research using competing visualizations of environmental issues as a means to go beyond our "naturalized" perception of images. The link between the level of foreign environmental policy and socionatures remains to be examined more closely. This will have to be done in empirical case studies that explore the formulation of specific foreign policy agendas as part of the co-production of socionatures. While we insist on not ontologizing "socionatures" but understand them as constantly manufactured, the concept as developed here remains too broad to grasp many phenomena at the meso and micro levels, especially regarding the overlap of different socionatures.

As social scientists have become part of the international endeavor of global environmental politics, they have to reflect the way in which the dominant hybrid natural science objectifies, globalizes, homogenizes and thus reduces climate change to both a challenge for management and a problem of efficiency. A fairly good starting point might be to elaborate "southern concerns" more comprehensively, especially the marginalized perspectives of adversely affected indigenous peoples (Fogel 2004; Smith 2007). The alienation effect that such research can produce is exactly in line with the aim of this chapter.

## Notes

1 The media and the public in most developing countries seem to be much less concerned about the issue of climate change, especially in comparison to other political, social, economic or environmental questions.

2 For an account of the history of Earth images and their effects on worldviews, see Jasanoff (2004a) and Sachs (1999).
3 This grouping does not imply firm blocs, but in fact the positions of southern countries regarding climate change have been remarkably similar (Najam *et al.* 2003).
4 The *Summary* shows only two graphs that locally differentiate sources of global $CO_2$ emissions, namely (1) the average regional per capita GHG emissions and total regional GHG emissions; and (2) the average regional GHG emissions per US$GDPPPP, both as of the year 2004.
5 The four most recent *Summaries for Policymakers* (IPCC 2007a, 2007b, 2007c, 2007d) do not use the terms "justice," "fairness" or "responsibility." Nor, although mentioned in the main third part of the report, did the *Summaries* devote a special section to equity issues.
6 It is important to stress that socionature essentially is process-based und does not resemble static entities such as "culture" or "civilization" as they are often perceived.
7 In a similar way, the term is used in political ecology and geography (Swyngedouw 1999). For a discussion of both usages, see Castree (2002).
8 See Böschen *et al.* (2006), Latour (1993), Jasanoff and Wynne (1998), and Wynne (1994).
9 Glover (2006) even suggests that the IPCC's practice resembles a "postnormal" concept of science, effectively integrating laymen into the review processes.
10 Interview, Kunming, June 2008.
11 In fact, the assumption of such a "pure" view is in itself an example of constructing the pre-modern "other" (the "noble savage," so to speak), thereby reinforcing the modern divide.
12 Interviews in Kunming, June 2008 and Beijing, June 2008.
13 Even if at the Bali conference non-Annex I developing countries accepted actions on mitigation "in a measurable, reportable and verifiable manner" (what some experts view as a breakthrough), developing countries committed themselves to reductions only to the extent that these are "nationally appropriate" (FCCC/CP/2007/6/Add.1, p. 3). The harsh critique that was brought about by the "sectoral approach" by the Japanese government during the UN climate talks in Bangkok again showed the opposing stance of China and the G77 regarding homogeneous treatment of reduction targets and commitments.
14 Interview, Kunming, June 2008.
15 See, e.g. for the Chinese case, Bjorkum (2005), Jeon and Yoon (2006), Kobayashi (2003) and Yu (2004).

# References

Adam, Barbara (1998) *Timescapes of Modernity: The Environment and Invisible Hazards*, London: Routledge.
Adger, Neil W. *et al.* (2003) "Adaptation to Climate Change in the Developing World," *Progress in Development Studies*, 3(3): 179–95.
Adger, Neil W., Paalova, Jouni, Huq, Saleemul and Mace, M.J. (eds) (2006) *Fairness in Adaptation to Climate Change*, Cambridge, MA: MIT Press.
Agarwal, Anil and Narain, Sunita (1991) *Global Warming in an Unequal World: A Case of Ecocolonialism*, New Delhi: Center for Science and Environment.
Alley, Richard B. (2003) "Palaeoclimatic Insights into Future Climate Challenges," *Philosophical Transactions of the Royal Society*, 362(1810): 1831–48.
Bjorkum, Ida (2005) *China in the International Politics of Climate Change: A Foreign Policy Analysis*, FNI Report 12, Lysaker: Fridtjof Nansen Institute.

Böschen, Stefan, Kratzer, Nick and May, Stefan (2006) "Einleitung: die Renaissance des Nebenfolgentheorems in der Analyse moderner Gesellschaften," in Stefan Böschen, Nick Kratzer and Stefan May (eds) *Nebenfolgen. Analysen zur Konstruktion und Transformation moderner Gesellschaften*, Weilerswist: Velbrück, pp. 7–38.

Boykoff, Maxwell T. and Roberts, J. Timmons (2007) "Media Coverage of Climate Change: Current Trends, Strengths, Weaknesses," United Nations Development Programme, Human Development Report 2007/3, background paper.

Byrne, John and Glover, Leigh (2005) "Ellul and the Weather," *Bulletin of Science, Technology & Society*, 25(1): 4–16.

Castree, Noel (2002) "False Antitheses? Marxism, Nature and Actor-Networks," *Antipode*, 34: 111–46.

*China Daily* (2007) "China Urges Accommodation to 'Emissions of Subsistence,'" Xinhua, 2.8.2007. Online. Available: http://www.chinadaily.com.cn/china/2007–8/02/content_5447300.htm.

Demeritt, David (2001) "The Construction of Global Warming and the Politics of Science," *Annals of the Association of American Geographers*, 91(2): 307–37.

*Down to Earth* (2007) "Rich Polluters' Beach Party," 16(14): 7–64.

Doyle, Julie (2007) "Picturing the Clima(c)tic: Greenpeace and the Representational Politics of Climate Change Communication," *Science as Culture*, 16(2): 129–50.

Fogel, Cathleen (2004) "The Local, the Global, and the Kyoto Protocol," in Sheila Jasanoff and Marybeth L. Martello (eds) *Earthly Politics: Local and Global in Environmental Governance*, Cambridge, MA: MIT Press, pp. 103–25.

Fuery, Patrick and Fuery, Kelli (2003) *Visual Cultures and Critical Theory*, London: Arnold.

Glover, Leigh (2006) *Postmodern Climate Change*, London: Routledge.

Government of India (2007) "India: Addressing Energy Security and Climate Change," Online. Available: http://envfor.nic.in/divisions/ccd/Addressing_CC_09-10-07.pdf.

Gramelsberger, Gabriele (2006) "Story Telling with Code: Archaeology of Climate Modelling," *TeamEthno-online*, 2: 77–84. Online. Available: http://www.teamethno-online.org.uk/Issue2/.

Greenhalgh, Susan (2008) *Just One Child: Science and Policy in Deng's China*, Berkeley, CA: University of California Press.

Heggelund, Gørild (2004) *Environment and Resettlement Politics in China: The Three Gorges Project*, Burlington, VA: Ashgate.

Hulme, Mike (2008) "The Conquering of Climate: Discourses of Fear and their Dissolution," *Geographical Journal*, 174(1): 5–16.

IPCC (2001) "Summary for Policymakers," in *Climate Change 2001: The Scientific Basis*. Online. Available: http://www.ipcc.ch/ipccreports/tar/wg1/005.htm.

—— (2007a) "Summary for Policymakers," in *Climate Change 2007: The Physical Science Basis. Contribution of Working Group I to the Fourth Assessment Report of the Intergovernmental Panel on Climate Change*, Cambridge: Cambridge University Press.

—— (2007b) "Summary for Policymakers," in *Climate Change 2007: Impacts, Adaptation and Vulnerability. Contribution of Working Group II to the Fourth Assessment Report of the Intergovernmental Panel on Climate Change*, Cambridge: Cambridge University Press.

—— (2007c) "Summary for Policymakers," in *Climate Change 2007: Mitigation. Contribution of Working Group III to the Fourth Assessment Report of the Intergovernmental Panel on Climate Change*, Cambridge: Cambridge University Press.

—— (2007d) "Summary for Policy Makers. Synthesis Report." Online. Available: http://www.ipcc.ch/pdf/assessment-report/ar4/syr/ar4_syr_spm.pdf.

—— (2007e) "About IPCC." Online. Available HTTP: http://www.ipcc.ch/about/index.htm.

Jasanoff, Sheila (2004a) "Heaven and Earth: The Politics of Environmental Images," in Sheila Jasanoff and Marybeth L. Martello (eds) *Earthly Politics: Local and Global in Environmental Governance*, Cambridge, MA: MIT Press, pp. 31–52.

—— (2004b) "The Idiom of Co-Production," in Sheila Jasanoff (ed.) *States of Knowledge. The Co-production of Science and Social Order*, London: Routledge, pp. 1–12.

Jasanoff, Sheila and Wynne, Brian (1998) "Science and Decisionmaking," in Steve Rayner and Elizabeth L. Malone (eds) *Human Choice and Climate Change*, vol. 1, Columbus, OH: Batalle Press, pp. 1–87.

Jeon, Hyung-kwon and Yoon, Seong-Suk (2006) "From International Linkages to Internal Divisions in China: The Political Response to Climate Change Negotiations,"*Asian Survey*, 46(6): 846–66.

Kameyama, Yasuko (2004) "The Future Climate Regime: A Regional Comparison of Proposals," *International Environmental Agreements: Politics, Law and Economics*, 4: 307–26.

Kobayashi, Yuka (2003) "Navigating between 'Luxury' and 'Survival' Emissions: Tensions in China's Multilateral and Bilateral Climate Change Diplomacy," in Paul G. Harris (ed.) *Global Warming and East Asia: The Domestic and International Politics of Climate Change*, London: Routledge, pp. 86–108.

Kropp, Cordula, Schiller, Frank and Wagner, Jost (2007) "Agrarwissenschaftliche Expertise an der Schnittstelle von Wissenschaft und Politik: Möglichkeiten und Grenzen des Wissensaustauschs," MPS-Ergebnisbroschüre. Online. Available: http://sozialforschung.org/de/literatur/Ergebnisbrosch%FCre_Schnittstellenkommunikation_kurz.pdf.

Lahsen, Myanna (2007) "Trust Through Participation? Problems of Knowledge in Climate Decision Making," in Mary E. Pettenger (ed.) *The Social Construction of Climate Change*, Burlington, VA: Ashgate, pp. 173–96.

Lan, Xinzhen (2007) "Curbing Global Warming," *Beijing Review* 46, November 15. Online. Available: http://www.bjreview.com.cn/print/txt/2007–11/12/content_85453.htm.

Latour, Bruno (1993) *We Have Never Been Modern*, Cambridge, MA: Harvard University Press.

—— (2004a) "Visualisation and Cognition: Drawing Things Together." Online. Available: http://www.bruno-latour.fr/articles/article/21-DRAWING-THINGS-TOGETHER.pdf.

—— (2004b) *Politics of Nature. How to Bring the Sciences into Democracy*, Cambridge, MA: Harvard University Press.

Litfin, Karen (2000) "Environment, Wealth and Authority: Global Climate Change and Emerging Modes of Legitimation," *International Studies Review*, 2(2): 199–248.

Liverman, Diana M. (2009) "Conventions of climate change: constructions of danger and the dispossession of the atmosphere," *Journal of Historical Geography*, 35(2): 279–96.

Macnaughton, Phil and Urry, John (1998) *Contested Natures*, London: Sage.

Mersch, Dieter (2006) "Visuelle Argumente. Zur Rolle der Bilder in den Naturwissenschaften," in Sabine Maasen, Torsten Mayerhauser and Cornelia Renggli (eds) *Bilder als Diskurse, Bilddiskurse*, Weilerswist: Velbrück, pp. 95–116.

Miller, Clark, A. (2004) "Climate Science and the Making of a Global Political Order," in Sheila Jasanoff (ed.) *States of Knowledge: The Co-production of Science and Social Order*, London: Routledge, pp. 46–66.

Müller, Benito (2002) *Equity in Climate Change: The Great Divide*, Oxford: Institute for Energy Studies.

Najam, Adil, Huq, Saleemul and Sokona, Youba (2003) "Climate Negotiations Beyond Kyoto: Developing Countries' Concerns and Interests," *Climate Policy*, 3: 221–31.

Narain, Sunita (2007) "Global Warming in an Unequal World: A Global Deal for Effective Action," presentation at the Commonwealth Finance Ministers Meeting, Georgetown, Guyana, October 16. Online. Available: http://www.slideshare.net/equitywatch/climate-equity-for-commonwealth-2007 (accessed 14 December 2007).

Oels, Angela (2005) "Rendering Climate Change Governable: From Biopower to Advanced Liberal Government?" *Journal of Environmental Policy & Planning*, 7(3): 185–207.

Permanent Mission of India to the United Nations (2007) Statement by Hon. Mr. P. Chidambaram, Finance Minister of India and Special Envoy of the Prime Minister of India during the high-level event on climate change, 24 September.

Pettenger, Mary E. (ed.) (2007) *The Social Construction of Climate Change. Power, Knowledge, Norms, Discourses*, Burlington, VA: Ashgate.

Pörksen, Uwe (1997) *Weltmarkt der Bilder. Eine Philosophie der Visiotype*, Stuttgart: Klett-Cotta.

Ramajani, Lavanya (2008) "Indiens internationale Klimapolitik," *Aus Politik und Zeitgeschichte*, 22: 19–25.

Rayner, John N. (2001) *Dynamic Climatology. Basis in Mathematics and Physics*, Oxford: Wiley-Blackwell.

Roetz, Heiner (2008) "On Nature and Culture in Zhou China," in Günter Dux and Hans Ulrich Vogel (eds) *Concepts of Nature in Traditional China: Comparative Approaches*, Leiden: Brill.

Sachs, Wolfgang (1999) *Planet Dialectics*. London: Zed Books.

Schellnhuber, Hans-Joachim and Wenzel, Volker (eds) (1998) *Earth System Analysis: Integrating Science for Sustainability*, Berlin: Springer.

Schneider, Stephen H. (2001) "Earth Systems Engineering and Management," *Nature*, 409: 417–21.

Shapiro, Judith (2001) *Mao's War against Nature: Politics and the Environment in Revolutionary China*, Cambridge: Cambridge University Press.

Smith, William D. (2007) "Presence of Mind as Working Climate Change Knowledge: A Totonac Cosmopolitics," in Mary E. Pettenger (ed.) *The Social Construction of Climate Change. Power, Knowledge, Norms, Discourses*, Burlington, VA: Ashgate, pp. 217–34.

Swyngedouw, Erik (1999) "Modernity and Hybridity: Nature, Regeneracionismo, and the Production of the Spanish Waterscape, 1890–1930," *Annals of the Association of American Geographers*, 89(3): 443–65.

Von Storch, Jin-Song (1999) "Natural Climate Variability and Concepts of Natural Climate Variability," in Hans von Storch and Götz Flöser (eds) *Anthropogenic Climate Change*, Berlin: Springer, pp. 83–135.

Weart, Spencer (2005) "Spencer Weart on Depicting Global Warming," *Environmental History*, 10(4): 770–5.

Weller, Robert P. (2006) *Discovering Nature. Globalization and Environmental Culture in China and Taiwan*, Cambridge: Cambridge University Press.

Wynne, Brian (1994) "Scientific Knowledge and the Global Environment," in Michel Redclift and Ted Benton (eds) *Social Theory and the Global Environment*, London: Routledge, pp. 169–89.

Yu, Hongyuan (2004) "Knowledge and Climate Change, Policy Coordination in China," *East Asia*, 21(3): 58–77.

Yue, Pan (2006) "Economic Development and Environmental Protection," lecture given at the 21st Century Chinese Economy Annual Meeting, 20 Dec. 2006. Online. Available: http://www.sepa.gov.cn/hjyw/200612/t20061220_97538.htm (accessed 12 November 2007).

Zhang, Zhihong (2003) "The Forces Behind China's Climate Change Policy: Interests, Sovereignty, and Prestige," in Paul G. Harris (ed.) *Global Warming and East Asia: The Domestic and International Politics of Climate Change*, London: Routledge, pp. 66–85.

# Part II
# Practice

# 6 The domestication of international environmental conventions

## Biodiversity in Ugandan foreign policy

*David R. Mutekanga*

This chapter examines the incorporation of international environmental conventions into Ugandan law and explores how this affects the country's foreign policy. Uganda is a land-locked developing country in East Africa. It lies to the south of Sudan, east of the Democratic Republic of Congo, west of Kenya, north of Rwanda and across the equator from Tanzania. It covers an area of 241,039 square kilometers and has a population of 30 million (2007 estimates) with a 3.4 per cent annual birth rate. Since 1995, it has had an annual economic growth rate of over 5 per cent. Politically, Uganda practices a decentralized administration with most political and administrative decisions taken and implemented at the level of its 72 districts (UNDP Uganda 2007). It operates a parliamentary system with a constitution that allows for multiparty activities and elections every five years.

In 1986, Uganda experienced a dramatic change. Internal conflicts and the breakdown of law and order gave way to a government that respected law and order, and which enabled democratization. This change included both discussion and formulation of a constitution through a consultative process and national elections for parliament and president. The National Resistance Movement (NRM) leadership, which spearheaded this dramatic change, came to power in 1986 after a protracted bush war. After the establishment of the new constitution in 1996 and with multi-party democracy established, the NRM changed into a political party, the National Resistance Movement Organization (NRM-O), and has won subsequent parliamentary and presidential elections.

This chapter expands on the two-dimensional topology of foreign policy variables described in the theoretical chapter by Barkdull and Harris (Chapter 2) by showing that, at the national level, Uganda's environmental policies tend to operate at the intersection of state-, power- and interest-based variables. This chapter further shows that Uganda's environmental *foreign* policy development is largely described by state-centric theory, and to a lesser extent by society-centric theory.

This chapter is divided into four main sections. The first outlines the history of the development of Uganda's foreign policy, the major players in environmental foreign policy in Uganda, and the major factors affecting the determination of foreign policy. The second provides a very brief introduction to the Convention on Biological Diversity (CBD) and the status of its implementation in Uganda. The CBD is used as an example of the relationship between the environment and foreign policy in Uganda, which is discussed in the third section of the chapter. Here we also analyze the relationship between environment and foreign policy, identifying factors influencing environmental concerns in the foreign policy of Uganda. The final section presents general recommendations on how best to implement international environmental policies within Uganda and other developing countries, in the process avoiding policy contradictions and conflicts.

## Uganda's foreign policy

### A brief history and background

Uganda is a land-locked Sub-Saharan East African country, which lies across the equator, and is divided into three main zones: swampy lowlands, a fertile plateau with wooded hills, and a dry land region. Uganda, which was a British colony from 1890 until it achieved independence in 1962, is rich in natural resources including wild life and minerals. Uganda's foreign policy since independence in 1962 has changed over time depending entirely on the changing regimes, especially when these changes have not been peaceful and/or democratic. Immediately after independence, for example, Uganda was not interested in the then world power "blocs" such as those of Casablanca and Monrovia groups of countries (Kironde 1962). The argument at that time was the need to develop a pro-African foreign policy but with some countries still under colonial rule and others pro-West (Europe and America) and others pro-East (then USSR, China and other Socialistic Asian countries), this was not very easy for emerging countries like Uganda.

Ocheng (1962) argued that the foreign policy of any country especially those emerging from colonialism was dictated and influenced by two factors: economic and political policies. This was true at that time and indeed to a very large extent Uganda's foreign policy immediately after independence was among those affected by these factors. Economically, Ocheng surmises that the search to enhance its trade would greatly influence a country's approach towards its neighboring states (for Uganda, then Kenya and Tanganyika). Elsewhere the search for enhanced trade relations influenced Uganda to take steps to draw closer to its other African neighbors such as the Sudan, the Congo, Rwanda and Burundi. Uganda's foreign policy was directed towards establishing new trade markets in Europe, Asia, the Middle East and South-east Asia, as well as expanding its trade within its existing markets especially India, Japan and China, and later expanding to include the United States. There was no reference at this stage in Uganda's foreign policy development to the need to consider the environment or environmental factors. In short, at that time, the environment played no role in the development of Uganda's foreign policy.

In the period immediately after independence, there was plenty of open discussion on how foreign policy should be developed. Policy-makers emphasized cooperation with Uganda's neighbors and the superpowers, participation in international organizations and the non-alignment movement in order to protect the state's sovereignty and support African countries as much as possible. However, Uganda's foreign policy objectives changed dramatically after the military coup in 1971. It then followed a more aggressive, militaristic and unpredictable policy, which was inevitably unsustainable. This situation did not change much during the regimes that came to power following the end of Amin's rule 1979. Most of the country's foreign policy depended on pronouncements by the presidents. The civil service worked to keep up with ever changing and unpredictable pronouncements and tried to explain it in one way or another to the outside world. This therefore did not take into account the environmental needs of the country or those of the region (Byrnes 1990).

### Foreign policy after 1986

However, after 1986, when the National Resistance Movement (NRM) Government came to power, there was a dramatic change both in the foreign policy and the administration of government. Gradually when law and order was re-established and a new constitution (1995) came into force, the process of foreign policy development also changed. Due to the need to pay greater attention to remedying the economic plight of the local people, the government sought to meet these needs before considering other related issues. It was only after the new constitution came into force that issues related to environment were to some extent considered.

In 2007 the mission of the Ministry of Foreign Affairs (MOFA) was "to promote and protect Uganda's national interests abroad"; and its mandate was "To ensure maximum benefits from the harmonization of Uganda's foreign and domestic objectives" (Government of Uganda 2007a). The ministry's key functions then included among others, "fostering a conducive environment for promoting trade, tourism and investment [and] collating and disseminating information relating to trade, investment and tourism opportunities" (ibid.). These were the two functions that had greatest relevance to the environment of the major 12 functions of the ministry in 2007.

The process of policy development in Uganda follows a number of steps. First, an issue may arise from either the Foreign Ministry or outside the ministry. It is then internally discussed in the ministry that develops the first draft of a Ministerial Paper. The ministry normally circulates this first draft to various forums and stakeholders for open discussion before preparing a final Ministerial Paper. This final paper is then presented and discussed in the Cabinet. At this stage, the proposal or initiative may be changed, removed, withdrawn or passed. After this stage, political and other socio-economic and scientific issues are also considered, especially at the national level. The Cabinet may send the document back for further consultation and input especially by other government departments and experts and/or for further public discussion. If the Cabinet accepts the policy, the paper goes to the parliament and undergoes the Uganda parliamentary rules of procedures (based on the British parliamentary system). This includes presenting it as a bill to the parliament, circulated to all members of the parliament and read at least three times before it is passed. After the first reading, the bill is sent to an appropriate committee of parliament. The committee examines the bill in detail and makes necessary inquiries, after which it reports back to the parliament. This is the second reading of the bill and it may be followed by debate depending on the report of the Committee. After this debate, the bill may be sent back to the Committee for further scrutiny or may be passed for presentation to the Committee of the whole House for the third reading before being passed. This process enables the public to have some input into policy development both directly and also through their representatives and other organizations.

Environmental issues came into the limelight in Uganda after 1990 when the process of developing a new overall managing authority began with support from the World Bank. Between 2000 and 2007, the Ugandan government was reported to have gradually taken on a new foreign policy, influenced by both the views of the general public and its desire to transform the country's economy. The country's foreign policy was expected to reflect the agenda of the ordinary citizens (Gitelson 1977; Stratfor 2002; Xinhua 2007), and therefore it was considered dynamic. For example, the foreign policy of 2006/2007 had seven major objectives, three of which directly or indirectly were related to the environment (Government of Uganda 2006):

- to promote regional and international cooperation, including meeting the relevant annual contributions to international organizations;
- to promote investments by encouraging foreign businesses and entrepreneurs especially in agro-processing industries;
- to promote tourism through the presentation of Uganda as a tourist destination.

While these policy objectives fall short of directly relating to the environment, they refer to the need to attract tourists and increase the numbers of visitors to Uganda. This can only be achieved if Uganda takes very good care of its environment, from protected areas to meeting industrial and operational environmental standards for investors. For example, in 2006, Uganda had 10 National Parks (fully protected conservation areas) which brought in a total of over 600,000 tourists in 2006, and this was projected to increase by 85 per cent in 2007 (Cohen 2007). The tourism industry brought in about 47 per cent (about US$ 4.1 million) of the total income of the Uganda Wildlife Authority (UWA) per year during the 2004/2005 financial year (Uganda Wildlife Authority 2007). This was a very significant portion of income for the UWA at this time. But the tourist income to the country certainly goes beyond entrance fees to the national parks and includes transport and accommodation in cities and towns outside the national parks, and tourists visit other areas not under UWA's jurisdiction like the source of the River Nile in Jinja.

This is also related to the invitation of foreign investments, which are expected to meet national environmental standards. In Uganda, the National Environment Management Authority (NEMA) is the principal agency for the management of the environment and it coordinates, monitors and supervises all activities in the field of environment. Its mission is to promote and ensure sound environmental management practices for sustainable development. NEMA was set up by a statutory instrument, the National Environment Management Statute of 1996 (Government of Uganda 1995c).

NEMA's policy statement states that it has four objectives: (1) greening work practices which include complying with environmental laws, regulations, standards and other requirements; (2) greening the workplaces; (3) contributing to the local community; and (4) contributing to the global community (Government of Uganda 1995b). To fulfill this policy and its legal mandate, and in conjunction with the lead agencies and ministries, NEMA developed a number of regulations including the General Guidelines for Management of Resources, Hilly and Mountainous Areas Regulations, 2000, the Wetlands, Riverbanks and Lakeshores Regulations, 1999, the Environment Impact Assessment (EIA) Regulations, 1998, the EIA Public Hearings Guidelines and the Final Guidelines to Conventions (NEMA 2007). For example, while the EIA guidelines clearly stated that all industrial investments from external or internal sources had to prepare and undergo an environmental impact assessment which might also at one stage necessitate undergoing a public hearing, the 2007 foreign policy did not explicitly say this when encouraging and urging foreign investors to come to Uganda. This is important because many investors wish to reduce the costs of their establishments and operations, and hence tend to overlook EIA requirements and this has inevitably resulted in many foreign-backed industries failing to meet the national environment standards. This is evidenced by the increasing number of cases in which investors and industrialists have been taken to court by NGOs and individuals (Greenwatch Uganda 2007). This is despite the fact that the NEMA statute prevails over the foreign policy.

In order to appreciate the link between the environment and foreign policy in Uganda, the following discussion uses the signing, domestic incorporation and application of the Convention on Biological Diversity in Uganda as an example.

### *Major players in Uganda's environmental foreign policy*

It has been correctly argued that a state's definition of its foreign policy is basically a result of its domestic factors, which include political, economic and socio-cultural factors among others (Chasek *et al.* 2006). In Uganda, the major players include the executive, the legislature, the NGOs, the private sector, the government bureaucrats and the general public. All the above groups are highly affected by domestic factors, and, to a lesser extent, by regional and international factors, such as multilateral environmental agreements (MAEs), bilateral agreements and other arrangements, political instability and insecurity among their neighbors, or regional bodies like the East African Community (EAC) and the African Union (AU).

In Uganda, these major players can be both the initiators and implementers of policies, depending on the type of policy. However, in respect of environmental and foreign policy, the executive and in particular the presidency have been the major players. These policies have also been heavily influenced by external factors especially instability in neighboring countries, and trade policy which encourages increased external investment. Both these issues are of great personal interest to the president. For example, in 2007, the Ugandan president personally took the lead in the setting up and execution of Uganda's export strategy, according to the Uganda Exports Promotion Board (Nakawesi 2007).

As described earlier, the process of introducing and implementing a policy remains the same even when the presidency is the source of the interest on a policy issue. However, because of the president's actual and perceived authority and his ability to lobby, in most cases, the Cabinet endorses the president's suggestions. Nevertheless, depending on the issue, it is either presented to the parliament for discussion by the relevant ministry and/or immediately passed on to the relevant ministry for follow up. All policies, however, are sent to the parliament and go through the parliamentary process as described above. One of the major challenges in Uganda has been that some policies are sent to the ministries for implementation from the Cabinet without going to parliament. This inevitably results in poor implementation and acceptance by both the local communities and political leaders.

The other players are the ministers and the government bureaucrats. Usually when policies or laws are developed as the result of an initiative by the bureaucracy or a minister, there is very wide public participation, including participation by NGOs, the private sector and even academia, depending on the type of policy. After several wide consultations, a policy document is then re-drafted and a Cabinet Paper is developed for Cabinet discussion. It then basically follows the same process as outlined above. The other avenue is when the policy originates from either an ordinary citizen or an NGO or the private sector. It could be accepted and taken up by the ministry which then takes the lead on the process or it may be taken up by one or more Members of Parliament who present it as a private/individual member's motion in parliament.

However, apart from the President and the Cabinet, it is not usual for the same people to have the chance to effectively participate in the initial development of both environmental policy and foreign policy (Table 6.1). This means initially only the President or the Cabinet can systematically integrate environment in foreign policy. This to some extent explains why there are very few environment issues on the foreign policy agenda. The Uganda government established a National Planning Authority (NPA) in 2002. The NPA was established by the NPA Act (15 of 2002) (Government of Uganda National Planning Authority 2002), in accordance with Article 125 of the Constitution of the Republic of Uganda, 1995. Its aim was to address the nationwide lack of a consistent, efficient, coordinated and integrated planning framework and system of managing and planning for national development with the very limited resources. The NPA is responsible for the management of national and decentralized development planning in Uganda and its major functions include harmonizing and ensuring that policies and programs of the different ministries are complementary and synergistic. This authority has improved coordination between ministries as far as policy development is concerned and is expected to reduce the conflicts that may arise in policies. It should also be able to address the potential

*Table 6.1* Comparison of environment and foreign policy players

| | Foreign policy (number of individuals/ players) | Environmental policy (number of individuals/ players) | Comments |
|---|---|---|---|
| Executive/President | 1 | 1 | Most politically powerful and most influential. |
| Ministers | 3 | 4 | Make presentations to Cabinet and to parliament. Bound by Cabinet collective responsibility. |
| Legislature/MPs | Parliamentary Committee and whole parliament | Parliamentary Committee and whole parliament | Affected by which political party they belong to and the political influence by the president and their constituents. |
| Government Bureaucrats | Many | Many | Affected by their technical affiliations and political decisions by the executive. |
| NGOs | Few | Many | Affected by their donors and constituents. |
| Private sector | Many | Few | Affected by their business interests. |
| General public | Many | Many | Affected by their well being (socioeconomic and cultural interests) and the politics. |

loopholes that may exist, for example, lack of environmental issues in the foreign policy and advising the executive appropriately.

## Major factors in determining Uganda's foreign policy

### *Domestic factors*

A number of domestic factors affect the development of Uganda's foreign policy. These include political, economic and socio-cultural factors, the relationships between the different players (for example, between the executive and the parliament) and other issues such as corruption and poverty. Earlier we discussed the changing political climate in Uganda since independence and how it has affected the process of policy development at national level. We have shown that the changes and development of a constitution have had a positive effect on the process of policy development. It is envisaged that Uganda's foreign policy development will benefit from the improving transparency of the political system. In the situation where the president's political party has a majority in parliament, the most likely situation is that the president's ideas will be voted for. There will be little or no effective opposition, hence parliament will not have a major impact on the foreign policy development.

Following the development of the national Poverty Eradication Action Plan (PEAP) as the main strategic developmental policy for Uganda, the government's major policy and plan is for industrial investment and increasing income for local people and the government itself. This explains why trade, investment and tourism appear as major objectives in the foreign policy. These policies directly affect poverty eradication activities and are also directly related to the economic development of the country. Therefore at the domestic level, the economic situation is a very significant factor in determining Uganda's foreign policy.

An additional key economic question concerns access to and exploitation of natural resources. Uganda is very well endowed with natural resources, ranging from tropical rainforests, lowland and highland forests to lakes, rivers and wetlands with abundant biodiversity. It has large grasslands and semi-arid areas with a wide variety of animal and plant life. In this context the goal of sustainable utilization by developing a tourist industry has become one of the major objectives of Uganda's foreign policy. Similarly, Uganda is basically a small-scale agricultural country. It has in the past exported unprocessed agricultural produce to Europe, the USA and Japan among others. Due to its fertile soil, Uganda continues to grow and produce many different types of tropical and non-tropical crops. In order to increase the income of the local people and the government, a policy has been developed to try and attract agro-processing industrial investors to the country. This would then enable processed products to be exported, thereby earning the country more revenue and also ensuring the farmers get more for their produce. Hence attracting foreign investment is also one of the major objectives of the foreign policy (United Nations 2000). It is important to note, however, that despite the above two major objectives – tourism and investment – as part of foreign policy, environmental issues that relate directly to tourism and investment do not appear in this policy.

Since the instability of neighboring countries tends to spill over into Uganda, the issue of peace within and outwith these countries is also an important factor; hence peace appears as an objective in the foreign policy. This is also inevitably affected by international factors.

Since 1986, Uganda has developed several strategies and set up institutions to address the problem of corruption. Certainly corruption too is a major factor in the determination of the foreign policy. The aims of Uganda's foreign policy to encourage investment and tourism are greatly affected by the level of corruption, especially for the investors who want not only efficient services but at minimal cost. This explains why the Ugandan government has put in place several systems including the Inspectorate of Government (IGG) to directly address corruption and in 2008 set up special judicial courts to specifically address corruption cases.

Another domestic factor is the interest and contacts gained by government bureaucrats who attend international meetings and network with colleagues from other countries. Since they are officially representing Uganda, they are elected to various positions, for example, for the CBD's Conference of the Parties, Uganda was "a friend to the chair" for several consecutive years (2000–2006), while discussing the International Regime for Access and Benefit Sharing of Genetic Resources (ABS). With this type of international environment responsibility, it becomes necessary for the environment to be placed on the foreign policy agenda but, apparently in this case, only to meet the needs of Uganda's official delegation to such a meeting. Inevitably, following such meetings, government bureaucrats play a major role in trying to get environmental priorities expressed in foreign policy. They may be motivated by either national or personal interests. At the level of national interest, it is logical to argue that for Uganda to continue participating in international environmental meetings, the environment should feature on the foreign policy agenda. This is also related to the need to meet international obligations, which may include subscriptions and continuous participation in meetings.

At the personal level, government bureaucrats pressurize the government to put the environment as one of the priorities on the foreign policy agenda. However, often it is difficult to effectively distinguish the national from the personal interests as these two sometimes work interchangeably at some critical levels of debate and/or discussion.

## International factors

International political and diplomatic factors and considerations also play a major role in the determination of issues in the foreign policy. For Uganda, security and peace in the neighboring countries, the East African Community and the African Union are very important international factors in its foreign policy. Trade, especially with its traditional partners (Europe, the USA and Japan), international peace (and in particular dealing with issues associated with terrorism) and Ugandans working outside the country are very significant issues and have a large role to play in shaping the objectives of Uganda's foreign policy.

As a follow-up to the role that Uganda plays at international environment meetings such as the Conference of the Parties for the CBD, other countries can indirectly influence Uganda's foreign policy regarding environmental concerns. For example, one of the major influences on Uganda's foreign policy in this case is the development partners who provide overseas development assistance (ODA) such as Europe and the USA, the regional bodies which Uganda subscribes to such as the EAC, the Common Market of Eastern and Southern Africa (COMESA) and the AU. These groups of countries commonly develop a position on an issue and their member countries have to support this stand.

## The Convention on Biological Diversity (CBD)

The CBD is the most comprehensive internationally binding legal instrument on the conservation and sustainable use of biological resources. Opened for signature on 5 June 1992, during the United Nations Conference on Environment and Development (UNCED) in Rio de Janeiro, the CBD rapidly came into force after only 18 months (i.e. June 1992–29 December 1993) (Glowka *et al.* 1994; Synge 1995). The Parties to the CBD increased in number between 2000 and 2003 from 177 to 188 (Convention on Biological Diversity Secretariat 2000, 2003). The Convention places its guiding objectives of conservation, sustainable use and equitable sharing of benefits in a binding commitment in its substantive provisions contained in Articles 6 to 20 (Convention on Biological Diversity Secretariat 1998). Conceived as a practical tool for translating the principles of Agenda 21 into reality, the Convention recognizes that biological diversity is about more than plants, animals and micro organisms and their ecosystems – it is about people and the need for food security, medicines, fresh air and water, shelter, and a clean and healthy environment in which to live (Convention on Biological Diversity 2007).

Uganda signed the CBD on 12 June 1992. The CBD was ratified by the Ugandan parliament on 8 September 1993 and that is when it came into force in Uganda. The ratification process coincided with the process of formulating and establishing a new environment management policy, statute, regulations and coordinating authority. The Ugandan National Environment Policy came into existence in 1994 following a National Environment Action Plan (NEAP) process. The NEAP process was started due to the need for Uganda to fulfill its global requirements after the signing and ratification of the CBD in 1992 and 1993 respectively (Government of Uganda 1995a). This process, which started in 1992, culminated in the establishment of Uganda's first National Environment Policy in 1994 after wide stakeholder consultation (Government of Uganda 1995b), and the National Environment Regulations and the National Environment Statute in 1995. This statute gave birth to the National Environment Management Authority (NEMA), which is the overall national coordinating organization for environmental management in Uganda (Government of Uganda 1995c).

When the NRM government came to power in 1986, it immediately set up a Ministry of Environment Protection and as the foundation of this new ministry, it was important for the government to be seen, particularly at the international level, to be supporting the conservation of natural resources. This inevitably affected Uganda's foreign policy and partly led to Uganda signing and ratifying the CBD.

Following this brief background about Uganda's Foreign Policy and the CBD, it is useful now to turn to the issue of how these two are related and affect each other. This discussion will lead to an appreciation of the foreign policy process and how it addresses the environmental challenges faced by Uganda.

### Environment as an issue in Uganda's foreign policy: the CBD case study

This section analyzes the relationship between the two issues – the environment and foreign policy – and identifies the factors that affect the role of environmental issues in the development of foreign policy. As the above discussion concerning the development of Uganda's foreign policy and the factors which affect its objectives highlights, the environment has had very little to do with the main objectives of Uganda's foreign policy. However, increased globalization and the need for an increase in tourism and investment have had an inevitable impact on the way the makers of foreign policy are starting to view the environment. The drive for more investment and tourism, for example, implies the need to have not only environmental regulations for investors but also proper rules and regulations to ensure tourists are attracted to visit. The majority of tourists who visit Uganda are well-heeled and well-informed people whose interest in Uganda goes beyond just seeing the wildlife to encompass issues of conservation laws and regulations and how the local communities are gaining from the money earned by the Uganda Wildlife Authority. This means, if the environment in Uganda is destroyed, the result will not only be a decrease in the number of tourists but also the loss of income generated from these tourists. Since most of the tourists come from abroad, this means there is a need for the environment to be directly reflected in the foreign policy.

However, there are a number of factors that affect the role of the environment in Uganda's foreign policy:

1   *The increased rate of MEAs on the international scene*: By 2002, there were over 500 Multilateral Environmental Agreements (MEAs) (Crossen 2004; Environment Canada 2007). This increase and the need for Uganda, especially after 1986, to play a role not only in the region but also internationally, have inevitably led to the environment becoming a factor in the country's foreign policy. For example, of these 500 MEAs, Uganda is a signatory to only 28 of them (only 6 per cent).

2   *The increase in international funding available for environmental and conservation programs and projects*: The support by the World Bank and other developed countries for the National Environment Action Plan (NEAP) process and later for the National Environment Management Authority (NEMA) which is the environment policy and implementation watchdog in Uganda. These same donors also support other developmental activities and do not want to be seen contradicting their environment agenda and development programs. For example, the World Bank was involved in supporting the work of NEMA as the overall national environment coordinator and it also supported the building of a large hydroelectric power-generating dam across the River Nile. The World Bank did not want to support a project (UG-Bujagali Hydropower GU/FY02) that did not follow the environment impact assessment standards and other related regulations set up by NEMA, which it also supported (Second Environment Management and Capacity Building) (World Bank 2007). Also Uganda, as a developing country, has relied on international support for about 50 per cent of the national Government's annual budget in 2006/2007 which has declined to 38.7 per cent in 2007/2008 (Government of Uganda 2007b, 2007c). The ultimate consequence, if the environmental issues are ignored, is not only the potential loss of external budget support but unknown negative impacts on Uganda's unique and natural environment.

3   *The increase in the relationship between environment conservation and international politics as exemplified by issues related to global warming and $CO_2$ emissions*: Developing countries like Uganda cannot afford new clean technologies due to their lack of capacity to use, manage and/or regulate these technologies. They have tended to use second-hand and old technologies which in most cases produce $CO_2$ and other polluting gases, like $SO_2$. Since foreign policy does not directly mention this issue, the country has continued to import old technologies and equipments, which are environmentally unfriendly and tend to increase greenhouse gas emissions.

4   *Uganda's foreign policy has also encouraged external investment especially through the introduction of agro-processing industries among others*: International competition for these industries has led the government to increase the attractiveness of investment in Uganda. One of the major approaches to attract investors is the provision of "free" land to set up industries together with conducive environmental policies and laws for investment.

5 *The relationship between the environment, conservation and development, especially industrial development*: As indicated earlier, one of Uganda's foreign policy objectives is attracting agro-processing industries. However, these industries have to meet the environmental regulations and standards in Uganda as stipulated in the National Environment Management Act (Government of Uganda 1995c).

Achieving these goals will require that environmental goals are integrated into broader foreign policy.

In the case of the CBD, after its signature by Uganda in 1992, the leading ministry in this case, the (then) Ministry of Environment Protection developed a Cabinet Paper on the CBD prior to its ratification. This paper was presented and passed by the Cabinet and legislation was presented to the parliament. After discussion in parliament, a decision was made to ratify the convention. This was basically the beginning of the process of incorporation of the CBD into Ugandan law.

The signing of the CBD before the environment statute came into being in Uganda was good for the country. As outlined below, for the first time, a national environment statute recognized an international environment convention (Mutekanga 2005). This situation of Uganda signing the CBD before making a national statute on environment enabled the country to use experiences from other countries and also to include some of the CBD requirements in the national statute. Second, it also enabled Uganda to move very quickly on developing its environment statute and to gain international support for the development process of this statute. Finally, as a result, Uganda was among the first countries in the Eastern, Central and Southern African regions to develop a comprehensive environment statute, policy and relevant operational guidelines at a national level.

Uganda's international environmental obligations (including the CBD) are stipulated in the environment statute in Part XV – International Obligations, Section 107 – where the environment statute clearly stipulates the procedures to give it a force of law (Government of Uganda 1995c).

From the above analysis it is very clear that Uganda's Foreign Policy is affected by many domestic factors and international factors but that it does not explicitly refer to the environment. This is despite the fact that domestic regulations and laws do refer to and have to accommodate international/multilateral environmental agreements. Further, while foreign policy advances a number of clear objectives on investment and tourism, it does not relate these to the environment. Despite this, Uganda still plays a role in environment agreement-making at the international level and meets its global responsibilities. Uganda has, in the case of the CBD, written and presented its Environment Reports to the CBD Secretariat and Clearing House Mechanism. It has also developed and published the national State of Environment Reports every two years since 1994. Judging by this criteria, Uganda is certainly meeting its international environmental obligations.

## Conclusion

The preceding discussion suggests that Uganda has a strong state-centered approach to foreign policy as is evidenced by the influence of the presidency and ministries (executive) in policy-making. There is a small but quickly growing role played by society as evidenced by the role of civil society, the private sector and parliament. This also makes the process of domestic application of international environmental agreements basically state-led and hence reflect mainly if not solely the state's power, interests, ideas and emphasis. However, the chapter has also shown that there is a growing change from a sole state (executive) to a more societal (civil, private sector) influence in foreign policy development. In light of the above, a number of policy recommendations arise that are intended to help officials domestically implement international policies, while having due regard for environmental policies in developing countries, in ways that do not add to existing contradictions and conflicts.

First, there is a need for a national-level planning authority which would, among other things, examine and monitor the development and the processes of establishing the various national policies to ensure consistent and synergistic relationships between the various policies and across portfolios, for example, in this case between foreign and environment policies. This process of establishing a national planning authority has commenced within some developing Sub-Saharan African countries including Uganda, but it is still too early to make any significant analysis of their impact. Second, there is a need for a transparent process in developing national-level policies, including foreign policy. In most developing countries this is beginning to happen as evidenced by the Ugandan case where the Parliamentary Committee on Foreign Affairs comments and advises the government on current and new foreign policies, and by the fact that the Cabinet meets and discusses the draft policies before they are submitted to the parliament for further scrutiny and approval, and that the process involves public participation. Third, there is a need for a continuous review of the national policies in general but in particular a critical examination of foreign policy as the global issues emerge. This calls for a very dynamic foreign policy. Fourth, there is a need for countries to explicitly include environmental requirements in their foreign policy. The absence of environmental issues tends to negate the implementation of the national environment policies, laws and regulations. This is particularly important where there is increased level of external/foreign investments and trade.

## References

Byrnes, Rita (ed.) (1990) *Uganda: A Country Study – Foreign Relations*, Washington, DC: GPO for the Library of Congress. Online. Available: http://countrystudies.us/uganda/65.htm (accessed 28 September 2007).

Chasek, P.S., Downie, D.L. and Brown, J.W. (2006) "The Emergence of Environmental Politics," in *Global Environmental Politics*, 4th edn, Boulder, CO: Westview Press.

Cohen, Francine (2007) "Uganda Tourism Sector Lights up Dark Continent," Top Story *Hotel Interactive*. Online. Available: http://www.hotelinteractive.com/index. asp?lstr=dcrory@cendyn.com&page_id=5000&article_id=7494 (accessed 18 October 2007).

Convention on Biological Diversity (1998) "Convention on Biological Diversity: Text and Annexes," ICAO, Montreal: Secretariat of the Convention on Biological Diversity.

—— (2007) "The CBD: What It Is." Online. Available: http://www.cbd.int/convention/ default.shtml (accessed 9 October 2007).

Convention on Biological Diversity Secretariat (2000) "Background Documents to Conference of Parties V," Montreal: Secretariat of the CBD.

—— (2003) *Handbook of the Convention on Biological Diversity*, 2nd edn, Montreal: Secretariat of the CBD.

Crossen, Teall (2004) "Multilateral Environmental Agreements and the Compliance Continuum," *Georgetown International Environment Law Review*, 1 April 2004. Online. Available: http://findarticles.com/p/articles/mi_qa3970/is_200404/ai_n9406137 (accessed 26 September 2007).

Environment Canada (2007) *Compendium of International Environment Agreements*, 3rd Edition 2002. Online. Available: http://www.ec.gc.ca/international/multilat/ compendium_e.htm. (accessed 26 September 2007).

Gitelson, Susan Aurelia (1977) "Major Shifts in Recent Uganda Foreign Policy," *African Affairs*, 76: 359–80.

Glowka, Lyle, Burhenne, Guilmin and Synge, Hugh (1994) "A Guide to the Convention on Biological Diversity," *IUCN Environment Policy Paper*, No. 30. Gland and Cambridge: IUCN, The World Conservation Union.

Government of Uganda (1995a) *The National Environment Action Plan (NEAP) for Uganda*, Ministry of Natural Resources. Kampala, Uganda: The NEAP Secretariat.

—— (1995b) *The National Environment Management Policy, National Environment Action Plan*, Kampala: Ministry of Natural Resources.

—— (1995c) *The National Environment Statute*, Entebbe: UPPC.

—— (2006) "Ministerial Policy Statement, Presented to Parliament for the Budget Estimates for Financial Year 2006–2007," Ministry of Foreign Affairs, Headquarters, Kampala, Uganda. 30 June 2006.

—— (2007a) "The Ministry of Foreign Affairs – Uganda." Online. Available: www. mofa.go.ug/ministry.php?Table=ministry (accessed 19 July 2007).

—— (2007b) "Background to the Budget 2007/2008 Financial Year," Ministry of Finance, Planning and Economic Development. Online. Available: http://www. finance.go.ug/docs/BTTB_07.pdf (accessed 18 September 2007).

—— (2007c) "National Budget Speech – Financial Year 2007/2008," Ministry of Finance, Planning and Economic Development. Online. Available: http://www. finance.go.ug/docs/Budget_Speech_FY_2007_08_Final.pdf (accessed 18 September 2007).

Government of Uganda National Planning Authority (2002) "National Planning Act." Online. Available: http://www.finance.go.ug/autonomous.php#five (accessed 9 October 2007).

Greenwatch Uganda (2007) "Greenwatch Uganda Judgements." Online. Available: http://www.greenwatch.or.ug/greenwatch_judgements.htm (accessed 18 October 2007).

Kironde, Erisa (1962) "Towards a Definition of Foreign Policy," *In Transition*, 5 (July): 13.

Mutekanga, David Robinson (2005) "The Involvement of Environmental Non – Government Organizations in the Implementation of the Convention on Biological Diversity: The Case of Uganda," unpublished thesis, Makerere University, Kampala, Uganda.

Nakawesi, Dorothy (2007) "Government Sets Up Export Strategy," *Monitor*, 11 October, 2007. Online. Available: http://www.monitor.co.ug/business/bus10114.php (accessed 11 October 2007).

NEMA (2007) "National Environment Management Authority: Environmental Legislation." Online. Available: http://www.nemaug.org/law.php (accessed 9 October 2007).

Ocheng, Daudi (1962) "Economic Forces and Uganda's Foreign Policy," *In Transition*, 6/7 (Oct.): 27–9.

Stratfor (2002) "Uganda's Changing Geopolitical Reality." Online. Available: www.stratfor.com/products/premium/read_article.php?id=204269&selected=Country %20Profiles&showCountry=1&countryId=127&showMore=1 (accessed 7 October 2007).

Synge, Hugh. (1995) "The Biodiversity Convention Explained: Part 1 Introduction and Objectives," *PlantTalk*, March.

Uganda Wildlife Authority (2007) "UWA Annual Report 2004–2005," Uganda Wildlife Authority, Kampala, Uganda. Online. Available: http://www.uwa.or.ug/ Report2004–5.pdf (accessed 9 October 2007).

UNDP Uganda (2007) "About Uganda," United Nations Development Program. Online. Available: http://www.undp.or.ug/aboutug.php. (accessed 28 September 2007).

United Nations (2000) "United Nations Conference on Trade and Development: Investment policy review – Uganda." Online. Available: http://www.unctad.org/en/ docs/iteiipmisc17_en.pdf. (accessed 27 September 2007).

World Bank (2007) "Uganda: Active Project." Online. Available: http://web. worldbank.org/external/default/main?menuPK=374969&pagePK=141155&piPK=14 1124&theSitePK=374864 (accessed 11 October 2007).

Xinhua (2007) "Uganda Embarks on New Foreign Policy to Promote Economic Transformation," *People's Daily*. Online. Available: http://english.peopledaily.com. cn/200701/09/print20070109_339241.html (accessed 19 July 2007).

# 7 From local protest to the International Court of Justice

## Forging environmental foreign policy in Argentina

*Isabella Alcañiz and Ricardo A. Gutiérrez*

In 2005, neighbors of the small Argentine city of Gualeguaychú, located in the province of Entre Ríos, began protesting the planned construction of two pulp plants on the Uruguayan side of the shared Uruguay River.[1] Protesters, claiming pollution from the plants would devastate the local fishing and tourist industry, blocked the international bridges that connect the two countries and demanded that Uruguay cease construction. The demonstrations grew in size and intensity, and in spite of the low priority traditionally granted by government and media to environmental disputes, the conflict quickly reached the national scene. In May 2006, the government of Argentina filed suit against its neighbor before the International Court of Justice (ICJ), claiming violation of the 1975 bilateral Uruguay River Treaty (International Court of Justice 2007). While currently awaiting the ICJ final decision, the two countries have carried their dispute to other international organizations and strained the bilateral relationship to an unprecedented point. How did this small-scale protest by local neighbors, environmentalists, and NGOs quickly escalate into an international dispute between two historically allied states?

This case study answers this question, and in doing so traces the process through which Argentina has forged its present environmental foreign policy. The argument advanced in this chapter is based on the convergence of four logics: social mobilization, water policy, issue salience and institutional context (Table 7.1). Specifically, we argue that the sustained radical tactics adopted by the protesters, coupled with the nature of water management – a policy area with overlapping and competing authorities – pushed the conflict onto

*Table 7.1* Explaining executive involvement and policy: four logics

| Dispute escalation | Government policy |
| --- | --- |
| Middle-class mobilization (radical tactics) | Issue salience (incentive to settle dispute legally) |
| Water policy (overlapping authorities and networks) | Institutional context (weak national agency-international treaty) |

the national scene. By closing off land traffic between Argentina and Uruguay, the protesters guaranteed extensive nation-wide coverage by the media, which in turn put pressure on President Néstor Kirchner (2003–7) to decide on a course of action, either in support of the protesters (and against Uruguay) or against the protesters (and in favor of Uruguay). Finally, the institutional weakness of the domestic agency charged with environmental policy in Argentina allowed local NGOs to push their agenda forward without resistance, and a pre-existing international treaty regulating the use of the Uruguay River gave the Argentine government a "roadmap" to tackle the crisis.

Interestingly, each side interprets the on-going conflict as resulting from the violation of rights. Argentina argues its environmental rights are being threatened by the plants, while Uruguay claims the bridges blockades encroach on the country's right to pursue economic development. Both countries claim to defend their right to *sustainable development*, but they conceive of it as protecting very different interests. Uruguay claims to uphold the country's economic interests and its right to seek foreign direct investment, whereas Argentina maintains both its environmental and economic rights are at risk.

By analyzing how local civil society can affect the foreign policy choices made by top decision-makers in Argentina, this chapter contributes to the study of the domestic determinants of environmental foreign policy. In so doing, it departs from systemic approaches and locates itself at the intersection between the society- and state-levels of analysis as defined by Barkdull and Harris in Chapter 2. Our chapter seeks to show the connection between the views and preferences of civil society actors and the policy choices of top decision-makers.

Finally, on a more practical stance, we believe both policy-makers and advocates engaged in institutional-building and management of shared natural resources can benefit from the lessons drawn from this case study. One of the main findings of this study is that local activists were successful in reaching top decision-makers partly because of the kind of ties they forged with their allies. Specifically, local activists sought ties with different social, economic, and political actors, which resulted in the development of broad "green" networks. This, in turn, helped forge a powerful all-inclusive coalition rallied around the goal of pursuing environmental rights by stopping the construction of the plants.

In the remainder of this chapter, we first analyze the case at hand through the analytical framework offered by contentious politics, water policy, issue salience, and environmental institutions in Argentina. Second, we explain why Argentina pursued an "international" strategy to deal with the conflict. We conclude by discussing some of the implications of this study for environmental advocacy and environmental foreign policy.

## Environmental advocates and radical tactics

One of the most relevant questions in the literature on social movements regards the determinants of advocacy success (Keck and Sikkink 1998;

McAdams *et al.* 2001; Goodwin and Jasper 2003). Given that all advocates want to affect policy (Keck and Sikkink 1998), and that advocates often lack the resources and clout of material-based groups (the power of exit, for example), what are the factors that translate into political influence? We address this theoretical discussion by answering two key questions regarding the case at hand. First, how did a local environmental protest escalate to the national level and force the executive to decide on a course of action? Second, why did the executive take up the protesters' agenda? The first question, we argue, is explained both by the nature of water policy (as one with many overlapping authorities) and the radical tactics chosen by the protesters. The answer to the second question, our argument continues, is due to the salience of the *"papeleras"*[2] issue and the weakness of existing environmental state institutions in Argentina.

Available resources, strategies, and tactics are crucial in explaining the possibility of political organization and sustained action by advocates and NGOs. In this case study, we find that in particular the radical tactic of blocking roads and the international bridges between Argentina and Uruguay immediately elevated the profile of the protesters' cause.[3] In adopting this tactic, the Gualeguaychú protesters, now commonly known as *asambleístas*,[4] mimicked the *piqueteros*; that is, the organizations of unemployed workers in Argentina that block roads in order to force authorities to negotiate their withdrawal in exchange for jobs or government subsidies.[5]

How did the *asambleístas* come together and organize? In the first half of 2003, environmentalists from Gualeguaychú and other Entre Ríos cities began to exchange information on the projected pulp mills that had already been discussed in Uruguay. In September of that year, they organized the first local demonstration to oppose construction and made public the Gualeguaychú Declaration, in which they expressed "the most absolute opposition to the installation of a pulp mill [in] Fray Bentos, Republic of Uruguay," rejecting "the environmental impact studies submitted by the foreign investors, which on the other hand have already been criticized by non-governmental organizations before the Uruguayan National Office for the Environment."[6]

After this first protest rally, the Gualeguaychú environmentalists focused on building a wider coalition with other social and political actors, targeting city associations and local government officials. In February 2005, they interrupted the Gualeguaychú Carnival (the most popular carnival in Argentina) to distribute surgical masks in order to call attention to the potential pollution hazards of the projected plants. In the words of one of the protestors, at that time, they were "no more than 10 nuts distributing surgical masks. Nobody paid much attention to us, we thought that our fight would end up being a failure" (quoted in López Echagüe 2006: 61).

In March 2005, Gualeguaychú environmentalists invited local organizations and neighbors to meet in order to debate Uruguay's pulp mill projects. With high attendance, participants decided to demonstrate on the Gualeguaychú–Fray Bentos international bridge on 30 April. Some 40,000 people (half of Gualeguaychú's 80,000 population) marched over the international bridge, blocking all traffic between the two cities. That same day the Environmental Assembly of the Citizens of Gualeguaychú (*Asamblea Ciudadana Ambiental de Gualeguaychú*) was formed.

While copying the *piqueteros'* main tactic of blocking roads, the *asambleístas* differed from the organizations of unemployed workers in that they were not organized along class lines. Rather, the Gualeguaychú protestors showed a diverse composition, resulting from the ties forged among different social, economic, and political actors (including the city mayor), albeit with a predominance of local middle-class elements. In addition, the Assembly maintained bottom-up decision-making procedures, thus encouraging the incorporation of more participants.

The sustained mobilization of the neighbors of Gualeguaychú was, we argue, the trigger of the crisis with Uruguay. Extensive national media coverage followed the protests, in particular during the summer months, as Argentine tourists attempting to vacation in Uruguay could no longer use the Uruguay River bridges to reach their destination. These high profile protests, thus, made it impossible for the Kirchner administration to ignore the situation and forced the national government to address the activists' claim.

The broad coalition of Gualeguaychú protestors fits what Cotgrove and Duff call the new "middle-class radicalism" (2003: 72). That is "new social groups ... which cut across traditional class-based alignments and cleavages" that endorse "direct action, and the growth of outside politics, [and] a decline in partisan support for the traditional parties" (ibid.: 72). The authors argue that this new middle-class radicalism, organized mostly around environmental causes, reflects not just the members' ideological belief in the environment, but also their (negative) views on industrial capitalism (ibid. 75). Thus, according to these authors, the radical nature of these groups is explained by their somewhat anti-capitalist ideology.

In their seminal work on transnational advocacy networks, Keck and Sikkink argue that environmentalists "are not as clearly principled" as other activists (Keck and Sikkink 1998: 121). This is so because "environmentalism is less a set of universally agreed upon principles than it is a frame within which the relations among a variety of claims about resource use, property, rights, and power may be reconfigured" (ibid.: 121). Concurrently, in our own research, we find that the *asambleístas* adopt the radical *piquetero* tactics not because of ideological beliefs or an anti-capitalist worldview. Rather, the protesters strategically embraced the tactics that they believed would be most effective in bringing national attention to their environmental and economic concerns of how the plants would damage their local tourist and fishing industries.

## Water policy and overlapping authorities

Together with radical mobilization, the nature of water policy enabled the conflict to escalate to the national scene, for it allowed local protestors to bring provincial and national attention to their plight. Water, like other natural resources, is managed across different overlapping jurisdictions (Schneider *et al.* 2003). In this case study, Uruguay and Argentina share (international) jurisdiction over the river; in Argentina alone there are three (domestic) jurisdictions: municipal, provincial, and national. Overlapping jurisdictions have two important effects. First, they enable the growth of networks of environmental activists, which in turn allow a more effective and democratic sharing of information and resources to solve common problems (Schneider *et al.* 2003; Keck and Sikkink 1998).

For example, originally, Uruguayan NGOs informed Argentine environmentalists in Entre Ríos about their government's plan to build the two pulp plants (Vara forthcoming). As the conflict intensified, only Argentine protestors pushed on, carried on by a network of different neighborhood associations and environmental NGOs, gathered around the Environmental Assembly of the Citizens of Gualeguaychú. The Assembly would end up developing an advocacy network with other NGOs from Entre Ríos and the rest of the country. Within this network an important coalition was built early on between the *asambleístas* and the Center for Human Rights and the Environment (CEDHA). Connected to several local, national, and international environmental NGOs,[7] CEDHA provided crucial legal and organizational assistance to the neighbors of Gualeguaychú as well as other cities in the province that would join the protests at a later date.

Further, as local and national authorities have legal as well as political stakes in water policy, environmental advocates can hold them accountable. Indeed, early on, the protestors claimed that not just Uruguay, but also the Entre Ríos government and the Kirchner administration were accountable in the dispute over the projected pulp mills. This is consistent with Keck and Sikkink's "accountability politics" by which advocates attempt to pressure political actors into closing "the distance between discourse and practice" (Keck and Sikkink 1998: 24).

The success of this type of politics, however, is dependent on the nature of key domestic structures (ibid.). This leads us to the second part of our discussion, which explains why the Kirchner administration decided to pursue a foreign environmental policy favorable to the *asambleístas*. Two factors, we argue, were critical in persuading the Argentine president to take up the cause of the Gualeguaychú neighbors. First, the salience of the issue, as it was covered relentlessly by the national media, and second, weak environmental institutions – which offered little resistance to the policy agenda of the protestors.

## Issue salience

There is a vast literature that links issue salience – the relative prominence of an issue in the public mind – with environmental policy outcome (for example, Harrison 1996; Shipan and Lowry 2001). While several factors contributed to the prominence of the Entre Ríos environmentalists, such as the protestors' radical tactics and Uruguay's increasingly argumentative position, the role of Jorge Busti (the governor of the province of Entre Ríos) was critical in raising national awareness of the conflict. In particular, Governor Busti helped frame the controversy over the pulp mills not just as an environmental issue but also as an economic problem for Entre Ríos, linking the potential ecological impact of the mills to future economic losses for the province.[8] Furthermore, the governor increased the visibility of the neighborhood assemblies by filing, on their behalf, formal complaints against Uruguay and the pulp firms before the Inter-American Commission on Human Rights and the MERCOSUR (The Common Market of the South).

Further, the location of the protests, on the bridges over the Uruguay River, was critical in making the conflict salient at the national level. Approximately 70 per cent of trade between the countries is transported mostly over the bridge that connects Gualeguaychú, Argentina with Fray Bentos, Uruguay (*America Económica* 2006). In addition, the bridges are also critical for the tourism industry in both countries.

The numerous protests closing off the bridges between the two countries, the active participation of the governor, and the severe disruption in bilateral trade and tourism, thus guaranteed sustained media coverage of the conflict. This, in turn, put pressure on the Kirchner administration to address the activists' cause and attempt to settle the growing dispute with Uruguay. The creation in 2005 of a joint task force (the Bilateral High-Level Technical Group or GTAN) did not resolve the dispute between the two countries, so the Argentine president finally decided to tackle the issue directly.[9] Addressing the new 2006 congress, Kirchner blamed Uruguay for violating the Uruguay River Treaty, unilaterally authorizing the construction of the pulp mills, and thus impeding a resolution to the crisis (*Clarín Newspaper* 2006).

Recently, Allee and Huth (2006) have argued that national executives have increased incentives to settle bilateral disputes when domestic opposition on the issue is strong, "as well as when the dispute is highly salient to domestic audiences" (ibid.: 219). Further, they argue "that leaders will seek legal dispute settlement in situations where they anticipate sizable domestic political costs should they attempt to settle a dispute through the making of bilateral, negotiated concessions" (ibid.: 219). We argue that President Kirchner decided to pursue international legal venues to solve the Gualeguaychú conflict precisely for these reasons. In particular, as the conflict quickly became permeated with strong nationalist overtones, conceding to Uruguay would have been extremely problematic for the Argentine government. Instead, bringing the case before a *neutral* international organization would allow the Kirchner administration to avoid some of the inevitable political costs associated with a negotiated solution with Uruguay.

## Institutional context

The final explanatory factor in this case, we argue, is the institutional context in which the conflict over the pulp mills took place. Argentina, like many developing states, lacked a strong and centralized environmental agency. Until very recently, the top domestic institution in environmental policy was an under-secretariat, under the Ministry of Health and Sustainable Development. This made it possible for the *asambleístas* – rather than the government – to frame the issue in their own terms, primarily as a conflict threatening their environmental rights, and by extension, their economic rights.

As a direct result of the Gualeguaychú conflict, President Kirchner upgraded the existing agency to a secretariat directly under the Ministers Cabinet. More tellingly, the head of the CEDHA, one of the leading NGOs backing the Gualeguaychú protests, became the new secretary of Environmental Policy (Fundación Proteger 2006). Thus, a key activist in the conflict became the government official in charge of defining state environmental policy.

While the Kirchner government lacked strong state advisors regarding environmental policy, it had, on the other hand, an international treaty signed with its neighbor, regulating the common use of the Uruguay River. This treaty offered a possible road map to negotiate the crisis. Signed in 1975, the Treaty of the Uruguay River established "common mechanisms needed for the rational and optimal management of the Uruguay River" (Art. 1) (Espacios Jurídicos n.d.). The Treaty established the creation of the Uruguay River Administration Commission or CARU (made up of equal number of Argentines and Uruguayans) that would have a crucial role in the conflict.

The Treaty also establishes that "the Party that intends ... the realization of whatever works that may affect the river's navigation, hydrological regime, or water quality must inform the Commission (CARU), which will determine, in up to thirty days, whether the project may cause a damage to the other Party" (Art. 7). Furthermore, Article 13 specifies that the obligation to inform the other party also "applies to all works referred in Article 7, be they national or binational, that either Party intends to realize, within its jurisdiction, on the Uruguay River *outside the section defined as River* and the correspondent areas of influence" (our emphasis). Finally, Article 27 stresses that "each Party's right to use the river's water, within its jurisdiction, with sanitation, industrial, or agricultural purposes will be exerted without eluding the procedure established" by Article 7 when such an intervention may affect the river's regime or the waters' quality.

As early as 2002, Argentine CARU delegates requested that Uruguay share the environmental impact project prepared by the Spanish firm ENCE earlier that year. Once received, the Argentine National Water Institute (INA) assessed the report and concluded that the Fray Bentos pulp mills would have "considerable" environmental impact and recommended substituting TCF (Totally Chlorine Free) for ECF (Elementary Chlorine Free), which is less contaminating. TCF technology was also recommended by Greenpeace and embraced by the Gualeguaychú Assembly as the only acceptable technology (Greenpeace Argentina 2006).

## The internationalization of the Argentine–Uruguayan conflict

As the Gualeguaychú protests increased in intensity and media coverage, early attempts to reach an agreement within CARU ultimately failed. Both countries, thus, looked for international venues to settle the dispute. On April 18, 2006 (one week after the busy Easter holiday for tourists), Uruguay filed a demand with MERCOSUR accusing Argentina of not guaranteeing the freedom of circulation of goods and blaming its neighbor for the negative impact of the protests on their economy (URUGUAY Ministerio de Relaciones Exteriores 2006). In May of the same year, Argentina filed a demand with the International Court of Justice (ICJ) accusing Uruguay of having violated the Uruguay River Treaty and requested the construction of BOTNIA to be called off immediately (International Court of Justice). As the Treaty stipulated, CARU was to be the first arena of dispute-resolution between the parties. If no agreement were reached within CARU by a certain deadline, "any controversy ... may be presented by either Party before the International Court of Justice" (Art. 60).

As stated above, in July 2006, the Argentine government named Romina Picolotti – president of CEDHA and legal advisor to the state of Entre Ríos and the Gualeguaychú Assembly – as head of the new Secretariat of the Environment and Sustainable Development. Picolotti, already advising the *asambleístas*, represented Argentina before the Court. Also in July 2006, the ICJ delivered its first ruling on the case. The Court ruled against Argentina's claim that construction of the plants was causing irreversible damage to the local environment. However, it also ruled that Uruguay would be found liable if the pulp mills were to cause pollution in the future. These were partial rulings for the ICJ did not rule on the substantive matter – the claim, by Argentina, that Uruguay violated the Treaty of the Uruguay River. The Court is not expected to rule on this before late 2009.

In September 2006, Argentina received another problematic ruling in another international legal battle. The Arbitration Tribunal of the MERCOSUR – in agreement with Uruguay's claim – ruled that the Argentine government was not doing everything in its power to prevent the blockade of the international bridges. However, the Tribunal also rejected Uruguay's request that MERCOSUR intervene and prevent any future blockades from occurring.

A month later, the World Bank's International Finance Corporation (IFC) – the institution financing the construction of BOTNIA – released a final study on the expected environmental impact of the pulp mill. The study argued that the plant would not have any significant negative impact either on the environment or the tourist industry. Secretary Picolotti argued unsuccessfully before the Board of Governors of the World Bank against them lending the $170 million requested by BOTNIA; thus, in November 2006, the World Bank officially announced it would finance the BOTNIA project (International Finance Corporation 2006).

Also in November of 2006, Uruguay requested that the ICJ sanction a provisional measure against Argentina in order to force its government to stop the bridges blockades by the Entre Ríos activists. This time the Court ruled against Uruguay, in January 2007, affirming that the blockades were not causing irreparable damages. In the meantime, the Kirchner administration sought the mediation of the Spanish King. After numerous meetings in Buenos Aires, Madrid, Montevideo, New York and Santiago de Chile, the Spanish mediation proved unsuccessful and the two countries remain in a stalemate with no resolution to the dispute in sight.

## Conclusion

This chapter has examined the ongoing dispute between Argentina and Uruguay over shared waters. The two countries have attempted unsuccessfully to settle the dispute in numerous international organizations, including the International Court of Justice (ICJ), the World Bank, and the Common Market of the South (MERCOSUR), of which Argentina and Uruguay are both members. In Argentina, as in most developing states, environmental policy has traditionally ranked low on the foreign policy agenda. However, we believe this high profile dispute has given environmental policy greater priority within Argentine domestic and foreign politics. We see the new, upgraded secretariat charged with environmental policy as evidence of this.

While social advocacy triggered the change in (foreign) environmental policy in Argentina, we believe the dispute with Uruguay needs to be explained within the strategic interaction of societal actors and state institutions. That is, we do not argue a clear-cut society-centered approach to foreign policy in which the state is seen as a neutral referee or a passive arena for the "translation" of domestic civil society preferences and ideologies (see Chapter 2). Rather, we believe that if Argentina's new environmental foreign policy ended up "resembling" the local protesters' preferences, it is largely because of the type of national environmental institutions and the underdevelopment of environmental policy. Given the institutional circumstances, top decision-makers strategically *chose* to take up the protesters' agenda and legally challenge Uruguay. In addition, it is worth noting that social actors in Entre Ríos were joined by local political actors from the first protests. This suggests, we believe, that in dealing with the domestic determinants of foreign environmental policy, more attention should be paid to the interaction (and sometimes the blurring of boundaries) between state and non-state actors operating at different government levels.

As the conflict is ongoing, it is hard to draw definite conclusions from the case. However, some early lessons are apparent. In particular, regarding the cross-class alliance forged by the Gualeguaychú activists. By not limiting themselves to an ideology-based coalition, the *asambleístas* have been more effective in developing ties with different NGOs and political actors at the provincial and national level. We find these networks to be crucial arenas (and actors) in the struggle to influence government policy. Future research on this emblematic case study could focus more on the resources available to these activist networks that are necessary to sustain collective action in time.

Finally, it is interesting to note that Argentina and Uruguay are reproducing, on a much smaller scale, the kind of tensions that we observe between some developing and developed states, namely, the struggle between the goals of *economic development* and *sustainable development*. Often, all developing countries are assumed to prioritize the former over the latter. This conflict reminds us that within the developing world there are different ways in which countries conceive of these two objectives, which in turn produce very distinct foreign environmental policies.

## Notes

1 The two plants, the Spanish ENCE and Finnish BOTNIA, were to be built across the river from Gualeguaychú, just 300 kilometers (186 miles) west of Montevideo, the capital city of Uruguay. Both were expected to produce yearly around 1,000,000 tons of pulp. The total investment for building both plants was estimated in approximately 1,500,000 dollars. In 2006, ENCE decided to move the construction of its plant to a new location, away from the Uruguay River and closer to Montevideo (FARN 2006: 1–2).

2 *Papeleras* or *pasteras* (in English, paper or pulp mills) are the names commonly used by Argentines and Uruguayans to refer to the pulp plants.

3 Argentine tourists, seeking Uruguayan beach resorts, are critical to the economy of Uruguay. Besides the very expensive option of flying, there are essentially two ways to travel between Argentina and Uruguay. Either by the Buenos Aires–Montevideo ferry or by vehicle, using one of the three international bridges over the Uruguay River. These bridges connect Uruguay with three cities in the province of Entre Ríos: Gualeguaychú, Colón, and Concordia. The bridge connecting the cities of Gualeguaychú and Fray Bentos (on the Uruguayan side) is the one most used.

4 In English, assembly members. In 2005, the Environmental Assembly of the Citizens of Gualeguaychú was formed to fight the construction of the plants.

5 For more on the *piqueteros*, see Auyero (2003) and Alcañiz and Scheier (2007).

6 *Cronista* Digital Newspaper, 1 June 2007.

7 Among those NGOs was Greenpeace Argentina, which provided the Assembly with important logistics support on specific occasions and also developed its own protest mechanisms. See www.greenpeace.org.ar.

8 As Governor Busti once stated in an interview: "nobody wants to buy from a polluted province." *La Nación*, 24 January 2006. At www.lanacion.com.ar.

9 In May of 2005 the Presidents of Argentina and Uruguay met in Buenos Aires and agreed on the creation of the GTAN in order to exchange information and develop monitoring mechanisms. Devised as a technical solution to the bilateral controversy, the GTAN was charged with carrying out an environmental study.

The GTAN first met in August of 2005. By 31 January 2006, however, when the first report was due, the Argentine and the Uruguayan delegation in the GTAN could not produce a common report and each delegation announced that separate reports would be presented. Released on February of that year, the Argentine report strongly criticized Uruguay for the lack of accurate studies on the environmental impact of the pulp mills and the violation of the Uruguay River Treaty (Argentina Ministerio de Relaciones Exteriores 2006).

## References

Alcañiz, Isabella and Scheier, Melissa (2007) "New Social Movements with Old Party Politics: The MTL *Piqueteros* and the Communist Party in Argentina," *Latin American Perspectives*, 34(2).

Allee, Todd L. and Huth, Paul K. (2006) "Legitimizing Dispute Settlement: International Legal Rulings as Domestic Political Cover," *American Political Science Review*, 100(2): 219–34.

*America Económica* (2006) March 24. Online. Available: http://www.americaeconomica. com.

ARGENTINA JGM (2005) *Memoria Anual del Estado de la Nación*, Buenos Aires: Jefatura de Gabinete de Ministros.

Argentina Ministerio de Relaciones Exteriores, Comercio Internacional y Culto de Argentina (2006) "Informe de la Delegación Argentina al Grupo de Trabajo de Alto Nivel." Online. Available: http://www.mrecic.gov.ar/ (accessed 5 May 2007).

Auyero, Javier (2003) *Contentious Lives: Two Argentine Women, Two Protests and the Quest for Recognition*, Durham, NC: Duke University Press.

*Clarín Newspaper* (2006) 2 May. Online. Available: http://www.clarin.com.ar

Cotgrove, Stephen and Duff, Andrew (2003) "Middle-Class Radicalism and Environmentalism," in Jeff Goodwin and James M. Jasper (eds) *The Social Movements Reader: Cases and Concepts*, Oxford: Blackwell.

*Cronista* Digital Newspaper (2007) 1 June. Online. Available; http://www.cronistadigital. com.ar.

Espacios Jurídicos (n.d.) "Estatuto del Río Uruguay de 1975." Online. Available: http://www.espaciosjuridicos.com/datos/ (accessed 15 July 2007).

FARN (2006) *Las plantas de celulosa en el Río Uruguay: el Análisis de la Normativa para una Posible Resolución del Conflicto*, Buenos Aires: Fundación Argentina para los Recursos Naturales.

Fundación Proteger (2006) "Romina Picolotti Named Head of Argentina's Environmental Secretariat." Online. Available: http://www.proteger.org.ar/home (accessed 3 May 2007).

Goodwin, Jeff and Jasper, James M. (2003) *The Social Movements Reader: Cases and Concepts*, Oxford: Blackwell.

Greenpeace Argentina (2006) "Plantas de Celulosa: Cómo Construir una Solución Sustentable." Online. Available: http://www.greenpeace.org/argentina/ (accessed 1 June 2007).

Harrison, Kathryn (1996) *Passing the Buck: Federalism and Canadian Environmental Policy*, Vancouver: University of British Columbia Press.

International Court of Justice (2007) "Pulp Mills on the River Uruguay (Argentina v. Uruguay)." Online. Available: http://www.icj-cij.org/ (accessed 1 June 2007).

International Finance Corporation (2006) "Summary of Project Information on BOTNIA," World Bank. Online. Available: http://www.ifc.org/ (accessed 1 June 2007).

Keck, Margaret and Sikkink, Kathryn (1998) *Activists beyond Borders, Advocacy Networks in International Politics*, Ithaca, New York: Cornell University Press.

López Echagüe, Hernán (2006) *Crónica del Ocaso: Apuntes sobre las Papeleras y la Devastación del Litoral Argentino y Uruguayo*, Buenos Aires: Grupo Editorial Norma.

McAdams, Doug, Tarrow, Sidney and Tilly, Charles (2001) *Dynamics of Contention*, Cambridge: Cambridge University Press.

Schneider, Mark, Scholz, John, Lubell, Mark, Mindruta, Denisa and Edwardsen, Matthew (2003) "Building Consensual Institutions: Networks and the National Estuary Program," *American Journal of Political Science*, 47(1): 143–58.

Shipan, Charles R. and Lowry, William R. (2001) "Environmental Policy and Party Divergence in Congress," *Political Research Quarterly*, 54(2): 245–63.

Uruguay Ministerio de Relaciones Exteriores (2006) "Laudo Tribunal Arbitral Ad Hoc del Mercosur, Controversia con Argentina, Derivada de los Cortes de Ruta." Online. Available: http://www.mrree.gub.uy/mrree/home.htm (accessed 1 June 2007).

Vara, Ana María (forthcoming) "Si a la Vida, No a las Papeleras: En Torno a una Controversia Ambiental Inédita en América Latina," *Revista Redes*.

# 8 Finnish environment and foreign policy

## Supranationalism, pragmatism, and consensus building

*Mika Merviö*

Finnish environmental policy brings together a mix of traditional realist foreign policy dominated by an analysis of Russian and wider European political situation and oligarchic decision-making, an interplay between well-established bureaucratic state and citizens trying to make their concerns better heard, and an increased awareness of environmental issues, having started from epistemic communities but now increasingly shaping the core political discourses and even the cultural construction of being Finnish. The Finnish environmental policy is heavily influenced by both the geographic location and the historical experiences of the people. The Finns have learned the hard way that as a small nation they have to pay close attention to the political aspirations of others rather than perceive foreign policy as a very separate political realm. Consequently, Finnish foreign policy may occasionally appear to contain contradictory elements combining Czarist (presidential) self-righteous decision-making with Nordic transparency and plebeian equalitarian values or narrow concerns of immediate national interests with world-embracing attempts to shape the international/regional system into a better one. Furthermore, the history of living with a foreign policy that has included a fair amount of double talk and contradictions has left many Finns quite skeptical of most ideologies and changing foreign policy goals. In short, Finnish foreign policy fits nicely into several boxes in terms of its theoretical orientations, but just as many Finns find it difficult to place themselves clearly in cultural and political reference groups in Europe or the world, they also find it difficult to categorize the Finnish foreign policy in terms of the broader universal trends and processes (see Chapter 2 by Barkdull and Harris in this chapter and, for a more universal picture, Kütting 2000: 11–22).

Although historical experiences greatly influence the Finnish attitudes toward foreign policy, the issue area of environmental foreign policy is most interesting, since it offers opportunities to break free from the constraints of history and make use of new regional and international systems, and in the process reorient and rethink the whole Finnish foreign policy and its priorities. The Finns tend to have a very close emotional, cultural, historical and economic relationship with their environment, and, in particular, with forests, whereas foreign policy has traditionally been concerned with very different priorities, mostly related to the Russian/Soviet threat scenarios. The older realist orientation may occasionally be supported by new attention to environmental security and new environmental threat scenarios that do not fall much short of national (or global) survival. In other words, both foreign policy and environment are serious matters for the Finns. However, the approach of neoliberal institutionalism and its reliance on international law also has an appeal to the Finns who are keen to seek allies and cooperation and who through centuries of rule by Sweden were brought to appreciate the strict rule by law and legalism.

### Finnish environment: culture and politics

In terms of natural environment, the Nordic countries are an interesting group. Finland and Sweden both possess relatively large amounts of territory, while Denmark (with Greenland), Norway and Iceland have huge maritime resources and areas under their control. While forests define the essence of nature and typical natural habitats in Sweden and Finland, in Norway and Denmark forests are rare and in Iceland it is difficult to even find any full-grown trees. Most Finns and Swedes find the Norwegian and Icelandic slaughter of whales just as barbaric as do the average Australians or Brits. However, for many Norwegians, their traditions in whaling seem to be an important part of making sense of their national experience and relationship with Nature. Thus, Nordic people do not have to go far to find other Nordic people who find it almost impossible to comprehend what they mean by sustainable forestry or fishing/whaling since their own neighbors within the Nordic countries are likely to have very different ideas/personal experiences relating to the environment. As Finns have learned to be skeptical about the environmentalist merits and blind spots of their neighbors, this experience has prepared them for European Union level environmental policy, where even more fundamental differences in environmental thinking are to be found.

The population of Finland at the end of 2006 was 5,276,955.[1] Finns make up 35 per cent of the world's population north of latitude 60°N, which tells something about the unique environment of the Finns. Finland is sparsely populated, with only 17 people per km². Finns for a long time combined hunting and fishing with relatively ineffective agriculture. Historically the Finnish population increased rapidly from about 400,000 in the seventeenth century. The rapid development of agriculture and modern urban economic development made it possible to maintain a far larger population (Peltonen 2002).

Modernization changed the attitudes of Finns toward nature and the environment. In the nineteenth century, forestry rapidly added value to forests and brought new prosperity to a large number of people. Most Finnish farmers have traditionally owned their land and forestry brought new prosperity to both landowners and to people working in the new industry. The Finnish economic and industrial growth from the latter part of the nineteenth century to the 1940s was largely dependent on forestry. Gradually all the forestry resources in the whole nation were brought to satisfy the needs of industry. In the Northern environment it takes a long time for the trees to grow and sustainability in forestry requires good planning and knowledge about forests. What helped to bring home the lesson about the sustainability of forestry was that forests were largely owned by farmers and most farmers were used to thinking in terms of the long-term management of their land for the good of their families. In any case, the ownership of land has been clear for centuries and has been far more equally distributed than in most other parts of Europe or elsewhere. The Finnish forestry companies were largely built by local people with local capital. While industrialists were worried about the sustainability of their resource management, there were fairly early on also voices raised about the need to save at least pieces of original natural environment for present and future generations. The internationally best-known Finnish early supporter of environmental protection was Nils Adolf Erik Nordenskiöld (who was exiled to Sweden by the Russians and became famous as the first person to navigate the North-east Passage from Europe to Japan). In 1880, Nordenskiöld published an influential article, which argued in favor of establishing natural parks in the Nordic countries.

In the late nineteenth century the idea of preserving the most typical or spectacular natural wonders was closely related to the rising political movement of nationalism and national independence. The Finnish nationalist movement was characteristically cultural in nature and as such was easier for the Russians to tolerate than, for instance, the Polish openly political challenges. Finnish nature became the main source of inspiration and symbolism for Finnish national Romanticism. Finnish visual arts, music (especially Jean Sibélius) and literature all in their so-called Golden Age in the decades before independence (1917) created stereotypical images of Finnish nature and the Finnish national relationship with nature. The collection, publishing and popularization of the ancient Finnish epic poetry, Kalevala, served an important role in this process. Forests have for thousands of years played a pivotal role in the lives of Finns, but from the late nineteenth century forests were also made the icons of Finnish culture. The pine trees in the paintings of Akseli Gallén-Kallela and the birch trees of Pekka Halonen are something that every educated Finn should always recognize.

These forests remain largely in private ownership (Sievänen 1998: 56–7; Ripatti 1998: 60). The ownership of forests reflects the fact that urbanization came relatively late to Finland and that many forests remain in family ownership even after the people have moved to the cities. People tend to be emotionally attached to family land and it is seldom seen merely as an investment. In 1996, some 380,000 families (17 per cent of the total) in Finland owned forest (Ripatti 1998: 60). In addition, there are 475,000 summer homes in Finland (Tilastokeskus 2006). This means that there is roughly one cottage for every 11 people. The ideal summer home is in a forest and has a sauna next to a lake or sea shore. The summer homes are largely for the city dwellers as rural people are surrounded by nature all year round. The Finnish lifestyle maintains an active relationship with Finnish nature. For instance, some 60 per cent of the population pick wild berries in the forests and 40 per cent fish for themselves (Sievänen 1998: 55). The legal principle of everyman's right established in the Swedish era gives everyone a right to walk freely and to pick berries and mushrooms, even on other people's private property (except gardens). In short, the Finns actually live in the forests and even the city dwellers make an effort to spend time in the Finnish rural areas and get into the countryside.

The city dwellers in Finland also tend on average to be more concerned about global environmental issues in the sense of reflexive modernization (cf. Beck 1986). However, the specific environmental issues that concern individuals tend to be very different among the people living in large cities, small cities and in rural areas. Konttinen's (1999: 117–20) survey of environmental activists reveals that in the urban areas the issues of urban planning and traffic are far more important for the activists than those of protecting endangered species and natural habitat, which are important local political issues in many rural areas. Konttinen (ibid.: 63) also notes that in some locations, especially in Northern Finland, environmental activism itself is still a subject of political repression for those representing values that they regard as more traditional (both the conservatives and communists being strong in these areas). This is a very different situation from large cities where the Greens have support levels near or over 20 per cent and where most political parties and politicians have learned to avoid the stigma of being ignorant on environmental issues.

The Finnish environmental movement from its inception has been very much influenced by the academic elite. The aforementioned romantic attachment to Finnish nature first politicized and idealized Finnish Nature and secured it an important role in the independent republic (1917–) as its symbol. From the outset there was also a strong trend to save nature in order to protect it for science. It is most likely that many scientists felt personal attachment to natural values, but it apparently sounded better to speak about international scientific interests, even when the significance of biodiversity protection was not yet fully understood. In the first half of the last century Finland had quite a few brilliant natural scientists, who were pioneers in many fields of biology by systematically studying Finnish nature. However, there were few voices in favor of more coordinated efforts to protect the environment while the economy was rapidly modernizing and increasingly dependent on natural resources and especially forestry. In the young republic, a Law on Nature Protection was passed in 1923 and new natural parks were established. The next qualitative change was in the 1950s when the interests of hydroelectric power companies clashed with the wishes to save the remaining unharnessed rivers. After an intense political battle 19 new natural or national parks with some of the most beautiful free waterfalls were established in 1956 (Luoma 2002: 158).

The period from the 1950s to the 1970s was a very interesting time as several authors, with mostly natural science backgrounds, were writing books that could be described as representing the Finnish ecosophia school. Among these writers were Pentti Linkola, Pekka Nuorteva, Olli Järvinen, Rauno Ruuhijärvi, Pentti Seiskari and Erkki Pulliainen (cf. Massa 1998: 63–4). They all added elements of environmental philosophy and social analysis and had already a fully developed global vision. Their writing greatly influenced the Finnish environmental discourses. In short, Finland had a strong and original discourse on environmental philosophy at the time when translations of similar books started to appear. In addition, there were also popular writers with an environmentalist message that proved to be truly popular. The nature author Yrjö Kokko is widely accredited with having almost single-handedly by his books saved the Whooper swan population in Finland from extinction and with making it thrive as the national symbol.

Pentti Linkola, a researcher-turned-fisherman, constitutes a category of his own among the Finnish environmental thinkers. Most people agree that his uncompromising and brilliant style makes his books and articles stand apart from the rest. However, his message is very pessimistic: democracy is a mistake, only radical change can save the environment from catastrophes and Linkola does not seem to believe that any change is possible. In his writing Linkola describes with emotion and in detail the destruction he has witnessed during his lifetime. He famously dedicated his best-known book *Toisinajattelijan päiväkirjasta* (From the Diary of a Dissident) "To Andreas Baader and Ulrike Meinhof for their absoluteness and for their few companions in arms. They are the signposts – not Jesus of Nazareth or Albert Schweitzer" (Linkola 1979). As one of the most famous ornithologists in Finland, he abandoned his easy life and research career and started to live as a fisherman without any modern luxuries, more or less the way he teaches. Most environmentalists in Finland have renounced all connections with him, but everyone concerned about the environment avidly reads everything that he writes. Linkola in a way represents a very Finnish and dark version of "an inconvenient truth."

Politically the green political agenda has been most effectively promoted by the Green League, which has its roots in various environmental and social movements of the 1970s and 1980s. The movement organized itself as a party in 1987, but won its first two parliamentary seats in 1983. The support rate in the 1980s was already relatively high in most large cities and since then the Greens have been able to gradually increase their number of seats in parliament. Being regarded as being somewhere in the middle of the party spectrum, the Greens are in a good tactical position to join a government coalition. The first Finnish and Western European Green minister on

Cabinet level was Pekka Haavisto, who served as Minister of the Environment and Foreign Aid from 1995 to 1999 in Paavo Lipponen's Social Democrat-led coalition. In the next Cabinet, the Greens had two Ministers, Satu Hassi and Osmo Soininvaara, representing the Environment and Foreign Aid and Basic Social Services. In 2002, the Green League quit the government coalition on its own initiative over the issue of nuclear energy.

However, in the March 2007 elections, the Greens did well and entered the four party center-right coalition, where they were given two portfolios, Labor for Tarja Cronberg and Justice for Tuija Brax. The *de facto* threshold in small-sized election districts has made it difficult to successfully enter Parliament from smaller, largely rural, districts. As a result the Green Party leader Cronberg with her some 8,000 votes did not make it into Parliament in 2007 from Northern Karielia while from the Uusimaa near Helsinki it was possible to enter Parliament with 1,000 votes. This did not prevent Cronberg from becoming a Minister and in December 2007 the government decided to level off the vote disparities by introducing four new "Counting areas" (while keeping the election district borders intact) in the next national parliamentary elections (Kymäläinen 2007). For the Greens, this is a big issue, because so far the party has suffered in rural areas from the image that it is a party of city-dwellers. Cronberg is the only prominent Green leader, who comes from outside the big cities. Regarding the extent of Green influence in Finnish government policies, there are different opinions: some dismiss their government participation as having provided an ecomark for governments that have not been fully committed to environmental goals, while the Greens are quick to claim that their ideas have been central in making the government adopt greener policies, for instance, in energy and tax issues. The Finnish Greens have also been active at the EU level, in particular in the European Parliament.

The modern environmental administration was established with the Ministry of the Environment in 1983 and a law in 1986, which made municipal environmental committees compulsory. The environmental administration has steadily increased in size and significance, becoming a major player in the Finnish political process, which is characterized by consensus seeking and the involvement of many interest groups, and by internationally exceptionally low levels of corruption (for more, see Tirkkonen and Jokinen 2001: 65–77). The most recent Ministers of the Environment have represented the Center Party, the Swedish People's Party and the Greens, but the actual policies of the Ministry or even the rhetoric of the ministers have not varied significantly, which says a lot about stability in policy-making and environmental issues not being regarded as particularly divisive political issues. Due to the relatively long roots of environmental thinking among the academic community, the environmental administration has enjoyed a close relationship both with the epistemic community of environmental scientists and with activists. There are also many cases of academics and activists, who have joined the bureaucracy.

## Finnish environmental foreign policy

As a relatively small country, there are limits to how much Finland can shape the global environment and its governance. Finland can either set a positive example or be a model for other countries to follow or work in concert with other countries with similar interests. Most Finns assume that Finland is and should be among the environmentally most progressive countries. The leader-laggard dynamic (cf. McCormick 2001: 88–90) helps to keep Finland in the 'progressive' group of EU countries in environmental issues. However, the environmental activists are often quick to note that the Finnish record often is far from perfect. However, if there is a broad consensus emerging on the Nordic or European Union level, the initial reaction among decision-makers would be to steer clear of falling behind others. For individual politicians the global environmental issues also provide a field where they can demonstrate their global responsibility and knowledge, and where opinions are less divided ideologically than, for instance, on defense issues and hard foreign policy issues (such as NATO membership/cooperation). Behind this rationale there is an understanding that Finland benefits from better and deeper multilateral cooperation in all fields and that the global environmental problems simply need an array of global and local solutions, even new powerful supranational institutions. In international environmental policy there is also an opportunity to justify action by self-interest, more than in the global human rights issues. In foreign policy liturgy Finland has, being a Nordic democracy, tightly linked human rights, social justice, human security and the environment. However, Finland has traditionally avoided condemning human rights violations as strongly as, for instance, Sweden, and has in its refugee policy shown cold-heartedness. Therefore, the global environment may be the field, where the Finns have few reservations about making a positive contribution.

The present President, Tarja Halonen, a Social Democrat, is regarded among the top politicians as being most genuinely concerned about global social issues. Her brand of environmentalism is clearly anthropocentric and always subject to human solidarity. Most other key politicians, such as the present Prime Minister, Matti Vanhanen, Center Party, and the Minister of Foreign Affairs, Alexander Stubb, National Coalition Party, do not hide their far closer commitment to Finnish national interests. However, the Finnish conservative politicians in most cases are not ideologically against human rights issues or global environmental cooperation and in the National Coalition Party (the right wing of the party spectrum) there are quite a few politicians who specialize in environmental issues. In short, no Finnish party or politician can monopolize environmental or human rights awareness, although the political opponents are quick to question the motives of their rivals.

It has also been realized that their neighbor with the longest border, Russia, is falling behind in most European standards of environmental cooperation and environmental awareness. In order to persuade Russians to do more, Finland should first set a good example and also give moderate rewards. However, in the issue of buying timber from Russia for Finnish industry the environmental issues are mixed with economic interests and Finland has tried its best (with little success) to use the EU to pressure Russia from raising it tariffs. In this issue, Finnish government has clearly indicated that national economic interests surpass other concerns. By being a major buyer of Russian timber and also increasingly establishing factories in Russia (due to the new tariffs) Finnish paper and pulp industry already is a major player in Russian forestry sector and, therefore, shares a responsibility for the protection of forest nature in Russia.

There are also a few topics that have caused friction in the otherwise smooth environmental cooperation between Finland and Brussels and that could be used to question Finnish dedication to common environmental standards. One typical case is the attitude (and orders) of the European Commission related to wolf hunting in Finland. The Finnish media especially have given the impression that the European bureaucrats in Brussels have no real understanding of how best to manage the wolf or bear populations in Finland. There is a broad consensus in Finland on the need to save these populations from extinction, but as these animals are potentially dangerous to people and domesticated animals, there are different opinions about the sufficient numbers and many Finns do not like to receive advice from Brussels on how to deal with the issue.

Among the internationally important state policy initiatives where Finland has played an important role are focus on the Baltic Sea marine environment protection, neighboring area cooperation, the Northern dimension, the Kyoto Protocol and the development of sustainable development indices. In the first three the obvious policy goal is to help the neighboring (post-socialist) countries to take care of their environment in order to prevent harmful impacts on Finland or its vicinity. As for the Baltic Sea, the Helsinki Convention of 1974 by then comprising seven member states, was at the time the first convention to cover all sources of pollution around an entire sea. There has been a long process to improve the Convention to cover all countries and accommodate new legal principles as well as to extend the Convention to the inland waters. The new Convention was signed in 1992, but came into force only in January 2000. The current Helsinki Commission (Helcom) action plan ambitiously seeks to restore the good ecological status of the Baltic marine environment by 2021. The reality today is one of algal blooms, dead sea-beds, and depletion of fish stocks. The efforts so far have already been able to reduce nitrogen and phosphorus emissions by some 40 per cent, but much still remains to be done. Significant progress can be achieved by building water purification plants, especially in Russia, and by more rigid controls on emissions from farms as well as from shipping. The Helsinki Commission has in recent years shifted its focus to that of a clear set of "ecological objectives" and "good ecological status" (for more, see

Helsinki Commission). EU-level cooperation may give weight to some of these initiatives. Meanwhile, the opinion of most Finns, especially those who living in coastal areas, is rather skeptical about the ability of the Helsinki Commission to restore the quality of Baltic Sea ecosystem.

In the years from 1990 to 2006, Finland allocated approximately 1,193 million Euros to the promotion of the economic and political process of change in the partner countries (Russia, the Baltic States, Central and East European countries and certain CIS countries) in the framework of its Action Plan for Neighboring Area Cooperation. The hard core of the program is to help transformation to environmentally less harmful practices. In the Baltic countries as well as in Central and Eastern Europe, the environment soon became a domestic priority and cooperation from abroad was warmly welcomed. This cooperation also fitted nicely into the framework of these countries entering the European Union, where they were obliged to meet the EU standards. The cooperation with Russia has been less straightforward, since Russian domestic priorities have changed during the period and still today in Russia there are few politicians who are interested in the environment. The cooperation focuses strongly on areas bordering Finland, including the city of St. Petersburg (Finnish Ministry of Foreign Affairs 2007). For the Finnish government, it is an increasingly sensitive issue to explain to its citizens why Finland continues to pay for cleaning up Russia while the Russian government puts its petro-euros elsewhere.

The Northern Dimension is linked to the EU–Russia cooperation framework and Finland has under this program tried to generate more interest and resources for various kinds of welfare, research and security projects in Northern Europe. In a way, the Northern Dimension can been seen as an attempt to balance the EU's heavy investments in the Mediterranean region, but there is also an idea to improve relations between the EU and Russia, as well as to get local benefits for Finland, if major funding starts coming from Brussels. The non-EU countries, Iceland and Norway have also been glad to join the project. However, so far it has proved difficult to sell the idea to the rest of the EU.

Finland has strongly supported the Kyoto Protocol throughout the process. Within the EU it was decided that Finland was required to stabilize its emissions to the 1990 level. The EU directives are now directing emission rights and emissions trading. In its national Kyoto strategy, Finland is somehow trying to solve the difficult equation of stabilizing its $CO_2$ emissions while the economy has been enjoying phenomenal growth and energy consumption has been rising. The taxation system is being changed to encourage energy saving and changing to less harmful energy alternatives and renewable energy forms, especially bio-fuels, are being developed. In a way Finland is copying one more Swedish strategy in a diluted form, although it remains to be seen whether it is realistic to rapidly increase the use of bio-fuels. Meanwhile, it is expected that the government will need to rely heavily on emissions trading (see http://www.ilmasto.org). While Sweden boasts its record as the most climate-friendly country and criticizes the other countries for doing too little (see e.g. Lewenhagen 2007 and *Dagens Nyheter* 2007), Finland has (also) in its climate policy adopted a more conciliatory posture, but has avoided falling too far behind Sweden. During the Bali meeting all the key Swedish politicians denounced the climate efforts of all other countries. Interestingly the Swedish Minister of Enterprise and Energy, Maud Olofsson, praised both Sweden and Finland when she denounced the records of all other countries in their bio-fuel policies (Larsson 2007).

Finland's National Program to Promote Sustainable Consumption and Production is interesting because it has set up a clear measurable government plan to make a whole society "sustainable." The program was drawn up in 2005 by a broad-based committee and aims, through long-term policy-making, to make Finland one of the most eco-efficient and competitive societies in the world by 2025. The program includes 73 policy measures. The first evaluation report came out in autumn 2007 and included information, for instance, on a new material research center and on forthcoming rules for public procurement, both of which should significantly improve eco-efficiency (see Ympäristöministeriö 2007). What makes this program interesting is that the new indices could be promoted within the EU or even globally. However, the effectiveness and implementation of the program are dependent on the strong tradition of central government in Finland and its close cooperation with the industry. The Finnish project fits nicely into the Johannesburg WSSD Conference aims and into the EU's Lisbon Process, and right now can be used by the Finnish government to demonstrate that Finland is doing its part.

## Constructing identities in foreign policy: who are the Finns?

Most Nordic people are quick to admit the existence of similarities in social institutions and in cultural and social values. However, the Nordic identity is ultimately difficult to define as most individuals would come up with very different lists of what is essentially "Nordic" for them. It is rather symptomatic that the Nordic Council decided in its report on Sustainable Development to glorify such abstract and relative virtues as political stability, rule of law and educational levels to sum up what unites the Nordic countries in their separate ways to sustainability (Nordic Council of Ministers 2004: 10).

The most obvious similarity in the Nordic countries relates to the linguistic similarities between the Scandinavian languages. The Finnish language as a non-Indo-European language, however, is not related to these languages and, instead, the linguistic affinity reminds the Finns of their links with the Estonians and Hungarians, both nowadays fellow members of the European Union, and linguistic roots even occasionally help the Finns to get a warm welcome as far away as in Turkey and Korea. No wonder that most Finns would gladly see Turkey join the EU. Finland, however, has in its Constitution since 1919 given official status to both Finnish and Swedish, which serves as a basis for maintaining far-reaching parity in terms of providing services to both language groups and for teaching both languages to the whole population (with the exception of the monolingual Swedish-speaking Åland islands). At the end of 2006 those with Finnish as their first language accounted for 91.5 per cent and those with Swedish as their first language accounted for 5.5 per cent of the total population (Tilastokeskus 2006). The use of Swedish in Finland has helped the Finns to follow the social developments in other Nordic countries. Its unique membership in the Nordic community plays an important part in Finnish multiculturalism, while in the other Nordic countries multiculturalism is usually seen in the context of immigration and their policies have favored integration. The Finns, therefore, have chosen to be "Nordic" when it suits them, and while the other Nordics have never been fully convinced that the Finns really belong to the group. To some extent the Finnish model of constitutionally well-defined cultural rights is rather inflexible in modern Europe with increasing numbers of immigrants from multiple sources. It is not very tempting to immigrate to a country where everyone is expected to be more or less fluent in both Finnish and Swedish just to get a decent job.

The Nordic Council has been successful in focusing on practical policy cooperation with a direct impact on people. It was Nordic cooperation which first internationalized social policy, economic integration and environmental policy in the Nordic countries, and in these areas it proved possible to achieve results that were often among the most progressive in the world in terms of providing practical solutions to very similar issues that later were addressed by such larger organizations as the European Union and the United Nations. The political cooperation within the Nordic Council since 1955 has provided very good practice for the Nordic people for the even more creative political community of the European Union. Furthermore, for Finland, the Nordic cooperation provided a much appreciated way to associate itself with the Scandinavian countries during the Cold War when the Soviet Union wanted rather to dilute the Finnish policy of neutrality. When Nordic cooperation focused on social and economic integration and environmental issues, not even the Soviet Union could interpret this as being targeted against it, as the Nordic politics was somehow de-foreignized in avoiding defense issues and divisive issues of world politics. The Finnish foreign policy's threat scenarios have for a very long time been dominated by the Soviet Union and Russia and it suited the Finns well to pretend that Finland could remain outside divisive political issues. While the political elites in Sweden have been far freer to think about saving the world and meeting the global challenges, the Finnish foreign policy discourses have been far more insular and tied to the realism of coping with the changing Soviet Union/Russia and preparing for the eventuality of an even more difficult neighbor. The Finnish EU enthusiasm (compared to a far cooler attitude in Sweden and rejection in Norway and Iceland) has much to do with the perception of a need to build a safe and at the same time friendly relationship with Russia. Furthermore, the Finnish experience of having been part of the Swedish, Russian and now European empires is something that the other Nordic nationals have problems identifying with, and the Finns may have an easier time finding history-conscious friends in the Baltic countries and Central Europe, although the Finns there are bound to meet very different attitudes toward the Nordic countries, Russia and Europe.

The Finnish economic and social model has focused on building an economy that is competitive on a global scale. The Finnish welfare society has clearly adopted its basic ideas from Sweden, while the Finnish political culture and electoral system have favored more pragmatic and consensual solutions. The Swedish political debates in their *de facto* two-party system tend to be far more ideological, while in Finland all the parties in governing coalitions can always blame their shifting allies for delaying or blocking their good work. However, in all the Nordic countries there is a very wide consensus on the positive impacts of a well-functioning welfare society for a very wide range of positive things such as economic prosperity, a comprehensive environmental policy, a stable labor market, quality of life, equality, social justice, low levels of crime and social marginalization and high educational levels. In the past ten years, when the Finnish economy has done remarkably well largely due to internationally competitive IT companies, most notably Nokia, there have been books praising the Finnish socio-economic model of combining education, innovation, environment, welfare society and consensus-oriented political system (see e.g. Castells and Himanen 2002).

In some sectors Finland is doing clearly better than its Nordic neighbors. For instance, in the PISA studies on school achievements in 57 OECD countries among 15-year-olds, Finnish pupils have repeatedly come first while the other Nordic countries have failed to make the top 20 list (see e.g. Liiten 2007). However, while the Finnish economy may be competitive and relatively sustainable in environmental terms, the historic experiences, somewhat isolated geographic location and small numbers of immigrants together have contributed to a certain lack of international solidarity among Finns. The social values of Finns tend to be rather conservative, insular and selfish. In a recent survey on the priorities of Finns, when they had to rank the fundamental rights and whether these could be limited, it turned out that the rights of equality before the law, privacy, freedom of expression and the protection of private property were very dear to the Finns while the rights to a healthy environment and freedom of assembly were least valued (YLE 2007). It may be that the Finns take many of their rights for granted and see little reason for social activism or participation for the sake of the environment or society.

## Conclusion

Finland's environmental and foreign policies are firmly rooted in its history, culture and the Finnish understanding of the country's place in the world. In foreign policy the Finns constantly redefine their roles as a member of the EU, the UN, the Nordic group of countries, as speakers of a Finno-Ugric non-Indo-European language and as a neighbor of Russia. With their multiple cultural identities and relatively high awareness of global environmental problems the Finns are well placed to understand the need to build supranational institutions to deal with global environmental issues. It is widely understood in Finland that the European nation-state system is changing into a politically more centralized but culturally still pluralistic system, which in terms of foreign policy is far easier for the Finns than the former system, where Finland was left more or less alone to deal with Russia and all global challenges. Due to the historically rooted deep suspicions of the motives of others, Finnish foreign policy is far less "idealistic" or openly nationalistic than that of its Nordic neighbors and, as such, has a more pragmatist approach to global issues, including environmental ones. The Finnish political culture and party system contribute to pluralistic and consensual decision-making, which extends to foreign policy, and may often suit multilateral environmental cooperation. The Finnish model currently does not depend on individual leaders or strong leadership, as being politically successful in the Finnish system requires cooperative skills. Environmental policy has benefited greatly from the Ministry of the Environment having established its coordinating role and having close links with all relevant interest groups in the field. The Finnish consensus model in politics and environmental policy apparently is heavily dependent on the relatively small size of the relatively homogeneous population and on a strong public sector and welfare society.

## Note

1 Tilastokeskus (2007) Statistics Finland, http://www.stat.fi/tup/suoluk/suoluk_vaesto_en.html.

## References

Beck, Ulrich (1986) *Risikogesellschaft. Auf dem Weg in eine andere Moderne* [Risk Society: Towards a New Modernity], Frankfurt a.M.: Suhrkamp.

Castells, Manuel and Himanen, Pekka (2002) *The Information Society and Welfare State. The Finnish Model.* Oxford: Oxford University Press.

*Dagens Nyheter* (2007) "Nu måste resten av EU börja ta sitt klimatansvar" [Now must the rest of the EU start taking climate responsibility], 5 December. Online. Available: http://www.dn.se/DNet/jsp/polopoly.jsp?d=572&a=721740 (accessed 15 July 2008).

Finnish Ministry of Foreign Affairs (2007) "Finland's Cooperation with Neighbouring Areas." Online. Available: http://www.ulkoministerio.fi/public/default.aspx?nodeid=34823&contentlan=2&culture=en-US (accessed 15 July 2008).

Helsinki Commission. Online. Available: http://www.helcom.fi/ (accessed 15 July 2008).

*Ilmasto.org*. Online. Available: http://www.ilmasto.org/. This is the homepage edited by the Green Party MP and government's climate change policy advisor Oras Tynkkyen, where information from various NGOs and government agencies on global warming and Finland are collected.

Konttinen, Esa (1999) *Ympäristökansalaisuuden kyläsepät* [Village smiths of the environmental citizenship], Jyväskylä: SoPhi.

Kütting, Gabriela (2000) *Environment, Society and International Relations*. London and New York: Routledge.

Kymäläinen, Leena (2007) "Vaaliuudistus vie paikkoja eduskunnan isoilta puolueilta" [The Parliament election system reform will take seats from the big parties], *Aamulehti*, 30 November. Online: http://www.aamulehti.fi/uutiset/kotimaa/56365. shtml (accessed 15 July 2008).

Larsson, Lars (2007) "Sverige vill se andra göra mer för klimatet" [Sweden would like to see others do more for the climate], *Dagens Nyheter*, 3 December. Online. Available: http://www.dn.se/DNet/jsp/polopoly.jsp?d=1042&a=721389 (accessed 15 July 2008).

Lewenhagen, Jan (2007) "Sverige klimatvänligast i världen" [Sweden is the most climate-friendly country in the world], *Dagens Nyheter*, 7 December. Online. Available: http://www.dn.se/DNet/jsp/polopoly.jsp?d=597&a=722473 (accessed 15 July 2008).

Liiten, Marjukka (2007) "Suomi taas ykkönen OECD:n Pisa-tutkimuksessa" [Finland again number one in the OESD PISA research], *Helsingin Sanomat*, 30 November. Online. Available: http://www.hs.fi/kotimaa/artikkeli/Suomi+taas+ykkönen +OECDn+Pisa-tutkimuksessa/1135232200951 (accessed 15 July 2008).

Linkola, Pentti (1979) *Toisinjattelijan päiväkirjasta* [From the diary of a dissident], Porvoo, Helsinki and Juva: Werner Söderström Osakeyhtiö.

Luoma, Pentti (2002) "Vihreät viirit. Muutos ja pysyvyys Maa- ja metsätalous-tuottajain Keskusliiton ympäristöpoliittisissa näkemyksissä vuosina 1980–2000 Maataloustuottaja-lehden valossa" [The Green bannerettes. The change and constancy in the environmental views of the Central Association of the Farm and Forestry Producers, in the light of the Agricultural Producer Magazine], Kasva-tustieteiden ja opettajankoulutuksen yksikkö, Sosiologian, naistutkimuksen ja ympäristökasvatuksen jaos. Doctoral dissertation. Oulu: Oulun yliopisto.

Massa, Ilmo (1998) *Toinen ympäristötiede* [The second environmental science], Tampere: Gaudeamus.

McCormick, John (2001) *Environmental Policy in the European Union*, Houndmills and New York: Palgrave.

Nordic Council of Ministers (2004) *Sustainable Development New Bearings for the Nordic Countries. Revised Edition with Goals and Measures for 2005–2008. Principal Policy Points*, Copenhagen. Esbjerg: Rosendahls Bogtrykkeri AS. Online. Available: http://www.norden.org/pub/ovrigt/baeredygtig/uk/ANP2004782.pdf (accessed 15 July 2008).

Peltonen, Arvo (2002) "The Population in Finland," Online. Available: http://virtual. finland.fi/netcomm/news/showarticle.asp?intNWSAID=25785 (accessed 15 July 2008).

Ripatti, Pekka (1998) "Joka kuudes suomalainen perhe omistaa metsää" [Every sixth Finnish family owns forest], in Aarne Reunala, Ilpo Tikkanen and Esko Åsvik (eds) *Vihreä valtakunta. Suomen metsäklusteri* [The Green Realm. The Finnish Forest Cluster], Metsämiesten säätiö—. Keuruu: Otava, pp. 58–63.

Sievänen, Tuula (1998) "Yhdeksän kymmenestä ulkoilee luonnossa" [Nine out of ten hike in the wild], in Aarne Reunala, Ilpo Tikkanen and Esko Åsvik (eds) *Vihreä valtakunta. Suomen metsäklusteri* [The Green Realm. The Finnish Forest Cluster], Metsämiesten säätiö—. Keuruu: Otava, pp. 55–7.

*Suomen väestö* (2006) *Tilastokeskus 2007.* Online. Available: http://www.stat.fi/til/ vaerak/2006/ vaerak_2006_2007-03-23_tie_001.html (accessed 15 July 2008).

*Tilastokeskus* (Statistics Finland) (2006) "Kesämökit. Suomessa 475 000 kesämökkiä 2006" [Summer cottages. There are 475,000 summer cottages in Finland]. Online. Available: http://www.stat.fi/til/kmok/2006/kmok_2006_2007-05-23_tie_001. html (accessed 15 July 2008).

—— (2007) "Suomen väestö 2006" [The population of Finland 2006]. Online. Available: http://www.stat.fi/til/vaerak/2006/ vaerak_2006_2007-03-23_tie_001.html.

Tirkkonen, Juhani and Jokinen, Pekka (2001) "Ympäristöhallinnon vakiintuminen ja toimiala" [The establishment of the environmental administration and its line of activities], in Yrjö Haila and Pekka Jokinen (eds) *Ympäristöpolitiikka* [Environmental Politics], Tampere: Vastapaino, pp. 65–77.

*Yle* (Yleisradio, Finnish national broadcasting service) (2007) "Gallup: Suomalaiset väheksyvät poliittisia oikeuksiaan" [The Finns underrate their political rights], 6 December. Online. Available: http://www.yle.fi/uutiset/kotimaa/oikea/id76690.html (accessed 15 July 2008).

*Ympäristöministeriö* (Finnish Ministry for Environment) (2007) "Kestävä kulutus ja tuotanto (KULTU)" [The sustainable consumption and production]. Online. Available: http://www.ymparisto.fi/default.asp?node=7468&lan=fi (accessed 15 July 2008).

# 9 Canada's foreign policy on persistent organic pollutants

## The making of an environmental leader

### Ken Wilkening and Charles Thrift

Effective leader states are vital to international environmental problem-solving. But how and why do certain states become leaders and others not? What are the sources and secrets of effective state leadership on international environmental issues? In this chapter, we seek to answer this question in a case study of Canada's leadership role on the transboundary issue of persistent organic pollutants (POPs). Leadership is a complex and elusive concept. We focus on Canada's foreign policy-making process. Specifically, we ask: What actors and factors have influenced Canada's foreign policy on POPs and how did they contribute to its leadership on the issue?

More than any other state, Canada was responsible for scientifically identifying the transboundary POPs issue in the mid- to late-1980s. Canada also helped initiate and was heavily involved in negotiations for a POPs protocol under the United Nations Economic Commission for Europe's (UNECE) Convention on Long-range Transboundary Air Pollution (LRTAP), signed in 1998. This was the first international agreement to explicitly address POPs. Similarly, Canada was a prime mover to establish a global POPs treaty. These efforts culminated in the United Nations Stockholm Convention on Persistent Organic Pollutants (hereafter referred to as the Stockholm Convention), signed in 2001. Since 2001, Canada has remained active during the implementation phase of these agreements.

In the next section, a brief introduction to the transboundary POPs problem is presented. In the following section, Canada's foreign policy-making on POPs is described chronologically through four time-periods. Then we analyze "the making of an environmental leader" and codify the actors and factors that have shaped Canada's foreign policy on POPs and contributed to its leadership. The final section contains lessons for effective state leadership on international environmental issues derived from this case study.

## Persistent organic pollutants: a brief introduction

POPs are a group of hundreds of chemicals that are persistent in the natural environment, 'organic' (i.e., carbon-based), and pollutants because exposure to POPs has been linked to a wide variety of negative environmental and human health consequences. Some POPs are toxic in their original form while others transform into toxic products. The initial compounds covered under the Stockholm Convention were organochlorine pesticides (aldrin, chlordane, DDT, dieldrin, endrin, heptachlor, hexachlorobenzenes, mirex, and toxaphene), industrial chemicals (polychlorinated biphenyls (PCBs)), and byproducts of combustion (dioxins and furans). These are the so-called "dirty dozen." They are differentiated as intentionally produced (e.g., pesticides) or unintentionally produced (e.g., dioxins).

Due to their extreme stability, POPs can survive for long periods of time and travel to the far corners of the earth. They can be carried on atmospheric winds, marine currents, and in migratory animals, with the former being the dominant mode of transport. Because POPs are semivolatile they can condense and re-evaporate (or volatize) multiple times. Since evaporation takes place much less readily in cold regions, they tend to accumulate in these areas; specifically, in the polar regions and at high altitudes. POPs can also bioaccumulate (i.e., accumulate in biological organisms) and bio-magnify (i.e., concentrate or 'magnify' as they move up the food chain). They can reach toxic levels in top-of-the-food-chain animals such as polar bears, orcas, and humans.

POPs became an object of international environmental policy-making due to their ability to cross national boundaries. They are currently regulated directly under the LRTAP POPs Protocol and the Stockholm Convention, and indirectly through several other global and regional conventions. Social science literature analyzing international POPs policy includes Downie and Fenge (2003), Eckley and Selin (2003), Hough (2003), Selin and Eckley (2003), Eckley (2001), and Selin and Hjelm (1999). Few studies address Canada's role in international POPs policy; see Thrift *et al.* (submitted for publication).

## Origin and evolution of Canada's foreign policy on POPs: 1989–2007

We divided the development of Canada's foreign policy on POPs into four time-periods: (1) pre-1989, covering precursors to Canada's foreign policy on POPs and ending with its first foreign policy statements in 1989; (2) 1989–97, covering Canada's emergence as a leader and ending with the conclusion of negotiations on the LRTAP POPs Protocol; (3) 1997–2001, covering Canada's leadership role during the Stockholm Convention negotiations and ending with the signing of the Convention; and (4) 2001–present, covering Canada's activity during implementation. Each period is discussed below.

The term "persistent organic pollutants" did not come into common usage until the mid-1990s. However, we generally use this label throughout the chapter. Common terms prior to this time include organochlorines, polychlorinated hydrocarbons, and bioaccumulative chemicals of concern.

### Period I: pre-1989

Arctic Aboriginal people were likely the first to detect the accumulation of POPs when they noted changes in the flesh and organs of animals and fish they hunted (Myers 2001: 40). They knew something was wrong and attributed it to pollution. Years later scientists confirmed their suspicions. The first scientific knowledge about POPs-type chemicals appeared in the late 1800s in Europe. Between this time and the mid-1980s, disparate knowledge accrued but was never tied together as pertaining to an *international* environmental problem. An important premonition came from Rachel Carson's (1962) famous book, *Silent Spring*. Following publication, an abundance of research demonstrated the presence of organochlorine pesticides in multiple locations around the globe.

Organochlorines in the Canadian Arctic were first detected scientifically around 1970 (Holden 1970); however, the levels were considered low and relatively harmless. In the 1960s and 1970s "oil gushed from rigs, rivers caught fire, skies were blackened by soot and smog, songbirds dropped dead, and many species were on the verge of extinction" (Cone 2005: 27); the contaminant levels in the Canadian Arctic drew little notice.

Around 1985, Canadian scientists, in conjunction with mid-level bureaucrats, 'discovered' the international POPs problem. Or more accurately, they pieced together a new international perspective on already known information. The new perspective was triggered by concerns about POPs in wildlife in the seemingly pristine Canadian Arctic, and by identification, during cleanup of Canada's abandoned Distant Early Warning (DEW) line radar sites, of the potential for PCB contaminants in native diets. These concerns were taken up in 1984 by Indian and Northern Affairs Canada (INAC) which organized in 1985 the Technical Committee on Contaminants in Northern Ecosystems and Native Diets (hereafter, Technical Committee), consisting of scientists and bureaucrats from four federal departments – INAC, Environment Canada, Health Canada, and Fisheries and Oceans Canada, as well as the Government of the Northwest Territories. Subsequently, the Technical Committee organized cooperative research involving all agencies represented on the Committee, with INAC as the coordinating agency.

This research quickly produced new data that heightened concern. Norstrom *et al.* (1988) found POPs in polar bears throughout the Canadian Arctic, suggesting "long-range transport, rather than point-source input" as their route into the Arctic. They also found that contamination *increased* from south to north. Bidleman *et al.* (1989: 308) provided the "first direct evidence for an atmospheric link of [organochlorines] to arctic food chains." Muir *et al.* (1988) found higher levels of chlordane in Harp seals from northern Baffin Bay than in seals from the urban-industrial Gulf of St. Lawrence.

This research was trumped by two studies in the late 1980s related to health impacts on Arctic populations. Dewailly *et al.* (1989) came to the shocking conclusion that PCB levels in Inuit women were up to 10 times the levels found in women in southern Canadian urban areas. When Dewailly contacted an expert at the World Health Organization, he was told the levels he found were the highest ever identified (Cone 2005: 31). In the second study, Kinloch and Kuhnlein (1988) measured PCBs in the blood and breast milk of Inuit in the community of Broughton Island (now part of Nunavut). More than 18 per cent of the participants exceeded Canada's "tolerable daily intake" of PCBs in their diet. These results were leaked to the press, and caused the Arctic POPs issue to explode in the public eye. Toronto's *The Globe and Mail* (15 December 1988), for example, ran a front-page headline: "Soviet, European pollution threatens health in Arctic." (The reference to Soviet and European pollution comes from earlier Arctic haze research that identified these two areas as the dominant source of pollutants responsible for Arctic haze.) A government official was quoted as saying "the Inuit might have to go on a diet of chicken and beef." This sensationalist media attention not only thrust POPs onto the government's policy agenda but also triggered panic in some northern communities. Revelation of high POPs levels in indigenous peoples transformed the issue from one of general environmental pollution to one of human health. From this point on, Northern Aboriginal groups became key actors in Canada's foreign policy-making process.

In February 1989, INAC hosted a "Scientific Evaluation Meeting on Contaminants in the North" to synthesize and assess the state of scientific knowledge. The meeting was attended by over 30 Canadian scientists and a delegate from each of the other seven circumpolar countries. The meeting's assessment was contained in a brief report (Technical Committee 1989), the majority of which was devoted to Kinloch and Kuhnlein's research on Broughton Island.

The evaluation meeting set the stage for a strategy workshop in Toronto in December 1989. At this workshop a Strategic Action Plan on Northern Contaminants was formulated. The Action Plan laid the foundation for a long-term, interagency research program (the Northern Contaminants Program (NCP)) and contained Canada's first foreign policy statements on POPs. Canada committed itself to actively pursuing international cooperation and agreements on POPs.

## Period II: 1989–1997

During Period II, Canada emerged as an international scientific and political leader on POPs. The period begins with Canada's first foreign policy statements on POPs, proceeds through Canada's efforts to place POPs on the international political agenda, and ends with the successful conclusion of the regional LRTAP negotiations in 1997. The year 1997 marks the divide between regional (LRTAP) and global (Stockholm Convention) negotiations.

As backdrop to Period II, the global political context in which international environmental problems were situated dramatically changed in the late 1980s and early 1990s. The Cold War ended, transforming, among other areas, international relations of the Arctic. And environmental issues made a rapid ascent on the international political agenda. For example, the famous Montreal Protocol to the Vienna Convention for the Protection of the Ozone Layer was signed in 1987, and the 1992 Earth Summit in Rio de Janeiro yielded a rich harvest of international agreements. The most significant impacts of this changing context on Canada's foreign policy on POPs were, first, enhanced opportunities for cooperation in the Arctic, and second, greater attentiveness paid to international environmental issues. Neither factor was decisive in determining its POPs foreign policy but both contributed forward momentum.

During Period II, the scientific context also changed significantly. The endocrine disrupting potential of POPs was discovered, largely through the work of US scientist, Theo Colborn. She inferred that the majority of wildlife effects resulting in population decline in the Great Lakes region were related to developmental effects rather than cancer, as previously assumed, and that these effects were likely caused by tiny traces of synthetic chemicals that wrecked havoc on the endocrine system. Colborn popularized her ideas in the book, *Our Stolen Future* (Colborn *et al.* 1996), which generated widespread media, government, and public attention.

INAC and Environment Canada were initially the centers of foreign policy-making within the government, to be joined later by Foreign Affairs and International Trade Canada (FAITC). Canada's major policy decisions were, domestically, to create an Arctic Environmental Strategy and the NCP, and, internationally, to actively seek regulation of POPs. In 1990, the Canadian government launched a new national environmental plan, the Green Plan, which included a six-year CAN$100 million initiative known as the Arctic Environmental Strategy (AES), announced in 1991. It was managed by INAC and contained a contaminant component known as the AES Action Plan on Contaminants. Its main objectives were reduction and elimination of contaminants in traditional foods and "establishment of international controls through agreements and cooperation."

A scientific research arm, the NCP, was also established in 1991 and integrated into the AES. The NCP soon developed into a world-class center of POPs research. Its first phase lasted until 1997. Management was, and still is, achieved through a committee structure based on a "partnership approach" involving scientists, bureaucrats, and representatives of Aboriginal groups (Shearer and Han 2003). This broadly consultative approach was to become a hallmark of both the scientific and political dimensions of Canada's policy-making process on POPs.

Research emerging from the NCP confirmed, extended, and dramatized the threat of POPs. For example, Muir (1992) conducted a circumpolar survey of beluga whales that showed similar contaminant levels throughout the Arctic. Kidd *et al.* (1995) documented extremely high concentrations of toxaphene in Lake Laberge, Yukon Territory. Levels were so high that Health Canada put out fish consumption advisories and the native subsistence, sports, and commercial fisheries were closed. And Wania and Mackay (1993) developed a global model that explained the preferential accumulation of POPs in polar regions.

By 1989, the year the Berlin Wall fell, discussions had begun among the eight Arctic nations – Canada, Denmark, Finland, Iceland, Norway, Sweden, United States, and the USSR (now Russian Federation) – to develop a common strategy to address Arctic issues, including pollution. In 1990, Canada put forward a proposal for an Arctic Council, an Arctic-wide intergovernmental forum. The Council was formally established in the 1996 Ottawa Declaration. In 1991, the Arctic Eight established the Arctic Environmental Protection Strategy (AEPS) and its scientific arm, the Arctic Monitoring and Assessment Program (AMAP). POPs was designated the principal focus of AEPS and AMAP. Canada was front and center in Arctic initiatives. David Stone from INAC, for example, became the first chair of AMAP. Meanwhile, as early as 1989, Canadian officials from INAC had approached various international organizations, such as the United Nations Environment Program (UNEP), about regulating POPs. Nobody showed much interest. They "did not yet understand the scientific foundation of why POPs were a long-range pollution problem" (Selin and Eckley 2003: 23). Canadian officials were forced to look elsewhere.

They turned to a regional forum, the UNECE's LRTAP, which includes Europe, Canada, and the United States. Canada and Sweden suggested developing a POPs protocol at roughly the same time. Thereafter, the LRTAP Executive Body set up a Task Force on POPs in 1990 under the leadership of Canada and Sweden to prepare an assessment by 1994. Based on its assessment, the Task Force recommended creating a POPs protocol. Subsequently, an Ad Hoc Preparatory Working Group, chaired by Canada, was established in 1995. This group drew up a priority list of POPs (the so-called "dirty dozen") and a draft text for a protocol.

Formal negotiations began in January 1997 and continued throughout the year, concluding in December. Environment Canada chaired the Canadian delegation. The protocol was signed in June 1998 in Århus, Denmark. In December 1998, Canada became the first country to ratify the protocol. All members of the negotiating team were from Ottawa-based federal agencies. Environment Canada consulted with interested parties – industry (e.g., agriculture-related organizations), territorial governments, Aboriginal groups, and environmental groups (e.g., the World Wildlife Fund (WWF)-Canada) – primarily through conference calls, often with more than 20 participants.

Surprisingly, of these interest groups, Aboriginal groups were probably the most influential. They were already active in the NCP; however, their political involvement took a decided turn in March 1997 when five Aboriginal organizations formed a coalition called Canadian Arctic Indigenous Peoples Against POPs (CAIPAP) to influence Canada's position in negotiations. Environment Canada encouraged formation of the coalition and provided modest funding.

After the second LRTAP negotiating session held in June 1997, tension developed between the coalition and the government over characterization of the POPs issue, whether it was an economic or public health issue. For Aboriginal peoples, POPs was emphatically a health issue. They developed a position that spoke from "the high moral ground." They were not responsible for the creation or emission of POPs; however they, their land, and their traditional way of life bore the brunt of the negative consequences. As one spokeswoman stated, "Imagine our shock and concern as we discovered that our food that had nourished us for generations and kept us whole physically and spiritually was now poisoning us" (FAITC 2004). Throughout the LRTAP and global negotiations, the Aboriginal coalition repeatedly emphasized the Arctic, Aboriginal, and public health dimensions of the problem, which were at times lost in the minutiae of debate.

With encouragement from Canada, POPs finally reached the global environmental agenda when the UNEP Governing Council adopted Decision (18/32) in March 1995 which invited the Intergovernmental Forum on Chemical Safety (IFCS) and the International Program on Chemical Safety (IPCS) to assess a shortlist of 12 POPs (the "dirty dozen" of LRTAP's list) and to make recommendations on the need for global action. Canada served both as President of IFCS and as Chair of its POPs working group. The IPCS submitted a report (Ritter *et al.* 1995), authored by Canadian consultants, and, based on the report, the IFCS recommended to the UNEP in 1996 that "international action, including a global legally binding instrument, is required to reduce the risks to human health and the environment arising from the release of the 12 specified POPs" (IFCS 1996).

### Period III: 1997–2001

Period III spans the time between the first negotiations on a global POPs treaty and their successful conclusion with the signing of the Stockholm Convention in 2001. Much greater public attention was paid to the global negotiations than to the regional LRTAP activities. Canada built on and enhanced its international leadership role throughout the period. Indicative of this, Canada offered to host the first negotiation session, which was held in Montreal in June 1998, the same month and year that the LRTAP POPs Protocol was signed. Negotiations continued through four more sessions: Nairobi (January 1999), Geneva (September 1999), Bonn (March 2000), and Johannesburg (December 2000).

Domestically, Canada's major policy decision with respect to POPs was renewal of the NCP (phase II, 1998–2003) with funding of CAN$5.4 million per year. The main focus became human health. Renewal of the NCP ensured continuation of Canada's world-renowned science informing its foreign policy.

During Period III there were no major new scientific discoveries that altered Canada's policy direction, instead the fruits of interdisciplinary and international projects begun in previous periods were harvested. The NCP published a 460-page Phase I assessment report in 1997, *Canadian Arctic Contaminants Assessment Report* (NCP 1997) based on more than 100 scientific studies in Canada. AMAP published its massive *State of the Arctic Environment Report* (AMAP 1997), also in 1997, which reviewed the Arctic as a whole. Collectively, the reports provided strong scientific support for global regulation in general, and for Canada's foreign policy position in particular.

John Buccini of Environment Canada was chair of UNEP's Intergovernmental Negotiating Committee (INC) throughout the negotiations. FAITC and Environment Canada were co-chairs of the Canadian delegation, which included an Aboriginal woman and representatives from industry and environmental groups. Politicians' profile increased starting in 1997. In the summer of that year, the Parliamentary Standing Committee on Foreign Affairs and International Trade issued a report, *Canada and the Circumpolar World*, that called on the federal government to "redouble its efforts" related to POPs. Several Members of Parliament became visibly active on POPs, pressuring ministers to act on this "nationally important" issue, and even attending negotiation sessions.

Environmental NGOs mobilized for the global negotiations, making them far more colorful affairs than the quiet LRTAP sessions. The International POPs Elimination Network (IPEN), a global network of NGOs, was formally launched at the first session of the INC in Montreal in June 1998. Over the course of the five negotiating sessions, it grew to include more than 400 NGOs in 65 countries. Canadian NGOs, including WWF-Canada, the Canadian Arctic Resources Committee (CARC), and the Canadian Environmental Law Association (CELA), worked both within and outside of IPEN.

There also appeared on the scene an extremely able and highly effective spokeswoman for Aboriginal peoples, Sheila Watt-Cloutier, an Inuk from Nunavik (northern Quebec), who served as Vice-President of the Inuit Circumpolar Conference (ICC) and President of ICC Canada. At the 1999 Nairobi session, Watt-Cloutier presented the meeting with a soapstone carving of an Inuk mother and child which quickly became a symbol of the talks. Responding to this gift, Klaus Topfer, Executive Director of UNEP, commented that indigenous peoples were the conscience of the negotiations. Aboriginal groups urged elimination of POPs not "perpetual management" and assistance to developing countries. Both positions influenced the Canadian government. Indicative of this, in March 2000, Canada became the first country to provide financial support (CAN$20 million) for capacity-building in less developed countries to reduce emissions of POPs. The fund, administered by the World Bank, became known as the Canada POPs Fund.

Treaty negotiations lasted two years. The most serious rift was between developed and developing countries. Developed countries by and large had ceased use of, or otherwise controlled, the dirty dozen. The same was not true of many developing countries. However, promise of financial and technological help, and permission to allow their use for special applications, secured their agreement. The final treaty contained clear, legally-binding obligations and a goal of "virtual elimination." The preamble states: "Arctic ecosystems and indigenous communities are particularly at risk because of the biomagnification of persistent organic pollutants." No other region of the world is mentioned in the preamble. The strong and unequivocal language of the preamble and the treaty as a whole is, in part, a tribute to Canadian leadership. Canada was the first country to ratify the Convention, in May 2001.

### Period IV: 2001–2007

The Stockholm Convention obliges each Party to the Convention to develop and implement a National Implementation Plan (NIP). Canada completed and submitted its NIP in May 2006. Environment Canada was the lead agency in its development, and engaged in an extensive consultation process, including three regional multistakeholder meetings in 2004.

Canada's NIP (Environment Canada 2006) is a statement of its post-2001 implementation activities. By 2001, Canada had eliminated the production, use, import and export of all of the intentionally produced POPs under the Stockholm Convention. In addition, there were no stockpiles of POPs pesticides in Canada. "As a result of domestic actions, the majority of POPs entering Canada's environment now come from foreign sources" (ibid.: vii).

A key element of the NIP is a new Chemicals Management Plan (CMP). Under the 1999 Canadian Environmental Protection Act, chemical substances made in Canada or imported from other countries since 1994 are to be assessed. However, many pre-1994 "legacy chemicals" had never been examined to determine if their use posed a risk to human health and/or the environment. Between 1999 and 2006 Environment Canada and Health Canada systematically categorized approximately 23,000 legacy chemicals on the basis of their persistence, bioaccumulation, and toxicity to the environment. A total of 4,300 substances (POPs and non-POPs) were identified as requiring further attention. These substances are to be assessed and regulated under the CMP. The Prime Minister proudly stated, "Canada has now become the first country in the world to achieve full categorization of our legacy chemicals" (Office of the Prime Minister 2006). The CMP will help identify new candidate POPs to the Stockholm Convention; however, to date, Canada has not supported inclusion of any new substances.

In the post-2001 implementation period, a wide variety of interest groups continue to influence Canada's foreign and domestic policy on POPs, including provincial and territorial governments, northern Aboriginal organizations, industrial associations and businesses, and environmental and health NGOs, including organizations focusing on women's and children's health. Canada designated three positions for NGO representatives on its delegation to the Stockholm Convention's Conference of Parties. Few other countries have involved NGOs to this degree. Environment Canada has provided funds for these NGOs to sit as part of the delegation; although, according to one source, there is some grumbling in the NGO community that the resources are insufficient to meaningfully participate and that meetings meant for dialogue are becoming "informational updates" because the NGO community is not being briefed with sufficient time to do any analysis, or prepare comments or recommendations.

Canada's scientific research remains strong. The NCP Phase II continued from 1998 to 2003. In Phase II there was a decided shift toward human health. Traditional knowledge of the northern Aboriginal peoples became increasingly important, and greater effort went into developing effective communication of scientific research to local communities. A second assessment report was issued in 2003 (NCP 2003). Research revealed that Inuit contaminant levels were still of concern, and that subtle health effects were detected in Inuit children exposed to these contaminants. Phase III is now underway, although at a reduced funding level, and continues to focus on human health, although monitoring the effectiveness of the LRTAP POPs Protocol and the Stockholm Convention is included. Researchers working on an NCP-supported "Monitoring Our Mothers" study announced in October 2007 that the body burden of PCBs in Aboriginal mothers was dropping despite greater consumption of traditional foods (Weber 2007). Global regulation of POPs may be working.

## Analysis: actors and factors influencing Canada's foreign policy on POPs

To organize our analysis of the making of a POPs leader, we utilized a typology of "approaches to foreign policy" constructed by Barkdull and Harris (2002) and contained in Chapter 2 of this volume (see Table 2.1). The typology differentiates three levels of decision-making (system, state, and society) and three types of influence on the decision-making, or causal variables that motivate foreign policy related behavior (power, interests, and ideas). It does not focus on leadership. We used it to help isolate the actors and factors influencing Canada's foreign policy on POPs, which in turn contributed to its leadership status. Our analysis is organized by level.

### System level

Systemic analysis hypothesizes that systemic factors, i.e., those larger than the state, influence foreign policy. Power is one system level factor. Canada's foreign policy on POPs and leadership role cannot usefully be explained in terms of regional or global configurations of power. Canada is a middle power in world politics; however, it became a global leader on the POPs issue. It used a "soft power" approach typical of middle powers.

Interests can derive from the system level. Geography is one system level factor shaping Canada's foreign policy interests. Canada is steward to one-quarter of the world's Arctic region, and, because of the physics and chemistry of POPs, it turns out cold regions like the Arctic are "sinks" for POPs and hence are prone to their negative consequences. The Arctic is the world's major sink; it is in Canada's interest to protect itself from POPs damage.

Large-scale historical change is another systemic factor shaping interests. The end of the Cold War and the rise of international environmental issues around 1990 provided Canada with a window of opportunity that it seized; for instance, using newly created Arctic forums for pushing POPs regulation.

International ideas or norms are, collectively, another system level factor influencing foreign policy choice. International ideas, however, do not explain Canada's foreign policy on POPs. Canada was primarily a creator of system-wide ideas related to these chemicals, not a recipient of them.

In summary, system level factors provide a first-cut explanation for Canada's foreign policy and leadership on POPs. Geography dictated Canada's vulnerability to the negative impacts of POPs, and large-scale historical change enhanced the context for the exercise of leadership in the early stages of the development of the POPs issue.

### State level

State level analysis hypothesizes that a state can act independently of domestic interests. Thus, foreign policy can be a product of institution arrangements, for example, between the Parliament and federal bureaucracies. Power is one state level factor. Foreign policy outcomes can be explained by identifying which state-level actors dominate the foreign policy-making process. Canada's foreign policy on POPs cannot readily be explained in terms of state-level politics because, first, societal interests were not ignored and, second, there was a high level of cooperation among an amazingly wide range of federal organizations, strong and weak.

Federal ministries, as opposed to the Prime Minister and Parliament, dominated the foreign policy-making process on POPs. The three main ministries were Environment Canada, INAC, and FAITC. Environment Canada was the lead agency throughout our time-span of analysis from 1989 to 2007, with the exception of the earliest phase when INAC stood out. INAC, however, housed the NCP and hence played a decisive role in establishing Canada's scientific leadership on POPs. FAITC did not become significantly involved until 1997. Lesser state-level actors were the Prime Minister's Office and parliamentarians.

Besides "faceless bureaucracies," numerous state-level individuals contributed to Canada's leadership on POPs. These included David Stone of

INAC and the NCP, who performed yeoman's work in his multiple coordinating roles, including first chair of AMAP and co-chair of the LRTAP Task Force on POPs; John Buccini of Environment Canada, who skillfully chaired the global negotiation sessions from 1998 to 2001; and Ken McCartney of FAITC, who co-chaired the Canadian delegation during the same time period.

State interests that exist apart from society are another societal level factor. There is little evidence that bureaucratic interests operating separate from society were a significant factor. Rather than acting as aloof bureaucracies, the three dominant ministries have received accolades for their efforts to bring diverse groups together from both inside and outside government. Consultation was a central theme of the foreign policy process, as it was on Canada's domestic scientific process within the NCP. Consultation helped form and inform state interests, and, despite occasional difficulties and complaints, was one of the "secrets" behind Canada's leadership status.

Ideas influential on state-level policy-makers are another state-level level factor. Ideas were indeed highly influential on Canadian foreign policy-makers. Explaining Canada's POPs foreign policy is, in part, an exercise in explaining how and why certain ideas influenced key state-level actors. The most influential ideas are highlighted in the next section.

In summary, state level analysis helps pinpoint the key state-level actors in Canada's foreign policy-making process on POPs (federal ministries and, to a lesser degree, the Office of Prime Minister and Members of Parliament, in addition to influential individuals within these organizations) and the procedures they used (especially, interagency cooperation and multistakeholder consultation); however, it doesn't fully explain the making of an environmental leader. For this, we need turn to the society level.

### Society level

Society level analysis hypothesizes that interest group or class interactions translate into foreign policies. In other words, foreign policy results from the preferences of domestic actors. Power is one society level factor. Was Canada's foreign policy determined by the preferences of the most powerful actors in society, generally the elite and rich? No. Canadian industry and business leaders, for instance, were relatively passive actors, in large part because the intentionally produced dirty dozen POPs were not manufactured in Canada and were little used in the 1990s.

Domestic interests expressed through interest group bargaining and compromise are another society level factor. Thus, to explain foreign policy one must identify the groups that participated, their relative influence, and strategies and tactics they employed. "Interests in society" were a major influence on Canada's POPs foreign policy.

Scientists and mid-level bureaucrats were initially responsible for making POPs an object of foreign policy between 1985 and 1989. It was they, in conjunction with the mass media, who sparked societal actors' interests. Mass media coverage of scientific studies on the alarming contamination levels in the Arctic Aboriginal population catapulted POPs onto the national political agenda in 1989 and galvanized Aboriginal and environmental groups. Thereafter, with some fits and false starts, a process of consultation, bargaining, and compromise among a wide range of interest groups came to characterize Canada's foreign policy-making. While the various groups lobbied a wide range of interests, those of indigenous groups seem to have been the most influential; in particular, the primacy of an Arctic focus and protection of Aboriginal health.

Domestic ideas are another society level factor. Internally generated ideas shape the way actors within a state define, interpret, and value the object of foreign policy choice. "Ideas in society," especially ideas generated by Canadian scientists, were a major influence on Canada's POPs foreign policy.

Canadian scientists were generators of original and highly influential scientific knowledge, especially as organized under the NCP. For example, they helped establish POPs as an international problem and identified the Arctic as the world's POPs hot spot and discovered high POPs concentrations in the Aboriginal population. Scientists remained influential throughout the timespan of analysis. Some of the secrets of the NCP's success include its use of a multidisciplinary "integrated ecosystem approach," its top-quality assessments, and its highly effective "science–policy collaboration." The NCP produced credible, comprehensive, consensus-based, world-class science, and channeled it not only back and forth between scientists and bureaucrats, but also downward to the local level and upward to the international level.

Ideas also came from other actors. For example, environmental groups, from their work in the Great Lakes region stressed the importance of virtual elimination and application of the precautionary principle. And both scientific and non-scientific ideas and events were in general enthusiastically covered by Canada's mass media in a manner sympathetic to international action/regulation.

In summary, society level analysis, especially dynamics related to interests and ideas, add greatly to understanding Canada's foreign policy and leadership on POPs. Canada did not seek a lowest common denominator foreign policy position. Why? From our analysis, three factors go a long way toward explaining this: Aboriginal interests, scientists' ideas, and minimal opposition by domestic economic interest groups.

Table 9.1 contains a summary, following Barkdull and Harris' framework, of dominant influences on Canada's foreign policy on POPs. All three levels – system, state, and society – are relevant. Of the three types of influence, power played little or no role; interests and ideas dominated, especially Arctic interests and scientific ideas. Thus, a conjuncture of actors and factors explains Canada's foreign policy and scientific and political leadership on POPs. The key actors were federal ministries, the NCP, and Aboriginal and

*Table 9.1* Influential actors and factors in Canada's POPs foreign policy and leadership

|  | System | State | Society |
|---|---|---|---|
| Power | Little policy impact | Little policy impact | Little policy impact |
| Interests | *Factors*: | *Actors*: | *Actors*: |
|  | Physics and chemistry of POPs Geography End of Cold War Rise of international environmental issues | Federal ministries (especially, Environment Canada, INAC, FAITC) Individuals within these ministries Prime Ministers and Members of Parliament | Aboriginal Groups Sheila Watt-Cloutier Territorial governments Environmental and health NGOs Business and industry Mass media |
|  |  | *Factors*: | *Factors*: |
|  |  | Interagency cooperation Science–policy collaboration | Consultation with interest groups Minimal opposition by powerful economic interest groups Enthusiastic media coverage |
| Ideas | Little policy impact | *Actors*: | *Actors*: |
|  |  | NCP | Scientists |
|  |  | *Factors*: | *Factors*: |
|  |  | Effective system of researching, assessing, and communicating | Aboriginal participation |

environmental groups. The key factors that bound these actors were cooperation, consultation, and collaboration within the context of an issue that
did not become highly contentious within Canadian society as a whole. This
dynamic propelled Canada to leadership status.

## Conclusion

Sheila Watt-Cloutier explained Canada's leadership on POPs in terms of
three aspects: good science (the NCP and its cooperative structure), good
politics (proactive and cooperative approach of federal ministries), and good
people (such as John Buccini and David Stone) (ICC Canada 2001). This
scheme provides a convenient vehicle for offering lessons to potential

international environmental lead states and reflects our case study findings that causal variables related to internal cooperation and to interests and ideas at the state and society levels largely explain Canada's foreign policy and leadership.

1   *Science.* Develop a multidisciplinary, holistic approach to research that is cooperative and collaborative, and that meaningfully involves appropriate non-scientists in the science process. Emphasize not only the production of top-notch science but also its translation and transmission downward to the local level and upward to the global level.
2   *Politics.* Value multi-stakeholder consultation. The watchword is inclusion not exclusion, with the caveat that inclusion may not be a panacea for highly contentious issues. And be poised to take advantage of opportunities provided by changes in the systemic context.
3   *People.* Construct a community of leaders. Select, encourage, and organize individuals who are leaders, for they are ultimately what make a state a leader.

## Acknowledgments

We would like to thank the following individuals for providing information and/or granting interviews: Mehran Alaee (National Water Research Institute), Terry Bidleman (Meteorological Service of Canada), Sue Bonnyman (Northwest Territories Environmental Contaminants Committee), Birgit Braune (Canadian Wildlife Service), Neil Burgess (Canadian Wildlife Service), Ih Chu (Health Canada), Marlene Evans (National Hydrology Research Institute), Aaron Fisk (National Water Research Institute), Tom Harner (Meteorological Service of Canada), Fe de Leon (Canadian Environmental Law Association), Don Mackay (Trent University), Derek Muir (Environment Canada), Clive Tesar (Canadian Arctic Resources Committee), and Frank Wania (University of Toronto). In addition, we appreciate the useful comments offered by reviewers of the draft chapter. Ken Wilkening's portion of the research was funded by SSHRC grant #410-2006-2207.

## References

AMAP (Arctic Monitoring and Assessment Programme) (1997) *Arctic Pollution Issues: A State of the Arctic Environment Report*, Oslo: AMAP.
Barkdull, John and Harris, Paul G. (2002) "Environmental Change and Foreign Policy: A Survey of Theory," *Global Environmental Politics*, 2: 63–91.
Bidleman, T.F., Patton, G.W., Walla, M.D., Hargrave, B.T., Vass, W.P., Erickson, P., Fowler, B., Scott, V. and Gregor, D.J. (1989) "Toxaphene and Other Organochlorines in Arctic Ocean Fauna: Evidence for Atmospheric Delivery," *Arctic Bulletin*, 42: 307–13.
Carson, Rachel (1962) *Silent Spring*, Boston, MA: Houghton Mifflin.

Colborn, Theo, Dumanoski, Dianne and Myers, John Peterson (1996) *Our Stolen Future*, New York: Dutton.

Cone, Marla (2005) *Silent Snow*, New York: Grove Press.

Dewailly, Eric, Nantel, Albert, Weber, Jean-P. and Meyer, François. (1989) "High Levels of PCBs in Breast Milk of Inuit Women from Arctic Quebec," *Bulletin of Environmental Contamination and Toxicology*, 43: 641–6.

Downie, David Leonard and Fenge, Terry (eds) (2003) *Northern Lights Against POPs*, Montreal: McGill-Queen's University Press.

Eckley, Noelle (2001) "Traveling Toxics: The Science, Policy, and Management of Persistent Organic Pollutants," *Environment*, 43: 24–36.

Eckley, Noelle and Selin, Henrik (2003) "The Arctic at Risk: Arctic Pollution 2002," *Environment*, 45: 37–40.

Environment Canada (2006) *Canada's National Implementation Plan under the Stockholm Convention on Persistent Organic Pollutants*, Ottawa: Environment Canada.

FAITC (Foreign Affairs and International Trade Canada) (2004) "Taking Action on Northern Contaminants." Online. Available: http://maeci.gc.ca/canada-magazine/issue23/08-title-en.asp (accessed 19 December 2007).

Holden, A.V. (1970) "Monitoring Organochlorine Contamination of the Marine Environment by the Analysis of Residues in Seals," in M. Ruivo (ed.) *Marine Pollution and Sea Life*, Surrey: Fishing News Books.

Hough, Peter (2003) "Poisons in the System: The Global Regulation of Hazardous Pesticides," *Global Environmental Politics*, 3: 11–24.

ICC Canada (Inuit Circumpolar Council Canada) (2001) "Notes for Ms. Sheila Watt-Cloutier." Online. Available: http://inuitcircumpolar.com/index.php?ID=95&Lang=En (accessed 19 December 2007).

IFCS (Intergovernmental Forum on Chemical Safety) (1996) *Final Report of the IFCS Ad Hoc Working Group on Persistent Organic Pollutants (IFCS/WG.POPs/Report.1)*, Geneva: IFCS.

Kidd, Karen A., Schindler, David W., Muir, Derek C.G., Lockhart, W. Lyle and Hesslein, Raymond H. (1995) "High Concentrations of Toxaphene in Fishes from a Subarctic Lake," *Science*, 269: 240–2.

Kinloch, David and Kuhnlein, Harriet (1988) "Assessment of PCBs in Arctic Foods and Diets," *Arctic Medical Research*, 47: 159–62.

Muir, Derek C.G. (1992) "Circumpolar Survey of PCBs in Beluga," in Russel Shearer (ed.) *Synopsis of Research Conducted under the 1990/1991 Northern Contaminants Program*, Ottawa: Indian and Northern Affairs Canada.

Muir, Derek C.G., Norstrom, Ross and Simon, Mary (1988) "Organochlorine Contaminants in Arctic Marine Food Chains: Accumulation of Specific Polychlorinated Biphenyls and Chlordane-Related Compounds," *Environmental Science and Technology*, 22: 1071–9.

Myers, Heather (2001) "Changing Environment, Changing Times: Environmental Issues and Political Action in the Canadian North," *Environment*, 43: 32–44.

NCP (Northern Contaminants Program) (1997) *Canadian Arctic Contaminants Assessment Report*, Ottawa: Indian and Northern Affairs Canada.

—— (2003) *Canadian Arctic Contaminants Assessment Report II*, Ottawa: Indian and Northern Affairs Canada.

Norstrom, Ross J., Simon, Mary, Muir, Derek C.G. and Schweinsburg, Ray E. (1988) "Organochlorine Contaminants in Arctic Marine Food Chains: Identification,

Geographical Distribution, and Temporal Trends in Polar Bears," *Environmental Science and Technology*, 22: 1063–71.

Office of the Prime Minister (2006) "Prime Minister Announces Canada's New Chemicals Management Plan." Online. Available: http://pm.gc.ca/eng/media.asp?id=1452 (accessed 19 December 2007).

Ritter, L., Solomon, K.R., Forget, J., Stemeroff, M. and O'Leary, C. (1995) *Persistent Organic Pollutants. An Assessment Report on DDT, Aldrin, Dieldrin, Endrin, Chlordane, Heptachlor, Hexachlorobenzene, Mirex, Toxaphene, Polychlorinated Biphenyls, Dioxins and Furans*, Geneva: International Programme on Chemical Safety (IPCS).

Selin, Henrik and Eckley, Noelle (2003) "Science, Politics, and Persistent Organic Pollutants: The Role of Scientific Assessments in International Environmental Co-Operation," *International Environmental Agreements: Politics, Law and Economics*, 3: 17–42.

Selin, Henrik and Hjelm, Olof (1999) "The Role of Environmental Science and Politics in Identifying Persistent Organic Pollutants for International Regulatory Actions," *Environmental Review*, 7: 61–8.

Shearer, Russel and Han, Siu-Ling (2003) "Canadian Research and POPs: The Northern Contaminants Program (Ch 3)," in D.L. Downie and T. Fenge (eds) *Northern Lights Against POPs*, Montreal: McGill-Queen's University Press.

Technical Committee (Technical Committee on Contaminants in Northern Ecosystems and Native Diets) (1989) *Summary of the Findings and Conclusions of the Scientific Evaluation Meeting on Contaminants in the North*, Ottawa: Indian and Northern Affairs Canada.

Thrift, Charles, Wilkening, Ken, Myers, Heather and Bailey, Renata (submitted for publication) "Analyzing Science in Canada's Foreign Policy on Persistent Organic Pollutants (1985–2001)."

Wania, Frank and Mackay, Donald (1993) "Global Fractionation and Cold Condensation of Low Volatility Organochlorine Compounds in Polar Regions," *Ambio*, 22: 10–18.

Weber, Bob (2007) "Study: Efforts to Reduce Pollution in Arctic May Be Working." Online. Available: http://cnews.canoe.ca/CNEWS/Science/2007/09/28/4534363-cp.html (accessed 19 December 2007).

# 10 Greening the streams

## Water in EU and US foreign policy

*Sara Hughes and Lena Partzsch*

Developing sustainable governance strategies for water resources is of critical importance for the twenty-first century. Large-scale assessments of current governance strategies have demonstrated the unsustainable use patterns and pollution of global water resources they produce (Gleick 1993; Postel *et al.* 1996; UNEP 2006). The challenges to developing sustainable strategies have been receiving greater attention over the past fifteen years. International networks and programs on water governance have been developed, such as the Stockholm World Water Week and the World Water Forum. This mobilization at the global scale has drawn attention to the status of water resources and has helped improve knowledge in the field. We now know that worldwide water consumption rises twice as fast as population grows, often in places that are already experiencing water stress, i.e., water use exceeds natural supply (UNESCO 2006: 116); more than a billion people worldwide lack access to potable water and twice as many do not have basic sanitation; some 4,900 people die each day as a result of diarrhea (UNDP 2006). The ecological consequences of rising consumption have been equally severe: around the world, rivers, lakes and canals are severely polluted and the services they provide are compromised (UNEP 2006; UNESCO 2006).

Two particularly influential global networks have emerged and are proposing solutions to solve these water-related problems. Perhaps the greatest programmatic focus is provided by the United Nation's announcement of the International Water Decade from 2005–15 (The Decade). The Decade's objectives stress that greater priority should be given to the water-related Millennium Development Goals (MDGs). Specifically these goals are that by 2015 the proportion of people who are unable to reach or afford safe drinking water and the proportion of people without access to basic sanitation should be halved. In parallel with The Decade has been the emergence of new ideas for water governance, termed integrated water resources management (IWRM). Officially coined by the Global Water Partnership, "IWRM aims to ensure the coordinated development and management of water, land, and related resources by maximizing economic and social welfare without compromising the sustainability of vital environmental systems" (GWP 2000). The term has been incorporated in water planning strategies and policy around the world as a laudable goal for water governance. However, operationalizing the term has proven to be much more of a challenge (Biswas 2004). Table 10.1 compares the key features of IWRM with to the characteristic approaches of traditional water management (Partzsch 2007: 68–72).

Since the attention to the global nature of water resources paid by the Johannesburg Summit of 2002, water has gained an increasingly prominent place on the foreign policy agenda of many countries. However, the scope of academic inquiry in the issue area of water foreign policy is rather undeveloped and has largely consisted of explorations of environmental insecurity due to decreasing water quantity and quality and the public health impacts of these trends (Starr 1991; Lewis 2007). There are three focal areas for assessing issues related to water foreign policy: (1) quantity (where water is located and where it is distributed to in what volume); (2) quality (the degree to which water is polluted, saline, or bacteria and nutrient-loaded); and (3) infrastructure (the means by which water is transported and delivered to and from users). Translating these issue areas into an effective foreign policy program for water resources is a new and critically

*Table 10.1* Comparing integrated water resource management to conventional water planning

| Integrated water resource management | Conventional water planning |
| --- | --- |
| Holistic approach: water as integral part of the eco-system (besides soil, forest, air, flora and fauna) but also as social and economic good | Main objective: higher human wealth (national or regional economic development, environmental quality and social welfare) |
| River Basin Commission: administrative unit refers to natural scope/borders of the basin, not existing administrative units | Planning according to existing administrative units at the international as well as at the national, regional and local level |
| Process-oriented management, strategic operational phase are combined | Strategic planning based on system analysis |
| Recognizing water needs in relevant sectors | Water plans adapted to multi-sector planning, e.g. agriculture, land use planning |
| Participative approach, public hearings | "Top down" decisions by experts and politicians |
| Gender inclusion, specific recognition of women | Lack of gender sensitivity |
| Market mechanisms such as demand side management and cost-recovering water pricing | Offer orientation, water over-use as the case may be, solutions based on technology |

Source: Partzsch (2007: 71).

important area of water governance. Incorporating the complexity of water resources and governance into these programs and strategies is still in its infancy.

The aim of this chapter is to provide an overview and analysis of the water foreign policy of the United States and the European Union, two bodies of government that play a significant role in this emerging field. Specifically, we demonstrate the processes through which institutional structures interact with emerging ideas and bureaucratic interests in shaping water foreign policy. For example, while domestic water policies in the US, and EU policies for Member States, are largely integrated into the environmental policy agenda, the degradation of water eco-systems is largely neglected in water foreign policy in favor of geopolitical interests and international development targets. In asking why this is so, we situate water foreign policy as a conduit between domestic and global developments in water governance. We draw from a state-centric theory of environmental foreign policy which asserts that bureaucratic politics compete over policy preferences and impact outcomes (Barkdull and Harris, this volume). We begin with the premise that the US and the EU are both significantly shaping the nature of water resource issues through hydrological, financial, and political means, and therefore their actions and ideas will have a significant impact on the world's water resources. We develop concrete policy recommendations that could help move water foreign policy in these regions toward a more integrated and "green" policy stream.

## EU and US water foreign policy programs: overview and comparison

The United States and the European Union are crucial players in the global water arena for a variety of reasons. Citizens in these regions have per capita water consumption rates much higher than the global average and maintain consumption patterns that require major water resource use outside their borders. The people of the US have the largest water consumption per capita with 2,480 m³/yr while the global total average is 1,243 m³/cap/yr (Chapagain and Hoekstra 2004: 53–5). Western Europe is the largest net water importer if resources used for the production of goods and services are considered. Countries such as the Netherlands (1,223 m³/cap/yr) and the United Kingdom (1,245 m³/cap/yr) have extremely high water import dependency, requiring 82 per cent and 70 per cent of the water needed from production abroad (ibid.: 66–8). In addition, as major global donors and policy leaders the US and EU governments often have a leading role in international and foreign policy formulation of global programs and nation states (Deckwirth 2004: 16, 25; Stadler and Hoering 2003: 126). Indeed, the European Union claims that "European experience was essential in addressing an emerging global water crisis that … was threatening lives, sustainable development, peace and security" (Europeaid 2007). Collectively, the EU and its Member States have spent close to €1.5 billion per annum since 2002 on water foreign projects, with all of the funds having been acquired from national budgets (ibid.). US and EU foreign assistance programs are one of their most crucial sources of influence on water governance in other countries through infrastructure and technology improvements and political reform. These programs will be evaluated throughout this chapter in terms of how "green," and therefore sustainable over the long term, international water targets and policies are.

### The water foreign policy of the European Union

The heart of internal EU water policy is the Water Framework Directive (WFD) (Kaika 2003; Hödl 2005). The Directive has a primarily environmental background and motivation. It was prepared and negotiated by the environmental committees of the European Commission, the European Parliament and the European Council. The goals of the WFD include the prevention of environmental pollution and the establishment of ecologically sustainable water policy. These are targeted specifically at river basin management strategies. The aim is to keep European waters of "good status," and water quality should be improved by 2015.

Although the WFD was adopted as EU domestic legislation, which means that it applies only to the territory of EU Member (and Accession) States, it is also considered a worldwide model for Integrated Water Resource Management (IWRM) (Table 10.1) and promoted through foreign programs (Dimas 2005: 3). The key EU programmatic strategy for tackling global water issues is the EU Water Initiative (EUWI). The EUWI was adopted at the Johannesburg Summit in 2002 and further expanded and solidified existing commitments to aiding water development abroad, giving a platform to smaller projects of partners at regional, national and local level (European Commission 2002b; EUWI 2004). The initiative is expected to continue until 2015, which is when the MDGs are due to be reached. Four geographical regions are officially targeted: Africa; the Mediterranean; Latin America; and Eastern Europe, Caucasus and Central Asia.

The EUWI was developed by Member State governments and the European Commission. A significant difference from the WFD is the exclusion of the European Parliament as a player. An additional difference has been the involvement of several Directorate-Generals of the European Commission (and not only DG Environment). While originally only DG Development was in charge of water foreign strategies (European Commission 2002a), now also DG Environment, External Relations, Aid Cooperation and Research have become engaged through the EUWI. Further, the EUWI aims to improve coordination and cooperation of public and private activities at different levels (Dimas 2005; EUWI 2004). Three objectives were set, namely to do the following:

1 *Reinforce political will and commitment to action*: The initiative seeks to give global water problems a higher priority on the political agenda as water is considered essential for poverty eradication and sustainable development.

2 *Improve coordination and cooperation*: The initiative seeks to provide an umbrella for a range of existing state and non-state activities in order to create synergy effects in the field of water supply and sanitation. Furthermore, regional and sub-regional water cooperation is aimed to be enhanced whereby the EU Water Framework Directive (WFD), originally adopted as domestic legislation, is promoted as best practice and model for foreign countries.

3 *Increase the efficiency of existing EU aid flows*: The initiative does not seek to increase the amount but the efficiency of official development aid, especially by establishing water tariffs and private funding for water supply and sanitation (Dimas 2005).

These objectives have resulted in a diverse and complex set of policies and institutional arrangements linking the EU to partner governments abroad, nongovernmental organizations and the private sector. The EUWI is a strategic partnership, embedding civil society stakeholders and the private sector in the policy-making process, particularly European water corporations. Hence, a multi-party collaborative governance arrangement was chosen. Driving this was the mobilization of private investments in order to expand water infrastructure for the poor (European Commission 2002a: 3, 20) which was prompted in part by the development of the MDGs and their focus on water services.

As the EUWI failed to acquire new funding from private sources on its own, the EU subsequently established the Water Facility (the Facility) in 2004. The Facility is a funding instrument giving €500 million in total for projects in African, Caribbean and Pacific (ACP) countries (Figure 10.1) (Europeaid 2007). Thus the Facility applies to a far more limited geopolitical scope than the EUWI which, however, reflects the traditional focus of EU water aid programs (ibid.). This geographical focus can partly be explained by the history of European colonial ties to the region, especially those of France and the UK. The regional focus on ACP countries may also reflect the political priority of meeting the MDGs for water resources, as Sub-Saharan Africa has the highest percentage of population without access to potable water and sanitation and is considered the world's "water hotspot" (Figure 10.2).

The Water Facility requires co-finance from applicants, reflecting the goal of the EUWI to only mobilize finance and not provide new funds for infrastructure projects. As such, if projects apply for funding they must bring in additional funding from other, possibly private, sources. Therefore, the European Commission calculates twice the amount of money donated by the EU as being mobilized through the Facility, i.e. €1 billion in total from €500

*Figure 10.1* The ACP countries: focus of EU water funds
Source: Europeaid 2007.

*Figure 10.2* Coverage of improved drinking water resources
Source: UNESCO 2006: 222.

million in donations (EUWI 2005). In practice, however, very little of the co-finance funds required comes from the private sector but rather from other (national) public funds. Despite the fact that private sector funds remain a minor contributor to infrastructure projects, civil society groups often criticize the practice of private co-finance, accusing the Facility of channeling development aid into subsidies for European water corporations (Deckwirth 2004:

25). For this reason, they charge the EU with wielding "imperial power" (Barkdull and Harris, Chapter 2, this volume) because they claim the Water Initiative and Facility are exploiting vulnerable areas. The European Parliament also questions whether the European Commission's attempts actually benefit the poor and whether only French and German water corporations receive the benefits of approved projects (European Parliament 2003: 13). Nonetheless the European Parliament generally agrees with the collaborative or participative approach in water management, including the participation of both private stakeholders and civil society (ibid.: 12).

Ecological outcomes, which are the original objectives of the EU Water Framework Directive, are tangential to these EU water foreign programs. Although the EUWI partnerships established regional working groups on IWRM in each of the partner regions, the aim of improving, or at least not eroding, the sustainability of vital ecosystems remains imprecise and marginalized; environmental concerns are not mainstream. As an example, the EU Water Initiative on Africa aims to expand water infrastructure in a set of countries (Congo, Ethiopia, Ghana, Zambia) quite separate from those where it aims to establish IWRM strategies (Lake Chad, Lake Victoria, Orange, Niger, Volta) (Europeaid 2007: 32). Such simultaneous neglect of ecological aspects and the expansion of infrastructure could lead to environmentally harmful impacts if, for example, extended infrastructure results in unsustainable water use.

The EU's focus on expanding infrastructure for improved access and sanitation is clearly understandable for regions that remain "water hotspots" lacking services to meet basic needs, such as Sub-Saharan Africa. However, water over-use and pollution are also critical issues in these same regions, and reversing the degradation of aquatic ecosystems in Africa is a neglected area of development assistance. Such neglect can lead to social and political destabilization, compromising the resilience of the communities dependent on the services the ecosystems provide and the very infrastructure designed to improve their condition (Sachs and Santarius 2005: 110–12). There are alarming examples of ecological threats from the region, such as the precipitous decline of Lake Chad. From a size of 23,000 km$^2$ in the 1960s, Lake Chad has shrunk by more than 90 per cent to a size of 1,350 km$^2$ (UNEP 2004: 20). This depletion of water resources impacts not only natural ecosystems but also human activities and livelihoods dependent on the water. Investing in the expansion of infrastructure or sanitation facilities here will do little to address overuse in the basin.

## The water foreign policy of the United States

Water foreign policy in the United States is not as well developed as in the EU: the first highly relevant legislation was passed in 2005. Water foreign policy in the US is a largely decentralized field, as is becoming more common in many foreign policy areas (Pickering 2000). Decision-making rests primarily in the hands of Congress in the form of bills that specify budgetary allocations and priorities. However, implementation and responsibility for water projects are distributed among foreign affairs agencies (e.g., US Agency for International Development, Department of State, and Department of Defense) and domestic agencies (e.g., Environmental Protection Agency, Department of Agriculture, Department of Commerce, and Department of Health and Human Services), as many domestic agencies now have international project offices and programs.

Foreign and domestic water policy differs in the degree to which environmental objectives are included. At the domestic level, similar to the EU Water Framework Directive, the US Clean Water Act of 1972 gives some priority to ecological objectives in water quality protection and quantity management. In addition, the US Endangered Species Act often plays a role in allocating water to ecosystems requiring flows to support threatened or endangered species. Such ecological objectives are only of secondary concern in US water foreign policy, as the focus has largely been on technical and public health-related problems. Historically, there have been four components of US foreign policy on water: (1) clean water and sanitation; (2) financing and infrastructure development; (3) national level planning; and (4) resolving transnational water issues (Parker 2005). Until the Water for the Poor Act in 2005, the US did not have a coherent position on water foreign policy strategies or priority areas. The implications and development of the 2005 Water for the Poor Act are discussed in a later section of this chapter.

Like the EU, the US announced its intention to take steps toward improving governance of global water resources at the Johannesburg Summit in 2002 in the form of increasing federal investments. Following the Summit, the US Agency for International Development (USAID), the primary agency involved in water development projects abroad, was allocated $970 million over a three-year period in the hope that this would "accelerate and expand international efforts to achieve the UN Millennium Development goals and implement the Johannesburg Plan of Implementation" (USAID 2003). During this time USAID also underwent a three-year review process of its water resources investments and strategies as part of the Bush administration's Presidential Water for the Poor Initiative (2002). This review process was the beginning of several years of policy change and refocusing for Congress and the Department of State in the water sector, a policy area that had previously been quite marginal. During this review period USAID declared the "global water crisis" to be largely the lack of infrastructure and access to clean water and sanitation in developing countries (ibid.).

Foreign policy actions in the water sector have largely been taken through direct financial commitments to countries and projects. Through USAID, the US committed to invest $970 million over three years (2003–5). These commitments targeted three key areas: (1) access to clean water and sanitation services; (2) improving watershed management; and (3) increasing the productivity of water (ibid.). However, the majority of these funds were, and have been historically, directed to projects in Afghanistan, Iraq, Jordan, Egypt and the West Bank and Gaza through both USAID and the Department of Defense. According to USAID, "Jordan, the West Bank, Gaza, and Egypt, have represented a disproportionately large percentage of USAID's total water supply obligations over the last few years" (USAID 2006). In 2006, nearly one-tenth ($23.5 million) of the total water budget was spent in Iraq through supplemental support from the Iraq Relief and Reconstruction Fund. This increased the country's allocation while the overall water budget was cut. The likely explanation for this focus is US geo-strategic objectives in the Middle East including reconstruction and relief efforts here in other sectors. This redefines water foreign policy as an issue of environmental security and subsequently incorporates the bureaucratic interests and power associated with security as opposed to the environment.

Increasing attention from nongovernmental organizations and the media also helped launch water issues into the spotlight (Parker 2005). Stories of "water wars" captured the public's attention, like the *Newsweek* article from 23 May, 2005, entitled "Water, War, and Politics." In 2005, USAID submitted its report on the review process to Congress and called for increased action and investment in the water sector. Funds were subsequently doubled (from $100 million to $200 million) and were required to be committed to "drinking water supply projects and related activities" through the Foreign Assistance Appropriations Act in 2005 for fiscal year 2006 (Public Law 109–102).

Also in 2005, Congress passed the Water for the Poor Act, a significant landmark in US water foreign policy, making "access to safe water and sanitation for developing countries a specific policy objective of US foreign assistance programs" (US Department of State 2006). The significance of the Act has been its ability to help the US meet the challenges of the MDGs and provide safe drinking water and sanitation facilities to people who most need them. The Act maintains a focus on financial commitments, primarily through funding to USAID. According to USAID's 2006 Congressional Report:

> the Act requires the Secretary of State, in consultation with USAID and other US Government agencies, to develop a strategy to provide afford-able and equitable access to safe water and sanitation in developing countries within the context of sound water management in order to ensure water security and sustainability with equity.

Perhaps the most significant impact of the legislation is that it shifted the focus of water foreign policy from strategic investments in the Middle East to meeting sanitation and water access goals in areas with the greatest need. Investments in Sub-Saharan Africa, Asia and Latin America have doubled and new water programs have been developed (Table 10.2). Yearly reports delivered to Congress provide information on the progress that has been made toward meeting the MDGs.

*Table 10.2* Percentage of annual USAID budget allocated to various regions of the world

|  | Per cent of USAID Water Budget FY 2003 | Per cent of USAID Water Budget FY 2006 |
|---|---|---|
| Africa | 7 | 40 |
| Asia and Near East | 15 | 27 |
| Europe and Eurasia | 5 | 3 |
| Egypt, Jordan, Iraq, West Gaza | 50 | 20 |
| Central Programs | 8 | 3 |
| Latin American and Caribbean countries | 15 | 7 |

Source: Adapted from USAID (2003, 2007).

In addition to the funds committed through the Water for the Poor Act, the new focus of water foreign policy has mobilized additional revenue in private capital by development credit guarantees, similar to the EU Water Initiative and Facility. USAID investment projects abroad are often limited to US companies (BFAI 2005). The most significant example of a public–private partnership in this area has been the USAID/The Coca-Cola Company (TCCC) Global Development Alliance. Initiated in 2005, the partnership works with the Global Environment and Technology Foundation (a non-profit-making government-contracting organization based in Washington, DC) to direct more than $10 million in combined resources to water development projects in 16 countries where both organizations work (USAID 2007). Over 80 per cent of these resources have been invested in Sub-Saharan Africa.

While top priority is being given to clean water and sanitation, resources are also being committed to improving water and watershed management for community and ecosystem benefits. These efforts are largely guided by the principles of IWRM, particularly the broad-based participation and institutional strengthening recommendations (Table 10.1). An example is the Okavango Integrated River Basin Management Project that provided logistical support, training, equipment and technical assistance to institutions involved in the "management and protection of river basin resources" (ibid.). Since the Water for the Poor Act, USAID has committed over $55 million to improved watershed, coastal zone, and freshwater ecosystem management, which represents about one-quarter of the resources committed to improving access to drinking water and sanitation. These programs seem to be included in the reporting as a supplement to the high profile and well-funded programs for water access, sanitation, and water sector reform processes for national governments.

Environmental considerations and benefits are beginning to stake their claim in the crowded terrain of US water foreign policy, but this cannot always be measured in dollar terms. Water-related foreign policy now comes under the responsibility of the Bureau of Oceans and International Environmental Scientific Affairs, providing a favourable institutional context. USAID (2007) now claims the "preservation and environmentally sound development of the world's water resources" to be a top priority. The US has been involved in efforts to improve reporting and measurement standards among the global water community, efforts that may help to incorporate environmental outcomes into its own evaluation procedures.

## Comparing EU and US water foreign policy

Both US and EU water foreign policy have been significantly influenced by the targets set in the MDGs and the new ideas presented in IWRM. However, the institutional context within which they are translated at the domestic or internal level, and the bureaucratic politics and interests encompassed there, have meant that the foreign policy programs of the two governing bodies are quite different. The EU has focused on developing regional partnerships and project-specific funding to address regional needs with a concentrated focus on ACP countries. The US works largely bilaterally to invest in infrastructure and governance projects through the USAID and other foreign and domestic agencies. After having had a strong focus on the Middle East for geo-strategic objectives in the past, the USA has also shifted its attention to investments in infrastructure construction, particularly in Africa.

As outlined previously, there are three primary focal areas of water governance: quantity, quality, and infrastructure. Both the US and EU water foreign strategies have been highly concentrated on the expansion of infrastructure while domestic or internal water policies have mainly been concerned with environmental problems of quantitative and qualitative water reliability. In probing further into the origins of these differences, we use a state-centric approach and compare which institutions of government drive particular policies and what options may be available for improving the environmental sustainability of water foreign policy.

### *EU and US water foreign policy prioritize the Millennium Development Goals*

The formulation and evaluation of water foreign policies have largely been dominated by geo-political interests (the US focus on the Middle East and EU focus on ACP countries) and development targets of the MDGs (the EU and new US focus on Africa). The interests of water foreign policy-makers in the EU and US translate these according to their own particular interests, creating different policy paths. The EU focus on ACP countries and infrastructural expansion of water supply and sanitation for the poor clearly reflects preferences of DG Development, originally in charge of EU water foreign programs. Although other European Commission agencies became involved in foreign water initiatives after the Johannesburg Summit (e.g., DG Environment), the EU has continued to focus primarily on ACP countries by investing and nurturing the partnerships there through the EUWI and the Facility. The focus in the US is beginning to change with the passing of the Water for the Poor Act and investment becoming less targeted on meeting the needs of countries with geo-strategic importance (the Middle East) and more targeted on meeting the needs of the countries in greatest need of clean water and sanitation. This can be seen in the huge increase in funds to Africa, the global "water hotspot," between 2005 and 2006 (USAID 2007). The interests of the Department of Defense, which is involved in water foreign policies in the US (unlike in the EU), are clearly reflected in these strategies and the rhetoric of the threatening "global water crisis."

Since the Johannesburg Summit in 2002 and the re-commitment of countries to meeting the MDGs prompted by the UN announcement of the International Water Decade from 2005–15, both the US and the EU have shifted their water foreign policy goals accordingly. In the case of the EUWI, partnerships are focused on water and sanitation access and infrastructure, and the relevance of projects is judged against their ability to improve numbers in these areas. Even when conveying the lessons for the EUWI that are contained in the WFD, the links to MDGs are made explicit (EUWI 2005). For the US, annual reporting by USAID to Congress is largely meant to track dollars spent and number of people benefited (the 2006 report to Congress is entitled, "Investments in Drinking Water Supply Projects and Related Resources Activities"). Clearly, these are the criteria with which USAID is being evaluated by Congress when deciding the future of the programs.

## Idea of ecological sustainability used in EU and US water foreign policy formulation but neglected in evaluation

In both EU and US water foreign policy, at least some emphasis is placed on the importance of IWRM, environmental outcomes, and the sustainability of aquatic ecosystems. In the EU foreign programs, water is considered to be essential for sustainable development and the WFD, promoted as best practice for partner regions, has a clear focus on IWRM approaches to water governance. In the US, environmental considerations are included in the missions of USAID in the water sector. Environmentally competent agencies such as the Environmental Protection Agency are included in the Water for the Poor Act's assessment of US capacities in water resources abroad. However, very little evaluation includes environmental considerations.

Foreign water policy rhetoric increasingly emphasizes environmental concerns, and their practical subordination (or neglect) may be explained by examining state institutions. In both the EU and the US, domestic water policies are part of the environmental policy agenda: the EU Water Framework Directive was prepared and negotiated by the environmental sections of the European institutions. The US Clean Water Act is administered under the Environmental Protection Agency. As the European Commission DG Environment, among other institutions, becomes more engaged in EU water foreign programs, environmental concerns of qualitative and quantitative water reliability are attracting attention in foreign policies too. The same holds true for the involvement of the US Environmental Protection Agency in administering the Water for the Poor Act. However, water foreign policies remain focused on implementing the MDGs, which largely results in projects that expand infrastructure. Attempts to coordinate and establish steering mechanisms that bring together the environmental and development departments on foreign water issues also need evaluative criteria that include the environmental dimensions of water foreign policy.

## Lack of connection between foreign and domestic water policies

The domestic realm of water policy in the US and the EU is more sophisticated in its ability to address environmental considerations than the foreign realm. Both the EU Water Framework Directive and the US Clean Water Act have as their objective to restore and maintain the quality and integrity of waters within state borders. Such efforts to incorporate ecological objectives are only of secondary concern in water foreign policy, and little of this agency experience is being directly incorporated within water foreign policy.

## Conclusion

The general lack of environmental programs and targets in US and EU water foreign policy is the result of the interests and inexperience of the bureaucracies charged with this relatively new and complex task. Environmental actors who have interests contrary to the existing priorities of expanding infrastructure are marginalized and little investment is being made in expanding bureaucratic capacity and learning. However, we do notice a variety of actors playing an important role in collaborative problem-solving as both the EU and the US have begun to integrate non-state actors into water foreign policy. While there are a multitude of approaches to addressing environmental concerns in water policy, the IWRM framework is certainly the most developed and is already part of US and EU water foreign policy rhetoric. Operationalizing at least the principles of IWRM into practical policy measures will be fundamental to ensuring that integrated and environmentally conscious approaches gain a place in foreign policy. This does not mean that IWRM should replace policies that target the MDGs (nor can it be so), but, rather, policy development should incorporate IWRM approaches that can help meet MDGs and avoid projects that are completely target-driven at the risk of undermining the sustainability and integration of water governance.

How can water foreign policy better incorporate environmental dimensions of water governance? A significant hurdle to greening water foreign policy is the lack of evaluation criteria that measure and prioritize environmental outcomes. Environmental outcomes abroad are difficult to trace, not only in the formulation of policy but also in selecting evaluation and reporting criteria. Data provided by the US and EU are not easy to compare, nor are they particularly transparent. Reporting is in large part an exercise in listing where money was spent and how many people benefited. Both the EU and the US have been involved in efforts to improve reporting and measurement standards among the global water community, efforts that may help to incorporate environmental outcomes into evaluation procedures (Europeaid 2007; USAID, personal communication). However, there have also been significant advancements in this area from groups such as the International Water Management Institute and within academia that can provide guidance. Governments should have access to these advancements and incorporate their findings on a country- or climate-specific basis.

Two of the world's largest and most powerful players in the water arena, the US and the EU, would do well to learn from their own internal water policy development as well as the capacity that is likely to be found, but perhaps buried, in their programs and experts. If they were able to work together to improve in this area, their impact abroad could be significant. The strategies that each government adopts for water at home and abroad are likely to influence those of the other. Learning from successes and failures will help speed the process of greening policies and evaluation, and agreement among the two regions can set a powerful standard for other countries tackling these same issues. In this way, perhaps the MDGs would not only be reached but would have a lifespan beyond those of international funding cycles.

Ultimately, greening the streams of water foreign policy will take government commitment to addressing the challenges of water governance. It is possible to achieve this kind of commitment for water resources. The key will be finding ways to incorporate and measure the multiple benefits, stakeholders, and values of water that allows for critical poverty reduction as well as environmental benefits.

## References

BFAI (Bundesagentur für Außenwirtschaft) (2005) "Neuer Schwung in Ägyptens Wasserwirtschaft [New Drive for Egypt's Water Business]," 3 May. Online. Available: www.bfai.de (accessed 15 June 2007).
Biswas, Asit K. (2004) "Integrated Water Resources Management: A Reassessment," *Water International*, 29(2): 248–56.

Chapagain, A.K. and Hoekstra, A.J. (2004) *Water Footprints of Nations*, Vols 1 and 2: *Main Report*, UNESCO Institute for Water Education, Delft. Online. Available: http://www.waterfootprint.org/?page=files/WaterFootprints (accessed 15 November 2007).

Deckwirth, Christina (2004) *Sprudelnde Gewinne? Transnationale Konzerne im Wassersektor und die Rolle des GATS* [Effervescent gains? Transnational Corporations in the Water Sector and the Role of GATS]," Bonn: Weltwirtschaft, Ökologie und Entwicklung.

Dimas, Stavros (2005) "EU Water for Life Initiative," The European Commission Side Event. Meeting the MDGs and the JPOI Goals on Water and Sanitation, 21 April 2005, European Union Delegation of the European Commission to the United Nations, New York.

Europeaid (2007) *Europeaid Annual Report 2007 on the European Community's Development Policy and the Implementation of External Assistance in 2006*. Online. Available HTTP: http://ec.europa.eu/europeaid/multimedia/publications/documents/annual-reports/europeaid_annual_report_2007_en.pdf (accessed 15 November 2007).

European Commission (2002a) *Communication from the Commission to the Council and the European Parliament. Water Management in Developing Countries. Policy and Priorities for EU Development Cooperation*, (COM 2002–2132).Online. Available: http://eur-lex.europa.eu/LexUriServ/LexUriServ.do?uri=COM:2002:0132:FIN:EN:PDF (accessed 15 November 2007).

—— (2002b) *EU Water Initiative: Water for Life: Health, Livelihoods, Economic Development, Peace and Security*, Working Document, Draft 21.08.2002. Online. Available: http://www.johannesburgsummit.org/html/sustainable_dev/p2_managing_resources/2508_eu_water_initiative.pdf (accessed 1 June 2006).

—— (2003) *Initiative Européenne pour l'Eau. Composante «GIRE en Afrique»*. Document de travail 1: Identification de Bassins Transfrontaliers pour mise en œuvre de l'Initiative (working document), Brussels.

—— (2004) *EU Water Initiative: Water for Life*. Luxembourg. Online. Available: http://www.euwi.net/download_monitoring.php?id=399 (accessed 15 November 2007).

European Parliament (2003) *Report on the Commission communication on Water Management in Developing Countries and Priorities for EU Development Cooperation*, Rapporteur Paul A.A.J.G. Lannoye, A5–0273/200322, July 2003. Online. Available: http:///www.europarl.europa.eu/sides/getDoc.do?pubRef=-//EP//NONSGML+REPORT+A5-2003-0273+0+DOC+PDF+V0//EN&language=EN (accessed 15 November 2007).

EUWI (EU Water Initiative) (2004) *Participatory Observation at EUWI Multi-Stakeholder Forum 22–25 August 2005*, Stockholm.

Gleick, Peter (1993) *Water in Crisis: A Guide to the World's Freshwater Resources*, New York: Oxford University Press.

GWP (Global Water Partnership) (2000) "Integrated Water Resources Management," Technical Advisory Committee Background Paper No. 4, Stockholm. Online. Available: http://www.gwpforum.org/gwp/library/Tacno4.pdf (accessed 15 November 2007).

—— (2004) *Catalyzing Change: A Handbook for Developing Integrated Water Resources Management (IWRM) and Water Efficiency Strategies*, Stockholm: GWP.

Hödl, Edith (2005) *Wasserrahmenrichtlinie und Wasserrecht* [Water Framework Directive and Water Law], Juristische Monografien, vol. 32, Vienna: Neuer Wissenschaftlicher Verlag.

Kaika, Maria (2003) "The Water Framework Directive: A New Directive for a Changing Social, Political and Economic European Framework," *European Planning Studies*, 11(3): 299–316.

Lewis, Leo (2007) "Water Shortages Are Likely to Be Trigger for Wars, Says UN chief Ban Ki Moon," *The Times*, December 4. Online. Available: http://www.timesonline.co.uk/tol/news/world/asia/article2994650.ece (accessed 15 April 2008).

Parker, Serena (2005) "Water Issues Becoming Increasingly More Important in US Foreign Policy," *Voice of America*, March 17. Online. Available: http://www.voanews.com/english/archive/2005–03/2005-03-17-voa21.cfm?CFID=167273150&CFTOKEN=62262745 (accessed 15 November 2007).

Partzsch, Lena (2007) *Global Governance in Partnerschaft. Die EU-Initiative, Water for Life* [Global Governance in Partnership. The EU Initiative "Water for Life"], Baden-Baden: Nomos.

Pickering, Thomas R. (2000) "The Changing Dynamics of US Foreign Policy-Making: An interview with Under Secretary of State for Political Affairs Thomas R. Pickering," *US Foreign Policy Agenda*, 5(1).

Postel, Sandra L., Daily, Gretchen C. and Ehrlich, Paul R. (1996) "Human Appropriation of Renewable Fresh Water," *Science*, 271(5250): 785–8.

Sachs, Wolfgang and Santarius, Tilman (eds) (2005*)* *Fair Future. Ein Report des Wuppertal Instituts. Begrenzte Ressourcen und globale Gerechtigkeit* [Fair Future. A Report by the Wuppertal Institute. Limited Resources and Global Justice], Munich: C.H. Beck.

Stadler, Lisa and Hoering, Uwe (2003) *Das Wassermonopoly. Von einem Allgemeingut und seiner Privatisierung* [The Water Monopoly: From a Common Property to its Privatization], Zurich: Rotpunktverlag.

Starr, Joyce R. (1991) "Water Wars," *Foreign Policy*, 82: 17–36.

UNDP (UN Development Programme) (2006) *Human Development Report 2006: Beyond Scarcity – Power, Poverty and the Global Water Crisis*. Online. Available: http://hdr.undp.org/en/media/hdr06-complete.pdf (accessed 15 November 2007).

UNEP (UN Environment Programme) (2004) *Lake Chad Basin*, GIWA Regional assessment 43, Kalmar: University of Kalmar.

—— (2006) *Water Quality for Ecosystem and Human Health.* Global Environmental Monitoring System, Burlington, Ontario.

UNESCO (UN Educational, Scientific and Cultural Organization) (2006) *Water: A Shared Responsibility: The UN World Water Development Report 2*, World Water Assessment Programme, New York: Berghahn Books.

USAID (US Agency for International Development) (2003) *USAID's Water Portfolio: Promoting Clean Water and Efficient Use of Freshwater and Coastal Resources.* Report to Congress, July 2003, Washington, DC.

—— (2006) *USAID Investments in Drinking Water Supply Projects and Related Activities.* Final Report to Congress, fiscal year 2005, Washington, DC: US Department of State.

—— (2007) *USAID Investments in Drinking Water Supply Projects and Related Activities,* Final Report to Congress, fiscal year 2006, Washington, DC: US Department of State.

US Department of State (2006) *Senator Paul Simon Water for the Poor Act of 2005,* Report to Congress, June 2006, Washington, DC: US Department of State.

# 11 Trade and the environment

## Foreign policies of developing countries in Asia

*Yohei Harashima*

The issue of trade and the environment is becoming an important foreign policy agenda item. For many developing countries, international trade is the driving force of economic growth. At the same time, natural resources and the environment are also key considerations for these countries. Consequently, they need to realize sustainable development by way of mutually supportive trade and environmental policies. Since the 1970s, increasing attention has been paid to environmental issues in Asian developing countries due to rapid economic growth and industrialization in one nation after another (Harashima 2000: 34). The World Trade Organization (WTO) has dealt with the issue of trade and the environment since its inception, and the Committee on Trade and Environment (CTE), established within the WTO in 1995, has been a key forum for trade and the environment negotiations under the multilateral trading system.

After overcoming an economic crisis in the late 1990s, Asia has been swept by waves of globalization. This has brought about new movements, such as China's accession to the WTO and enhancements of free trade agreements (FTAs) within the Asian region. These developments have important implications for environmental foreign policy.

This chapter outlines the North–South conflict in trade and the environment negotiations. It identifies the positions of Asian developing countries at CTE negotiations in an attempt to understand the issue of trade and the environment in their foreign policies. Using key trade statistics, it also explores the relationship between these negotiating positions and changes in the countries' structure of trade. Finally, the chapter posits that the national economic interest of each country is the key variable that determines its environmental foreign policy behavior. Within the typology of theoretical approaches presented by Barkdull and Harris (see Chapter 2 in this volume), this chapter focuses on the systemic level and emphasizes *interests* as variables in the foreign policy of trade and environment.

## Conflict between North and South

The conflict between North and South has been a serious issue at CTE negotiations thus far and is expected to continue defining the nature of trade and environment negotiations in the future. Many developing countries were negative about the establishment of the CTE because they feared it could lead to an increase in so-called "green protectionism" and even disrupt the outcome of the Uruguay Round on improving market access. As Brack and Branczik point out, "developing countries as a whole also tend to be hostile to the trade-environment proposals of Northern countries, fearing that new environmentally directed trade restrictions will discriminate dispropor-tionately against their exports, and potentially lead on to other new bases for trade barriers, such as labour or animal welfare standards" (Brack and Branczik 2004: 10). Such resistance among developing countries was prob-ably the reason for the breakdown of the CTE negotiations in the run-up to the Singapore WTO Ministerial Conference in 1996.

As time went on, though, the conflict between North and South under-went considerable changes. At the Seattle WTO Ministerial Conference in 1999, for instance, citizens' groups from developed countries demonstrated against free trade, arguing that it could adversely affect environmental and labor conditions around the world. Trade and environment issues received a great deal of attention in the WTO negotiations, during which the South allowed itself to be seen as the scapegoat for the policy deadlock and "the main hurdle to any integration of trade, environment and development" (Najam and Robins 2001: 53). In a sense, though, the developing countries were misunderstood by the North. They were not in fact anti-environmental but simply had different priorities from the developed countries.

Developing countries have been consistently unsuccessful in their attempts to use the threat of nonparticipation to influence the outcomes of issues that are of great interest to key developed countries. And they now confront the reality that it is increasingly difficult to keep trade discussions uncoupled from those on the environment (ibid.: 54). There is also a growing need for both governments and private businesses in developing countries to respond to consumer preferences in the global market for ecologically friendly pro-ducts and to set and impose more stringent environmental standards (Khan 2002: 17). Linking trade and the environment, moreover, can offer new export opportunities and encourage investment. One must also keep in mind that some developing countries wish to retain the option of resorting to the environmental argument to protect themselves against surging imports from China and other Asian countries that make advances in economic growth (Veiga 2004: 18).

Environment-related cases under the dispute settlement mechanism of the General Agreement on Tariffs and Trade (GATT) and the WTO have been rapidly increasing since the 1990s. In the tuna–dolphin case brought to GATT, a panel found that a United States (US) import ban on tuna from Mexico for the purpose of marine mammal protection was not justified under GATT Article XX. However, in the shrimp–turtle case under the WTO, the Appellate Body found that the US import ban was justified under the provisions of Article XX (g) but that it failed to meet the requirements contained in the article's chapeau. This suggested the possibility that trade measures implemented for environmental reasons would be justified under WTO rules. Such an interpretative modification of WTO rules by a dispute settlement body was a surprise for developing countries. Developing countries that had been relying on litigations in lieu of using the CTE to clarify WTO rules on trade and the environment now faced the possibility that the Appellate Body could shift further towards environmentally friendly outcomes (Kufuor 2004: 49).

This situation forced developing countries to participate proactively in trade and environment negotiations in the CTE. For their own interests, they adopted a more positive position and began suggesting alternatives during CTE negotiations. Submissions to the CTE by developing countries, particularly those in Asia, have indeed been increasing: four were submitted in 2002, six in 2003, three in 2004, and four in 2005. These figures are almost equal to the number submitted by the European Union (EU), which is the most active region regarding trade and environment negotiations.

## Mandates for the CTE

There were few discussions on trade and the environment during the Uruguay Round. The Marrakesh Ministerial Decision on Trade and Environment of 1994, which was adopted by members at the end of the Uruguay Round, however, decided to establish the CTE and identified ten items as terms of reference for the CTE. Following this, the EU, supported by Japan, Norway, and Switzerland, pushed hard for its inclusion in the Doha Ministerial Declaration, which has been called the Doha Development Agenda, since the opening of the Doha Round in 2001.

Table 11.1 compares the CTE mandates stipulated in the Marrakesh Decision with those in the Doha Declaration. Because members had no particular concerns about some of the ten Marrakesh items, they were excluded from the Doha Declaration. The Doha Declaration focuses only on a few issues of trade and the environment and avoids the more controversial ones. As an important and additional mandate, though, the Doha Declaration requires the CTE to conduct negotiations on the liberalization of trade in environmental goods and services, a subject that had not been discussed separately in WTO negotiations. Moreover, the Doha Declaration newly set up the CTE Special Session as a negotiating group regarding mandates in Paragraph 31 of the Doha Declaration.

### The WTO-MEA relationship

Of the various points raised, the compatibility of environment-related trade measures with WTO rules is the most important one. This issue was discussed in several cases under the GATT/WTO dispute settlement mechanism, but they all concerned "unilateral" measures. So far no members have

Table 11.1 Mandates for the WTO/CTE

| | | Marrakesh Decision of 1994 | | Doha Declaration of 2001 |
|---|---|---|---|---|
| WTO-MEA Relationship | 1 | The relationship between the provisions of the multilateral trading system and trade measures for environmental purposes, including those pursuant to multilateral environmental agreements (MEAs) | 31 (i) | The relationship between existing WTO rules and specific trade obligations (STOs) set out in multilateral environmental agreements (MEAs) |
| Environmental Policies | 2 | The relationship between environmental policies relevant to trade and environmental measures with significant trade effects and the provisions of the multilateral trading system | | |
| Taxes | 3a | The relationship between the provisions of the multilateral trading system and charges and taxes for environmental purposes | | |
| Technical Regulations and Labelling | 3b | The relationship between the provisions of the multilateral trading system and requirements for environmental purposes relating to products, including standards and technical regulations, packaging, labelling and recycling | 32 (iii) | Labelling requirements for environmental purposes |
| Transparency | 4 | The provisions of the multilateral trading system with respect to the transparency of trade measures used for environmental purposes and environmental measures and requirements which have significant trade effects | 31 (ii) | Procedures for regular information exchange between MEA Secretariats and the relevant WTO committees, and the criteria for the granting of observer status |
| Dispute Settlement | 5 | The relationship between the dispute settlement mechanisms in the multilateral trading system and those found in multilateral environmental agreements (MEAs) | 31 (i) | See above |
| Market Access | 6 | The effect of environmental measures on market access, especially in relation to developing countries, in particular to the least developed among them | 32 (i) | The effect of environmental measures on market access, especially in relation to developing countries, in particular the least-developed among them |

Table 11.1 (continued)

| | | Marrakesh Decision of 1994 | | Doha Declaration of 2001 |
|---|---|---|---|---|
| Effect of Trade Liberalization on the Environment | 6 | The environmental benefits of removing trade restrictions and distortions | 32 (i) | The situations in which the elimination or reduction of trade restrictions and distortions would benefit trade, the environment and development |
| Domestically Prohibited Goods | 7 | The issue of exports of domestically ⬚ goods | | |
| Intellectual Property Rights | 8 | The relevant provisions of the Ag⬚ n Trade-Related Aspects of Intellectual Property Rights (TRIPS) | 32 (ii) | The relevant provisions of the Agreement on Trade-Related Aspects of Intellectual Property Rights (TRIPS) |
| Trade in Services | 9 | The work program envisaged in the Decision on Trade in Services and the Environment | | |
| Relations with NGOs | 10 | Input to the relevant bodies in respect of appropriate arrangements for relations with intergovernmental and nongovernmental organizations referred to in Article V of the WTO | 31 (ii) | See above |
| Environmental Goods and Services | | | 31 (iii) | The reduction or, as appropriate, elimination of tariff and non-tariff barriers to environmental goods and services |
| Capacity Building | | | 33 | The importance of technical assistance and capacity building in the field of trade and environment to developing countries, in particular the least-developed among them |

brought up cases concerning the compatibility of trade measures with mul-tilateral environmental agreements (MEAs). The issue of the WTO-MEA relationship is still controversial. Before the Singapore WTO Ministerial Conference in 1996, members exchanged their views on this issue at the CTE. On the one hand, the EU pressed for an amendment to GATT Article XX to create a presumption of compatibility with MEAs. On the other, developing countries argued to keep the status quo and also suggested applying waiver provisions of GATT when disputes arose.

The conflict between North and South remains an issue. In reality, it is virtually impossible to amend Article XX as suggested by the EU. Moreover, the Doha Declaration limits the negotiations on the WTO-MEA relation-ship "to the applicability of such existing WTO rules as among parties to the MEA in question" (Paragraph 31 (i)). Because it avoids controversial issues to reach a consensus, the Doha Declaration is not intended to deal with disputes between parties and non-parties to an MEA. Alternatively, Para-graph 31 (ii) of the Doha Declaration provides for negotiations on proce-dures for regular information exchange between MEA secretariats and the relevant WTO committees, as well as criteria for granting observer status in order to reduce the risk of conflict between WTO rules and MEAs.

The CTE Special Session has given a lot of time to discussions of the WTO-MEA relationship. Participants have been trying to come to a common understanding about the terms in Paragraph 31 (i) of the Doha Declaration. In this regard, there are two approaches: one group, including the EU and Switzerland, emphasizes conceptual issues, and the other group, including the United States and developing countries, focus on the identifi-cation of actual cases of specific trade obligations (STOs) as stipulated by MEAs in the Doha Declaration.

Many Asian developing countries have been paying close attention to the issue of the WTO-MEA relationship. China, Chinese Taipei, the Republic of Korea, Hong Kong, Malaysia, and India have, respectively, voiced their views during the CTE Special Session on the issue. They want to keep the CTE's mandate as narrow as possible and limit the scope of STOs in MEAs in the Doha Declaration. Indeed, India expressed its view that the criteria for con-sidering an environmental agreement as an MEA should have the following elements: (1) it should have been negotiated under the aegis of the United Nations or specialized agencies such as the United Nations Environment Program (UNEP); (2) its procedures should stipulate that participation in the negotiations is open to all countries; (3) there must have been effective participation in the negotiations by countries belonging to different geo-graphical regions and by countries at different stages of economic and social development: and (4) the agreement should provide for procedures for acces-sion of countries which are not its original members and on terms that are equitable in relation to those of its original participants (TN/TE/W/23: para. 4).

Trade measures can be categorized into the following four types: (1) both mandatory and specific in their entirety; (2) only the outcome to be achieved is identified with a list of appropriate measures that parties could implement to achieve the desired outcome; (3) the outcome to be achieved is identified, but the measures which could be implemented to achieve that outcome are not specified; and (4) additional and more stringent measures to achieve the overall objectives of the MEA that are more in the form of a right granted to a party as opposed to an obligation. Most developing countries argued that for any provision in an MEA to qualify as an STO, it must be "mandatory and specific" in character. Korea, Malaysia, Chinese Taipei, Hong Kong and China, respectively, identified STOs contained in key MEAs.

However, Asian developing countries have taken different stances on the more detailed questions of how to deal with the decisions, resolutions, and recommendations of the Conferences of the Parties (COP) of MEAs and regional MEAs. While India, China, and Malaysia were reluctant to treat STOs contained in such decisions as being set out in the MEAs, Korea and Chinese Taipei gave their support to do so due to the important role of COPs. As for regional MEAs, Malaysia strongly opposed their inclusion in MEA negotiations.

After the Cancun WTO Ministerial Conference in 2003, several new ideas were proposed to the CTE Special Session by the EU and Australia. Nevertheless, the CTE Special Session is still in the process of identifying its mandate and has not reached the stage of negotiation in earnest. It should be noted that, on the potential outcome of the negotiations, Chinese Taipei proposed that members could discuss an interpretative decision or an understanding that sets out conditions and principles for WTO compatibility of an STO provided for in an MEA (TN/TE/W/11: para. 15).

Asian developing countries as a rule have argued that the compatibility of MEAs with WTO rules must be interpreted as narrowly as possible. However, their stances on detailed points differ depending on country. Some developing countries in Asia have been making constructive proposals on the potential outcome of the negotiations.

*Environmental goods*

With regard to environmental goods in Paragraph 31 (iii) of the Doha Declaration, the questions of which committee or negotiating group within the WTO would be the appropriate forum for this issue was a matter of controversy in the beginning stages. It was agreed to shift this mandate to the Negotiating Group on Non-Agricultural Market Access (NAMA) and to the Council for Trade in Services Special Session. However, because the definition of these goods was not clear, the CTE Special Session was called to clarify the concept of environmental goods.

In the beginning of the CTE negotiations, members referred to lists of such goods compiled by the Organisation for Economic Cooperation and Development (OECD) and the Asia-Pacific Economic Cooperation (APEC) forum. While the APEC list focuses on pollution control and monitoring equipment, the OECD list broadly covers pollution control, clean technologies and products, and resource management.

In general, developing countries are net importers and developed countries are net exporters for the aggregate set of all goods on the OECD and APEC lists, and countries in Asia are no exception (Kim 2006: 534). Therefore, developing countries are at a great disadvantage in the liberalization of trade in environmental goods. Only developed countries would benefit from the trade liberalization of such goods.

Because there is no consensus on the definition of environmental goods, the CTE Special Session changed to a more practical approach in discussions about the list of products that members wanted considered as environmental goods. In addition, specific proposals have been submitted regarding the negotiation modalities for environmental goods by both developed and developing countries. Coming to the end of the Doha Round, the CTE Special Session focused its discussions on environmental goods in an attempt to achieve tangible results. Asian developing countries are increasingly voicing their views on this issue, particularly China, Chinese Taipei, and Korea. Because direct trade gains might flow largely to developed countries, China underscored the need for efforts to increase the potential for direct trade gains from trade liberalization in environmental goods and services for developing countries. China also sought further discussions on the definition issue, advancing an approach that would circumvent contentious problems during CTE deliberations (TN/TE/W/42: para. 3).

China proposed promoting the liberalization of trade in environmental goods by creating two lists: a "common list" and a "development list." The former is a list for all members consisting of specific product lines on which there is consensus that they constitute environmental goods. For the products on the common list, members are committed to reduce or eliminate tariff and non-tariff barriers. The development list, meanwhile, is made up of products needing "special and differential treatment" (S&D) from among those on the common list. The development list comprises those products selected by developing countries from the common list for exemption or for a lower level of reduction commitment as exceptions to the principle of full reciprocity, taking into consideration the needs of their economic development and the vulnerability of relevant domestic industries in the area of environmental goods. The importance of facilitating technology transfer to developing countries was also stressed in China's submissions.

Chinese Taipei, referring to the APEC list, argued that the "direct use" of goods is a practical and effective criterion for identifying environmental goods in the category of pollution management. It also nominated 78 specific items in the following product groupings: air pollution control; wastewater management; solid and hazardous waste management; remediation and clean-up of soil and water; noise and vibration abatement; and monitoring, analysis, and assessment (TN/TE/W/44: para. 5). Similarly, Korea suggested that the criteria for identifying environmental goods must be practical and simple, based on which it selected 89 products using both the OECD and the APEC lists. Most of them come under the pollution management category (TN/TE/W/48: para. 7).

India presented a different viewpoint from the above Asian countries. The CTE negotiations on the issue have mainly considered "industrial products," but India has utilized the concept of liberalizing the trade of "environmentally friendly products" to expand its exports of environment-related "agricultural products." India argued that exceptions to an importing country's environmental requirements should be provided for "environmentally friendly products" (WT/CTE/W/207: para. 9).

In the final stages of the Doha Round, India criticized the list approach in the CTE negotiations and offered the alternative proposal of an "environmental project approach" during CTE Special Session negotiations. Under this proposal, a project meeting certain criteria would be considered by a Designated National Authority (DNA). If approved, the goods and services included in the project would qualify for concessions for the duration of the project. This approach would solve the problems associated with the list method and also contribute positively to capacity building and technology transfer (TN/TE/W/51: paras. 12–13).

Several Asian countries, including China, Chinese Taipei, and Korea have made specific proposals that have pushed forward the negotiations on environmental goods. India, on the other hand, has taken a different stance and offered an alternative proposal, namely, the pursuit of an environmental project approach.

### Market access

Improved market access for products from developing countries is instrumental to achieving the goal of sustainable development in such countries. The issue of market access was incorporated into the Doha Declaration as a CTE mandate in consideration of developing countries, which feared their products would be excluded from the market due to environmental measures implemented by developed countries. In order to deal with this issue, agreement has been reached to examine how importing countries should design their environmental measures so that: (1) they are consistent with WTO rules; (2) they are inclusive; (3) they take into account the capabilities of developing countries; and (4) they meet the legitimate objectives of the importing country.

Owing to growing global concerns about the environment, developing countries should not overlook the fact that market access for their products could be reduced by environmental measures in developed countries. India in particular has actively engaged in negotiations on this issue. Its proposals were recognized to be worth serious consideration among members. In India's view, developing countries are most likely to feel the adverse effects of environmental measures on market access and competitiveness because they lack infrastructure, have limited technology choices, do not have adequate access to environmentally friendly raw materials and lack information access. Environmental requirements are highest in the export sectors that are of interest to developing countries and where they have comparative advantages, such as textiles and clothing, leather and leather products, footwear, forestry products, and food products. These requirements affect the market access of suppliers from developing countries. The effect is particularly felt by the small and medium-sized enterprises (SMEs) in developing countries, which have financial, managerial, and technological constraints and whose capacity to bear a higher cost of compliance is naturally quite limited (WT/CTE/W/207: para. 4).

For this reason, India made the following proposal to the CTE: Foreign producers should be given opportunities to participate in the early stages of the design of environmental requirements and have adequate time to adjust to new requirements. In addition, longer time frames for compliance should be accorded to products of interest to developing countries so as to maintain opportunities for their export.

More recently, some developing countries in Asia have turned their attention to the positive effects of environmental measures on market access. For instance, at a meeting of the CTE Special Session, the representative from China agreed that the Indian submission merited further discussion but noted, "there was also a need to reflect on the positive impacts of certain measures, such as technology transfer, financial or technical assistance, which were equally, or, in some cases, more important to developing country members to address issues related to market access or the protection of the environment" (WT/CTE/M/37: para. 5). Such views reflect the changing negotiating positions of Asian developing countries.

Many developing countries, including India, underscored the need for responses under WTO rules against reduced market access in developed countries due to environmental measures. On the other hand, some Asian countries, including China, focused their attention on the positive effects of such measures. On the issue of market access, too, there can be seen contrasting views among developing countries in Asia.

### *Effects of trade liberalization on the environment*

According to the latter part of Paragraph 32 (i) of the Doha Declaration, the CTE initiated a sector analysis of trade liberalization focusing on four sectors, namely, agriculture, energy, fisheries, and forestry, to create "win-win-win" opportunities for the environment, trade, and development. The issue of subsidies is the most critical in the sectoral analysis. Developing countries have criticized developed countries for introducing domestic subsidies. Indonesia, Malaysia, the Philippines, and Thailand are the key member countries of the Association of Southeast Asian Nations (ASEAN) and also are members of the Cairns Group of Agricultural Fair Traders. These four countries and India have been aggressively pursuing the goal of reducing and eventually eliminating agricultural export subsidies.

In contrast, Korea is of the view that a certain level of domestic support and subsidies is necessary to maintain the environmental and other benefits arising from agricultural activity. They emphasized the positive effects of such policies on the environment. Korea's experiences showed, for instance, that some fishery subsidies could play a positive role in conserving fishery resources and improving the marine environment. Korea also proposed a comprehensive approach that took into account the socioeconomic needs of the fishing industry and the unique domestic environment and development needs of various countries (WT/CTE/W/175: para. 20). Moreover, Chinese Taipei sympathized with Korea's view and stated that "the fishery subsidy which contributed to overcapacity, and illegal, unreported and unregulated fisheries should be prohibited, and those which contributed to the sustainable development of this sector should be permitted" at the CTE meeting (WT/CTE/M/37: para. 47).

Most Asian developing countries, including ASEAN countries and India, demanded the reduction and elimination of subsidies in developed countries. However, Korea and Chinese Taipei focused attention on the positive effect of such subsidies on the environment.

### Intellectual property rights

Several environment-related provisions are contained in the Agreement on Trade-Related Aspects of Intellectual Property Rights (TRIPS), which was concluded in the Uruguay Round after overcoming strong disagreement between the North and South. The Doha Declaration mandates the CTE to review the relevant provisions of the TRIPS Agreement. The focal point of negotiations on the issue is the relationship between the TRIPS Agreement and the Convention on Biological Diversity (CBD).

India has been one of the key drivers of the negotiations and has also made several important submissions to the CTE on the issue. According to India's proposal, there are two major contradictions between the provisions of the CBD and those of the TRIPS Agreement. The first is a lack of any conditions in patent applications on mentioning the origin of the biological/ genetic resources and indigenous/traditional knowledge used in biotechnological inventions. The second contradiction is a lack of provision in the TRIPS Agreement on prior informed consent of the country of origin and the knowledge-holder of the biological raw material meant for usage in a patentable invention (WT/CTE/W/65: paras. 13–14).

In order to resolve these contradictions, India suggested an amendment to the TRIPS Agreement to accommodate some essential elements of the CBD. Such an amendment could require that an applicant for a patent relating to biological materials or to traditional knowledge should: (1) disclose the source and country of origin of the biological resources and/or the traditional knowledge used in the invention; (2) give evidence of prior informed consent through the approval of authorities; and (3) give evidence of fair and equitable benefit sharing.

Another group, including several developing countries, is of the view that there is no conflict between the CBD and the TRIPS Agreement. Some members consider that, although the CBD and TRIPS are mutually supportive, their implementation could create conflicts. There is still disagreement among members over the issue (WT/CTE/8: para. 27 and IP/C/W/368: para. 6).

As mentioned above, India is actively seeking the amendment of the TRIPS Agreement itself. In contrast, China has refrained from openly expressing anything of substance. China merely stated generalities and platitudes about meeting the demands of developing countries (Endeshaw 2005: 223). The rest of the Asian developing countries have not expressed much concern about the issue, and have made few submissions and suggestions on the issue to the CTE.

### Environmental labelling

The number of environmental labelling schemes is rapidly increasing in various parts of the world. It was agreed that voluntary, participatory, market-based, and transparent environmental labelling schemes are potentially efficient economic instruments that can inform consumers about environmentally friendly products. Moreover, they tend to be less trade restrictive than other methods (WT/CTE/8: para. 30). Needless to say, these schemes need to be non-discriminatory and should not result in unnecessary barriers or disguised restrictions on international trade. It is imperative that prerequisites be clarified for WTO compatibility.

Although negotiations have continued since its inception, the CTE has produced few tangible results on the issue. Its work has been limited to information collection and analysis of environmental labelling. The root of the controversy surrounding the labelling debate is WTO compatibility of measures based on non-product-related processes and production methods (PPMs). Most developing countries take a negative stance on WTO compatibility with environmental labelling based on PPMs because they feel it could result in so-called green protectionism.

The assumption that comprehensive labelling schemes have a positive effect on achieving environmental goals was questioned by developing countries. The criteria of environmental labelling tend to focus on local concerns and do not address the views of foreign suppliers nor the specific environmental situation in the countries of these suppliers. Environmental labelling schemes that focus on environmental problems in developed countries do not always work effectively in developing countries because of differences in their priorities.

Asian developing countries have made few submissions to the CTE on this issue. However, some, including India, Indonesia, and the Philippines, have spoken out on the issue at CTE meetings and voiced their support for the position taken by other developing countries. That is, they were reluctant to agree to a broad interpretation of WTO compatibility for environmental labelling. Another group of Asian countries, including Korea and China, have shown little interest in the issue. For instance, China stressed "the need for more time to consider the issue" at the CTE meeting and did not clarify its stance (WT/CTE/M/34: para. 67). The issue of environmental labelling does not seem to be a critical concern for Asian developing countries. However, statements at CTE meetings have reflected subtle differences in the negotiating positions of such countries as India, Indonesia, the Philippines, China, and Korea.

## Negotiating positions and trade structure

Each country's position in trade negotiations is closely related to its structure of trade. Exploring the relationship between each country's negotiating positions at the CTE and changes in their structure of international trade can therefore provide valuable clues to an understanding of why they have had different foreign policies on trade and the environment in the context of the WTO.

### Changes in the structure of international trade

Figure 11.1 and Figure 11.2 classify eight Asian developing countries by trade structure based on both the shares of industrial and agricultural products in their exports and their percentage increase/decrease. Whether these figures are high or low is judged against the world average for each item. The target period is 1990–2005, when global concerns about trade and the environment were growing.

Asian countries have diverse trade structures. A notable difference can be seen, for instance, between China and India. Korea and Chinese Taipei, which are Newly Industrializing Economies (NIEs), are categorized into a similar pattern, but it is different from those of either China or India. In addition, there is a wide discrepancy among such ASEAN countries as Malaysia, Indonesia, Thailand, and the Philippines. A high share of the exports of NIEs like Korea and Chinese Taipei are industrial products. The Chinese economy is currently registering unprecedented rapid growth, mainly based on national development strategies for export-oriented industrialization. The share of agricultural products in China's exports is falling, while that of industrial products is rising sharply.

The pattern for India forms a striking contrast to that of China. Although the Indian economy began a process of development through its national strategies for economic liberalization in the early 1990s, this was not driven by exports of industrial products. Rather, India's national development strategy is focused on expanding domestic demand. Its exports are still

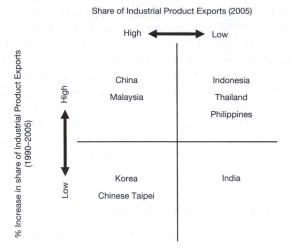

*Figure 11.1* Share of industrial product exports
Data source: World Development Indicators 2007.

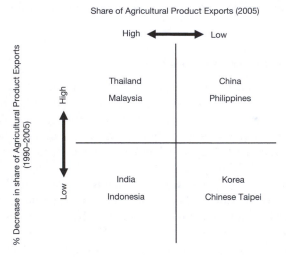

*Figure 11.2* Share of agricultural product exports
Data source: World Development Indicators 2007.

mostly agricultural products, as shown by the fact that the share of industrial products in its exports is broadly flat. It is worth noting, though, that the share of trade in services has risen dramatically. Table 11.2 shows the share of trade in services of key Asian countries. India's share rose 17 points from 20 per cent in 1990 to 37 per cent in 2005. It is a remarkable rise compared with the figures of other countries. India has a unique trade structure that depends not on the industrial sector but on the service sector, including software.

*Table 11.2* Share of trade in services

|  | 1990 (A) (%) | 2005 (B) (%) | B − A |
|---|---|---|---|
| Korea | 12 | 13 | 1 |
| China | 8 | 9 | 1 |
| India | 20 | 37 | 17 |
| Thailand | 21 | 16 | −5 |
| Malaysia | 11 | 12 | 1 |
| Indonesia | 9 | 13 | 4 |
| Philippines | 26 | 10 | −16 |
| World | 18 | 19 | 1 |

Source: World Bank (2007).

## Relationships between negotiating positions and trade structure

Asian developing countries have distinct negotiating positions at the CTE in keeping with their respective trade structure patterns. For instance, China takes a contrasting position to India in the CTE negotiations. The greatest concern for India is market access for agricultural products, and it fears that environmental measures by developed countries could reduce that access. As mentioned above, China's stance is the opposite of India's on the effect of environmental measures. China pays attention to the issue of trade liberalization of environmental goods, which could expand its export opportunities. China's proposal for negotiation modalities is thus designed to enable it to benefit from international trade. On the issues of intellectual property rights and environmental labelling as well, China and India assumed attitudes different from each other. China and NIEs, including Korea and Chinese Taipei, depend on industrial products in their trade and have actively participated together in negotiations on environmental goods. But while the share of industrial products in NIEs' exports has more or less plateaued, that for China has continued to rise.

From the mid-1980s to the early 1990s, NIEs sought to catch up with Western developed countries and Japan by implementing export-oriented development strategies through government intervention, a phenomenon known as the "East Asian Miracle." Today, however, NIEs find that their lead over China and other latecomers in economic growth is rapidly narrowing. Therefore, they often share the position of developed countries on trade and the environment. Indeed they are in sympathy with developed countries, including those in the EU, on the issues of the WTO-MEA relationship and subsidies, as mentioned previously.

No common pattern is to be found among four ASEAN countries. Although ASEAN countries jointly form a "loose-knit consultative body," each has adopted its national development strategies independently of each other in line with domestic conditions. Because they do not always have the same interests in CTE negotiations, it is difficult for them to take collective action at the CTE. Each of the key ASEAN countries made separate submissions and suggestions on each of the CTE mandates, and they have not taken a common position in CTE negotiations. In short, the negotiating positions of Asian developing countries at the CTE reflect the features of their respective trade structures, derived largely from the progress made in the pursuit of their national development strategies.

## Conclusion

While the CTE has not produced concrete results concerning its mandate, a definite change can be seen in the negotiating positions of developing countries, as many developing countries in Asia are now participating proactively in the CTE negotiations process. This chapter has shown that Asian countries' views on trade and the environment differ on issues of the WTO-MEA relationship, environmental goods, market access, effect of trade liberalization on the environment, intellectual property rights, and environmental labelling. In some cases, they have opposing views.

The negotiating positions of each Asian country in the CTE, moreover, are closely related to their trade structures, which are derived largely from the progress made in the pursuit of their national development strategies. In accordance with their respective trade structures, NIEs, such as Korea and Chinese Taipei, have distinct negotiating positions, as do China and India. ASEAN countries have taken varying positions in the CTE negotiations, each ASEAN member espousing its own views depending on issue.

This chapter provides evidence of employing interests as a factor in explaining environmental foreign policy outcomes, as described by Barkdull and Harris (Chapter 2). The trade structure of each country is a determinant of its negotiating position on trade and the environment. These positions can change in response to changes in the countries' structure of trade. National interests in trade make the distinctive differences in negotiating positions among countries. This indicates that each country's position in environmental foreign policy heavily depends on its national economic interests. Particularly for developing countries, their national development strategies have significant implications for formulating their foreign policies on trade and the environment.

## References

Brack, Duncan and Branczik, Thomas (2004) *Trade and Environment in the WTO: After Cancun* (Briefing Paper No. 9), London: The Royal Institute of International Affairs.

Endeshaw, Assafa (2005) "Asian Perspectives on Post-TRIPS Issues in Intellectual Property," *The Journal of World Intellectual Property*, 8(2): 211–35.

Harashima, Yohei (2000) "Effects of Economic Growth on Environmental Policies in Northeast Asia," *Environment*, 42(6): 28–40.

Khan, Shahrukh Rafi (ed.) (2002) *Trade and Environment: Difficult Policy Choices at the Interface*, London: Zed Books.

Kim, Joy A. (2006) "Opportunities and Challenges in Liberalizing the Environmental Goods and Services Market: The Case of Developing Countries in Asia," *Journal of World Trade*, 40(3): 527–48.

Kufuor, Kofi Oteng (2004) *World Trade Governance and Developing Countries: The GATT/WTO Code Committee System*, Oxford: Blackwell.

Najam, Adil and Robins, Nick (2001) "Seizing the Future: The South, Sustainable Development and International Trade," *International Affairs*, 77(1): 49–67.

Veiga, Pedro da Motta (2004) "Trade and Environment Negotiations: A Southern View", *Bridges*, 8(4): 18–20. Online. Available: http://www.ictsd.org/monthly/bridges/BRIDGES8-4.pdf (accessed 1 October 2007).

World Bank (2007) *World Development Indicators 2007*, Washington, DC: World Bank.

## WTO Official Documents

IP/C/W/368
TN/TE/W/11
TN/TE/W/23
TN/TE/W/42
TN/TE/W/44
TN/TE/W/48
TN/TE/W/51
WT/CTE/8
WT/CTE/M/34
WT/CTE/M/37
WT/CTE/W/65
WT/CTE/W/207
WT/CTE/W/175

# 12 Financing for the environment

## Explaining unequal burden sharing

*Aike Müller*

In the context of the Rio Earth Summit in 1992 and the establishment of several conventions related to the environment, industrialized countries accepted the notion of common but differentiated responsibilities when it comes to managing environmental change. Historically industrialized countries are disproportionately responsible for global environmental problems, but for the sake of future generations these problems can only be solved if developing countries are included within environmental solutions. As developing countries have few incentives to participate, ways to persuade them include financial concessions and technical assistance in the form of environmental aid that pays for the "full incremental costs" incurred by developing countries in their domestic policies that solve global environmental problems. These costs can be defined as the costs a country incurs in taking actions that generate global environmental benefits and that exceed what the country would otherwise do if guided purely by national self-interest (Kaul and Le Goulven 2003: 349). But once it comes to concrete policies and financial contributions needed to involve developing countries in protection measures, industrialized countries do not share an equal financial burden.

The chapter is therefore guided by this question: Why do industrialized OECD countries not share an equal financial burden when it comes to tackling global environmental change, now an important aspect of foreign policy (Harris 2001a, 2007)? Explanations for unequal burden sharing behavior can be found on the basis of different foreign policies and on the basis of the theoretical and empirical literature which has guided the discussion on traditional aid policies. As environmental aid is often simply a subcategory of official aid, the relevant aid and foreign policy literature will be briefly reviewed before an empirical section draws a detailed empirical account of bi- and multilateral financial flows to the environment, referred to as environmental aid. It will be shown that environmental aid burdens are indeed unequally shared. The remainder of this chapter, therefore, offers explanations that take into account different foreign policies and a multivariate regression analysis for bilateral environmental aid. In particular, this analysis considers the causal variables Power, Interests and Ideas from the $3 \times 3$ matrix introduced by Barkdull and Harris in Chapter 2 of this book (see Table 2.1). In fact, the variance is best explained by single foreign policies and a set of influential variables from the matrix including power- and interest-based indicators, as well as economic, norm-driven and partisan indicators.

### International aid, foreign policy, and the environment

The politics of aid have always been an important part of foreign policy analysis since the institutionalization of a formal aid system in the 1960s. The academic perception of foreign aid is strongly influenced by political science, international relations and economic theory, in which an interest-based relationship between donor interests and recipient countries' need has been shown for bilateral aid. Thus nation-states are likely to consider spending on international cooperation only if it is in their self-interest, with a risk that resource allocation will fall short of required funds (Kaul and Le Goulven 2003: 337).

In the early 1960s, Morgenthau (1962) published a controversial essay on the "Political Theory of Foreign Aid." In his article he makes a realist argument that much of the transfers under the name of foreign aid are effectively in the nature of bribes, a transferral of money and services from one government to another in the role of a price paid for political services, justified in terms of foreign aid for economic development. For Morgenthau, these bribes are less effective than traditional measures for purchasing political favors (ibid.: 303).

Influenced by such arguments, authors like McKinlay and Little (1977, 1978a, 1978b, 1978c) or Maizels and Nissanke (1984) investigated more systematically whether foreign aid is driven more by donors' political, strategic and economic interests than by recipient countries' need in terms of extreme poverty. This tendency turned out to be especially valid for bilateral aid which is subject to direct donor influence. It is less true for multilateral aid, traditionally regarded as "less political," since it is channeled through multilateral institutions that can act as arbitrators. Nonetheless, authors argue that, in some cases, multilateral aid commitments serve the perceived national interest of donors as effectively as bilateral arrangements. This is especially true when concerning problems of global consequences – such as environmental degradation – as they cannot be resolved through bilateral channels alone (Hook 1995: 29).

Confronting the view that donor interests matter most, Lumsdaine makes a strong argument in favor of a recipient need model. Although admitting that interests play a role, he argues that not all aid programs show patterns of self-interested behavior and that a growing number acknowledge the great need of recipients and are thus provided on altruistic grounds (Lumsdaine 1993). This study goes hand in hand with an article by Noël and Thérien (1995) who follow Lumsdaine's argument that foreign aid and welfare state policies express the same values. With reference to domestic social spending, partisan hypotheses and the attributes of Esping-Andersen's welfare state, the authors show that states with high social spending rates at the domestic level and with attributes of social democratic governments emerge as the best explanatory variable for foreign aid at international level. This explains why Scandinavian countries in particular share a higher burden of foreign aid and give more money for humanitarian purposes (ibid.). While a four-country qualitative case study analysis supports this view for the case of Sweden (Hook 1995: 103f), a systematic statistical analysis of four donor countries problematizes this argument, showing that Swedish aid is motivated by trade benefits and a positive relationship between aid levels and the socialist[1] ideology of the recipient country (Schraeder *et al.* 1998: 314f). A further study backs this finding but only partly. If the share of subsidies and transfers in total government expenditure is taken as an independent variable, a positive relationship does not exist (Round and Odedokun 2003: 18).

After the end of Cold War rationales, the debate shifted slightly as traditional strategic and defense interests became less relevant. Nevertheless, though the debate still supports the relevance of donor interest models, it concentrates less on strategic interests and more on the selectivity of aid in relation to democracy or human rights. Alesina and Dollar (2000: 56) show, for example, that a former non-democratic colony gets about twice as much aid as a democratic non-colony. Eric Neumayer makes the point that industrialized countries do not systematically reward countries which have improved their human rights situation with higher aid donations (Neumayer 2003a, 2003b). In recent studies, Dollar and Levin have shown that the selectivity of aid in targeting countries with a good rule of law and property rights is a rather new phenomenon. While they observed a negative relationship of bi- and multilateral aid with the rule of law in the 1984–89 period, this shifted to a positive relationship in early 2000 (Dollar and Levin 2006).

From a principal agent perspective Helen Milner (2006) investigates the differences between bi- and multilateral development aid. Inspired by the donor interest literature, she explores why countries would increasingly allocate foreign aid through multilateral channels rather than through bilateral ones as it is much harder for donors to exercise direct influence when using multilateral aid channels. In a statistical analysis that controls for a variety of factors, Milner isolates the public opinion in donor countries as an important determinant for the differences between bi- and multilateral aid allocation. While governments favor bilateral aid spending, the median voter is skeptical if a government spends limited aid resources to pursue political interests instead of aiding countries in need. As multilateral institutions limit the influence of donor countries and have a reputation as "fair" aid givers, the general public favors aid being spent multilaterally. A government interested in re-election cannot risk ignoring public opinion and always tends to spend some aid multilaterally (ibid.: 109).

Some authors question whether interest-based or altruist motives alone explain aid patterns. Influenced by the (global) public goods theory (Samuelson 1954; Kaul *et al.* 1999, 2003), Sandler and Arce (2007) recently argued that foreign aid assistance increasingly focuses on the provision of global public goods (GPG) which leads to a changing composition of aid and different spending patterns. As more public goods are financed through traditional aid, donor states use their aid to receive positive spillover effects. Thus aid is no longer driven by altruism or self-serving concerns, as some public good aid provides beneficial spillover effects to donor nations in addition to recipient private benefits: "This collective rationale can be exploited by the international community to educate donors about how augmenting their aid budget addresses their own interests" (ibid.: 542). Accordingly, the interest in positive cross-border effects of global public goods could lead to an increasing funding of GPG, which should not necessarily result in decreasing efforts for traditional aid. This positive assumption should not hide the fact that several authors see an increasing share of traditional aid purposes being placed under pressure due to increasing public good funding (Kaul and Le Goulven 2003; Anand 2002; te Velde *et al.* 2002).

The literature on environmental aid and burden sharing is less extensive. As environmental aid is largely financed or at least co-financed through traditional ODA (Official Development Assistance), donor interests could also play a role in environmental financing and could have an effect on the differences in the financial burden sharing arrangements towards environmental change. It is surprising that this question has still not been addressed by studies on aid, possibly due to inconsistent and unreliable data for environmental aid – a shortcoming which has begun to change in recent years.[2]

Two exceptions are worth mentioning here. Lewis refers to a donor interest's model in environmental aid and analyses the politics of USAID, US-based philanthropic foundations and the Global Environment Facility (GEF) towards environmental aid. She argues that "environmental aid is caught in the web of international politics that includes economic, political, and security interests" (Lewis 2003: 158). On the other hand, Harris compares EU and US policies in the area of environmental change and burden sharing and focuses on their different aid budgets. Although Harris does not distinguish environmental aid from traditional aid, he works out determinants for why the EU has been more generous than the USA in helping the world's poor and the environment and explains these differences with diverging public attitudes towards developing assistance, contrasting political and decision-making systems and political pluralism. Building on the arguments of Lumsdaine (1993) and Noël and Thérien (1995), Harris argues that "western European and EU foreign aid to a great degree reflects their relatively generous domestic welfare systems" (Harris 2002: 393). Though these explanations from the literature are contentious, they give us some hints as to why the burdens of environmental change could be unequally shared between different aid donors.

Concluding this review section, one can argue that states tend to spend their scarce financial resources on development aid only if it is in their national self-interest. This implies that resource allocations have a tendency to be under-funded and that financial burdens are unequally shared: states that follow a donor interest aid pattern have tighter aid budgets, which results in less aid on a relative basis, as aid is concentrated on selected strategic allies and trade partners. States following a recipient need aid pattern normally have wider and less concentrated aid budgets, resulting in higher burden sharing when measured on a relative capacity to pay basis. Bearing this in mind, the next section draws an empirical account of environmental aid transfers and financial burden sharing.

## Sharing the financial burden of environmental aid

Financial transfers from rich to poor countries or to multilateral institutions with the purpose of aiding the environment and compensating for the full incremental costs of developing countries are a relatively new phenomenon but lie at the heart of global environmental and foreign aid politics. Following Keohane (1996: 5), environmental aid can be defined as financial transfer from rich to poor countries or to multilateral institutions with specific environmental purposes. Financial burden sharing[3] is best measured as the amount given to environmental aid relative to the ability to pay and the strength of the economy, typically measured as a percentage of Gross National Income (GNI) or Gross Domestic Product (GDP). Though rarely acknowledged, the most important funding source for global environmental politics is official development assistance (ODA),[4] meaning that environmental aid is often simply a subcategory of official aid and, therefore, potentially as biased as the traditional forms of aid reviewed above.

At the 1992 Rio Summit, the UNCED Secretariat estimated the financial needs of the Agenda 21 as being $US 600 billion per year, including $US 125 billion per year on grant or concessional terms, at that time about 0.7 per cent of the GNI[5] of the developed world (Agenda 21: 33.18).[6] Instead of moving ahead to the so-called 0.7 per cent goal, the 22 members of the Development Assistance Committee (DAC) of the OECD departed from that goal. In the late 1980s the total DAC countries represented 0.33 per cent of DAC members' combined GNI. By the year 2000 this figure had declined to an historical all-time low of 0.22 per cent (OECD/DAC 2005b). It increased again in recent years and was 0.28 per cent in 2005, reaching in total terms $US 106.7 billion (OECD.Stat 2007).[7]

Although overall ODA flows have declined in relative terms, it is generally estimated that the share of ODA directed toward the environment or other global public goods has been rising (Porter *et al.* 2000: 158; Kaul and Le Goulven 2003: 329ff; Sandler and Arce 2007). This is true if measured in current US dollars without adjustment for inflation. On average, bilateral environmental aid accounts for about 6 per cent of ODA.

Since the early 1990s it has been possible to capture certain aspects of environmental aid efforts through the different purpose codes of the OECD/ DAC creditor reporting system (CRS). The database consists of 188 different purpose codes with the aim of providing a set of readily available basic data that enables analysis on where aid goes, what purposes it serves and what policies it aims to implement, on a comparable basis for all DAC members (OECD/DAC 2006; OECD.Stat 2007). Beyond the specific purpose codes the system also captures aspects of environmental sustainability (ES) through all aid activities and economic sectors through an environmental sustainability marker system.[8] With the CRS categorization, sustainability markers, hand inspection and preliminary research, it is possible to trace back bilateral environmental aid efforts for 22 OECD countries back to 1991.[9]

Total bilateral environmental aid from all donors varies between ~ $US 3.00 in 1991 and more than $US 4.5 by the end of 2005 and a significant increase in recent years. On a country level the absolute transfers vary considerably. Since 1991, Japan has spent an annual average of $US 1.1 bn on environmental aid, followed by the United States ($US 0.456 bn) and Germany ($US 0.255 bn). While absolute transfers tell us little about financial burden sharing, the picture looks rather different if the contributions of the 22 DAC countries are measured as a percentage of GNI which measures the ability to pay. Figure 12.1 shows an average generosity ratio[10] on the basis of bilateral environmental aid contributions between 1991 and 2005. It turns out that especially the "Nordic" countries and most surprisingly Japan share an above average burden and spent more on bilateral environmental aid than other countries.

While environmental aid from ODA sources is only one part of the environmental aid story, it is of great interest if the picture is any different for

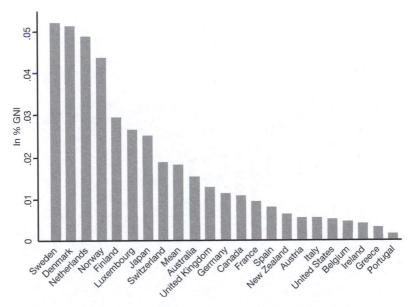

*Figure 12.1* Generosity ratio for Bilateral Environmental Aid, 1991–2005
Note: Own calculations
Source: OECD/DAC 2007b, OECD.Stat 2007, World Bank 2007.

multilateral environmental aid. As the multilateral institutions that are captured through the CRS system play a limited role in the area of environmental protection, transfers to the Global Environment Facility (GEF) seem to be more appropriate.

### The Global Environment Facility

The Global Environment Facility (GEF) is the most important and only new multilateral funding source that emerged from the Earth Summit in Rio de Janeiro 1992. It was set up "as a mechanism for international cooperation for the purpose of providing new and additional grant and concessional funding to meet the agreed incremental costs of measures to achieve agreed global environmental benefits" (GEF 2004: 10). Currently, the GEF finances actions in six priority areas of global concern and has been replenished four times after a pilot phase that started in 1991. Between 1991 and 2006 the major donors contributed $US 7.039 bn to the GEF (GEF 2003). The largest individual donors are the US ($US 1.5 bn), Japan ($US 1.2 bn) and Germany ($US 0.9 bn).[11] So far the GEF has financed more than 2,000 projects in 140 developing and transition countries (GEF 2007a).

Figure 12.2 displays an average donor states' generosity ratio to the GEF as a percentage of GNI for the years 1991–2006. This period includes the

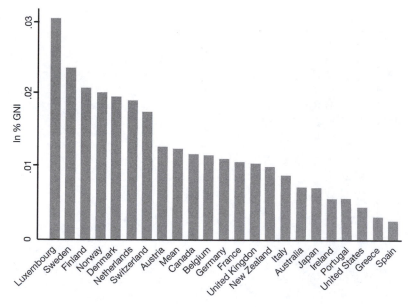

*Figure 12.2* Generosity ratio to the GEF, 1991–2006
Note: Own calculations
Source: GEF 2007b, GEF 2003, World Bank 2007.

pilot phase and three replenishments. Again, a familiar burden-sharing pattern is obvious with "northern" countries and Switzerland spending above average and countries like the USA, Italy or Ireland spending under average for environmental aid. An important difference, however, is the fact that Japan now lags behind after spending above average on bilateral environmental aid.

As will be shown for the case of Japan, financial transfers are a direct consequence of environmental foreign policy-making. Of particular interest, therefore, is to ask which factors might explain the picture of unequal burden sharing of environmental aid. This is the aim of the remainder of this chapter.

## Explanations for unequal burden sharing

There are several factors that determine unequal burden sharing, some of which are more obvious than others. The general trend of the burden sharing picture for environmental aid fits quite well with the assumptions made by Noël and Thérien (1995). With the exception of Japan and Switzerland, all countries with attributes of social democratic welfare states and comparatively high social spending rates at home also spend more on environmental purposes. It seems that international aid and domestic welfare state policies follow similar norms, ideas and values, an argument that fits well with a constructivist position that stresses the importance and the impact of norms and ideas for state behavior.

The somewhat unexpected high share of Japan's bilateral environmental aid is difficult to explain on the basis of the current aid literature but makes perfect sense when looking more closely at Japanese environmental foreign policy. At UNCED 1992, the Japanese Ministry of Foreign Affairs (MOFA) announced its intention to expand and strengthen environmental ODA and it has increased its disbursements substantially since 1993. As the ministry controls nearly half of the aid budget, this new policy soon had significant effects on Japan's environmental aid (Asuka-Zhang 2003: 154). At a special session of the UN General Assembly in June 1997, Japan's Prime Minister Ryutaro Hashimoto announced the "Initiative for Sustainable Development Toward the 21st Century" which was part of Japan's plan for future international development assistance. The plan includes a shift of Japan's ODA to environmentally sound projects. Kameyama suggests that "with this announcement, Japan incorporated global environmental issues in its foreign policy, at least on matters related to development assistance" (Kameyama 2003: 141).[12] These new foreign policy objectives are reflected in the bilateral environmental aid data shown above. As Japan spends comparatively less on multilateral environmental aid, in the case of the GEF, the country favors bilateral transfer channels rather than multilateral channels to transfer environmental aid. Japan also maintains a foreign policy that it cannot be the single largest donor to any multilateral fund and ties itself to the action of the USA, usually the largest donor in nominal terms (Clémençon 2006: 68).

Another factor accounting for unequal burden sharing could be the voluntary nature of contributions. Although the UN recommends 0.7 per cent of the GNI to be spent on aid, there is no binding obligation to do so. This is similarly true for the GEF, where an allocation formula follows adjusted IDA[13] shares with the option of voluntary contributions over and above the assessed amount (Sjöberg 1999: 36). The only environmental aid arrangement with a comparatively fair burden sharing agreement is the multilateral fund to protect the ozone layer. This could result from the fact that the replenishments for the multilateral fund are based on the United Nations key of contributions which itself uses GNI as the main indicator for determining contributions. This alone of course is not a sufficient explanation for equal burden sharing behavior in the case of ozone protection but the empirical observation fits well into the "success story" of the ozone case.

## Empirical analyses

In order to offer a more detailed analysis of the main determinants which are assumed to determine unequal burden sharing, the final section offers a statistical analysis of determinants of unequal burden sharing for bilateral environmental aid from ODA sources. Bilateral environmental aid (measured as an annual percentage of GNI) enters the model as dependent variable. Data on bilateral environmental aid has the advantage that it is available as time series data from 1991–2005 for 22 OECD/DAC countries.

Barkdull and Harris propose a 3 × 3 matrix that categorizes different approaches to the study of environmental foreign policy (see Table 2.1). This matrix introduces Power, Interest and Ideas as the basic causal variables involved in the study of environmental foreign policy. The following empirical analysis backs this assumption. On the basis of the literature review,

*Table 12.1* Regression results

| Coefficient | Bilateral environmental aid |
| --- | --- |
| SOCX | 0.00232*** (15.3) |
| GNI_pc | 0.00106*** (11.7) |
| MILIEX | 0.000340 (0.24) |
| GREENP_pc | 0.000538*** (3.75) |
| GREENSEATS | −0.00206*** (-4.36) |
| CONSTANT | −0.0556*** (-19.3) |
| Observations | 235 |
| Countries | 22 |
| R-squared | 0.53 |

Notes: Stata 9.1, (xtpcse), z statistics in parentheses. *** $p < 0.01$, ** $p < 0.05$, * $p < 0.1$

theoretical assumptions and the 3 × 3 matrix, five independent variables will enter the model:

1 Gross National Income per capita $(GNI\_pc)$[14] enters the model as a classic indicator for interest-based liberal theories of foreign policy. It is generally used to assess a society's wealth. Higher economic and social welfare leads to an increasing request for post-materialist goods like environmental protection, health, etc. (Bedarff *et al.* 1995: 318; Porter *et al.* 2000: 57f). Authors like Hopkins and others argue that growing government deficits and low economic growth lead to cuts both in foreign aid expenditures and in domestic expenditures (Hopkins 2000: 431). Economic growth and high per capita income should lead to the opposite. Therefore a positive relationship between GNI per capita and environmental aid burden sharing is expected.

2 Military expenditure (*MILIEX*) measured as a percentage of GDP (SIPRI 2007) is one of the most prominent power-based determinants which could also affect environmental aid levels. It is most commonly used in the "donor interest" aid literature which was reviewed above and follows a neorealist understanding of international relations and foreign policy. Countries with higher military spending rates provide aid only if it is of "strategic" interest for the donor. It is only provided to selected allies which results in little overall aid. A negative relationship is expected where higher percentages of military expenditures result in lower environmental aid.

3 Social Expenditure (*SOCX*) in percentage of GNI (OECD 2007b). This independent variable follows the assumptions made by Noël and Thérien (1995), Lumsdaine (1993) or Harris (2002). It is argued that international aid and domestic welfare policies express similar ideas, norms and values within a society. Countries that have higher social spending rates on the domestic level also tend to spend more on international aid which is also supported by the general public. Although this relation has not been tested for the environmental aid, it is expected that a positive relationship for environmental aid exists.

4 Greenpeace supporters per capita (*GREENP_pc*): The independent variables SOCX and *GREENP_pc* pay tribute to a growing body of constructivist research in international relations and international political economy. This literature stresses the importance of "norms, beliefs and rules that collectively provide the foundation for individuals' interests" (Perkins and Neumayer 2007: 23). Though norms are difficult to measure this chapter introduces Greenpeace supporter figures[15] as one feasible variable (Greenpeace International 2008; Greenpeace Nordic 2008). The supporter data per country and year are divided by the country's population (World Bank 2007). The variable captures the domestic strength of environmental NGOs and environmental norms of a society. A positive relationship is expected: More supporters reflect a growing social norm of aiding the environment which in turn should lead to

more environmental aid on the state level. A more appropriate measure would be to count membership of all environmental NGOs (ENGOs) which is beyond the scope of this chapter. Thus the Greenpeace measure has to be seen together with the social expenditure data.

5   The existence of green parties (*GREENSEATS*) in the parliament measured as the share of seats (Müller-Rommel 2002; Armingeon *et al.* 2006) is used as a partisan variable that could positively influence environmental aid levels. Similar to the GREENPEACE variable above, green parties represent certain ideas and a green ideology. As elected members of parliaments they push environmental topics onto the agenda and pressure governments to be more involved in global environmental politics and thus spend more money on environmental aid.

### Empirical results

Regarding the panel structure of the data, Prais-Winsten regression for correlated panels with corrected standard errors (PCSEs) are chosen as the most promising estimation technique. As the regression output from Table 12.1 shows, most independent variables are significant in determining unequal environmental burden sharing levels.

Overall, the analysis backs the causal relationships made above and explains about 50 per cent of the variance for bilateral environmental aid burden sharing. In particular, GNI per capita, social expenditure and Greenpeace supporter figures are highly significant on a 99 per cent level. So is the partisan variable greenseats, with an unexpected but interesting negative relationship. This means that bilateral environmental aid levels are decreasing with an increasing number of green seats in national parliaments. A plausible explanation is that green parties favor multilateral channels as the more adequate solution for global environmental problems, not subject to empirical testing in this chapter. Nonetheless early research results on multilateral environmental aid to the GEF show that green parties in national parliaments do have a positive and statistical significant impact on environmental aid to the GEF (Müller 2007). Green parties seem to pressure governments to channel environmental aid through multilateral institutions rather than bilateral channels. The inverse shaped relationship also makes sense on the basis of the priorities and public perception of green parties who generally favor international institutions over bilateral channels to settle disputes or solve global challenges.

The power-based variable military expenditure is of low explanatory power. In both cases military expenditure is a weak and statistically insignificant determinant for unequal burden sharing.

### Conclusion

This chapter has linked the literature on traditional foreign aid with a detailed empirical account of financial flows to the environment and illustrated an unequal distribution of burdens when it comes to financing global environmental politics. It has made evident that the smaller Nordic countries in particular but also Japan and Switzerland share an above average burden of environmental aid with differences between bi- and multilateral environmental aid. Unequal burden sharing can be explained on the basis of varying priorities in the individual foreign policies of the donor states and a set of influential variables including two power-based, one economic, two norm-driven and one partisan indicator. Apart from the power-based explanatory variables, all determinants offer good explanatory power of unequal environmental aid burden sharing. This is especially true for the variables that capture domestic and international norms.

Concerning the approaches to the study of environmental foreign policy introduced by Barkdull and Harris in Chapter 2 (see Table 2.1), it seems that ideas and norms have a significant impact on the environmental burden sharing picture when measured on the society level. As the indicators that capture the growing impact of norms in environmental governance turn out to be very promising, future research should concentrate on more robust indicators and a stronger theoretical connection to social constructivism.

The findings of this chapter also have some practical relevance as they give us some hints as to why states are not able or willing to share equal financial burdens once it comes to financing concrete environmental protection measures or the full incremental costs of developing countries. Acknowledging this is a necessary precondition for a discussion among scientists, policy-makers and practitioners on how to overcome current failures and weaknesses of environmental politics and resource allocation towards the environment.

## Acknowledgments

I would like to thank James E. Scorer, Christian W. Martin, Katharina Holzinger, Friedbert W. Rüb, Thomas Sommerer and an anonymous reviewer for comments on an earlier draft of this chapter.

## Notes

1 Schrader *et al.* use the term socialist to indicate that "Sweden demonstrated an ideological predilection to support progressive, socialist-oriented regimes such as Algeria, Tanzania, Uganda, and Zambia" (Schraeder *et al.* 1998: 315).
2 During the process of publication of this book a major step for consistent data availablility on environmental aid was undertaken with the publication of results from PLAID Project (Hicks *et al.* 2008).
3 For a more detailed approach, see Harris, who defines burden sharing or international equity as "a fair and just distribution among countries of benefits, burdens, and decision-making authority associated with international environmental relations" (Harris 2001b: 25).
4 In this chapter, ODA and aid are treated synonymously.

5 Gross national income. Early ratios used GDP as the denominator, giving way to GNI in later years as OECD changed their accounting guidelines and reporting directives for ODA (OECD 2002).
6 The financial Chapter 33 of the Agenda 21 was not even included in the document until final negotiations were concluded in Rio (Bryner 1999: 161).
7 This huge increase in recent years, however, results largely from flows to Iraq in the form of reconstruction, security aid and debt cancellation. In 2005, these flows accounted for $US 19.65 billion (OECD.Stat 2007; Foreign Policy 2006: 72).
8 For details, see OECD (2007a).
9 Mascarenhas and Sandler (2005: 1114f) identify ODA transfers that finance national and international environmental public goods. For further details, see: Mascarenhas and Sandler (2005), OECD/DAC (2002, 2005a, 2006, 2007a, 2007b).
10 The term generosity ratio follows a study by Addison *et al.* (2003).
11 Data source GEF (2003, 2006). Including the pledges for the current working phase (2007–10), this would amount to $US 9.235 bn. The amounts for the current working phase (2007–10) have still not been fully assigned but have been pledged at the last replenishment meeting.
12 See also MOFA (2003, 2007).
13 International Development Association.
14 World Bank (2007).
15 The Greenpeace indicator was recently used in an article that analyzed how international environmental agreements are best designed without deterring participation. It also investigated how international social networks and NGOs affect ratification (von Stein 2008).

# References

Addison, Tony, McGillivray, Mark and Odedokun, Matthew (2003) *Donor Funding of Multilateral Aid Agencies*, United Nations University (UNU)/World Institute for Development Economic Research (WIDER) Discussion Paper (17/2003), Helsinki: UNU/WIDER.
Alesina, Alberto and Dollar David (2000) "Who Gives Foreign Aid to Whom and Why?" *Journal of Economic Growth*, 5: 33–63.
Anand, Prathivadi B. (2002) "Financing the Provision of Global Public Goods," *World Economy*, 27: 215–37.
Armingeon, Klaus, Leimgruber, Philipp, Beyeler, Michelle and Menegale, Sarah (2006) *Comparative Political Data Set 1960–2004*, Berne: Institute of Political Science, University of Berne.
Asuka-Zhang, Shoughuan (2003) "Development Assistance and Japan's Climate Change Diplomacy: Priorities and Future Options," in Paul G. Harris (ed.) *Global Warming and East Asia. The Domestic and International Politics of Climate Change*, London: Routledge, pp. 152–66.
Bedarff, Hildegard, Bernauer, Thomas, Jakobeit, Cord and List, Martin (1995) "Transferzahlungen in der internationalen Umweltpolitik," *Zeitschrift für internationale Beziehungen*, 2: 317–45.
Bryner, Gary C. (1999) "Agenda 21: Myth or Reality?" in Norman J. Vig and Regina S. Axelrod (eds) *The Global Environment. Institutions, Law, and Policy*, Washington, DC: CQ Press, pp. 157–87.
Clémençon, Raymond (2006) "What Future for the Global Environment Facility?" *The Journal of Environment and Development*, 15: 50–74.

Dollar, David and Levin, Victoria (2006) "The Increasing Selectivity of Foreign Aid, 1984–2003," *World Development*, 34: 2034–46.

*Foreign Policy* (2006) "Ranking the Rich," *Foreign Policy*, September/October: 68–75.

GEF (2003) *GEF Annual Report 2003*, Washington, DC: GEF.

—— (2004) *Instrument for the Establishment of a Restructured Global Environment Facility*, Washington, DC: GEF.

—— (2006) *Summary of Negotiations on the Fourth Replenishment of the GEF Trust Fund*, GEF/C.29/3 Washington, DC: GEF.

—— (2007a) *GEF Project Database*, Washington, DC: GEF. Online. Available: http://www.gefonline.org/home.cfm (accessed 3 May 2007).

—— (2007b) *Trustee Report. GEF/C.31/Inf.3*. GEF Council Meeting, 12–15 June, Washington: GEF – Global Environment Facility.

Greenpeace International (2008) *Historic Supporter Figures Greenpeace Worldwide*, Amsterdam: Greenpeace International.

Greenpeace Nordic (2008) *Historic Supporter Figures Greenpeace Nordic*, Stockholm: Greenpeace Nordic.

Harris, Paul G. (ed.) (2001a) *The Environment, International Relations, and U.S. Foreign Policy*, Washington, DC: Georgetown University Press.

—— (2001b) *International Equity and Global Environmental Politics*, Aldershot: Ashgate.

—— (2002) "Sharing Burdens of Environmental Change: Comparing EU and U.S. Policies," *Journal of Environment & Development*, 11: 380–401.

—— (ed.) (2007) *Europe and Global Climate Change: Politics, Foreign Policy and Regional Cooperation*, Cheltenham: Edward Elgar.

Hicks, Robert L., Parks, Bradley C., Roberts, J. Timmons and Tierney, Michael J. (2008) *Greening Aid? Understanding the Environmental Impact of Development Assistance*, Oxford: Oxford University Press.

Hook, Steven W. (1995) *National Interest and Foreign Aid*, London: Lynne Rienner Publishers.

Hopkins, Raymond F. (2000) "Political Economy of Foreign Aid," in Finn Tarp (ed.) *Foreign Aid and Development. Lessons Learnt and Directions for the Future*, London: Routledge, 423–49.

Kameyama, Yasuko (2003) "Climate Change as Japanese Foreign Policy: From Reactive to Proactive," in Paul G. Harris (ed.) *Global Warming and East Asia. The Domestic and International Politics of Climate Change*, London: Routledge, pp. 135–51.

Kaul, Inge, Conceição, Pedro, Le Goulven, Katell and Mendoza, Ronald U. (eds) (2003) *Providing Global Public Goods. Managing Globalization*, Oxford: Oxford University Press.

Kaul, Inge, Grunberg, I. and Stern, Marc A. (eds) (1999) *Global Public Goods: International Cooperation in the 21st Century*, Oxford: Oxford University Press.

Kaul, Inge and Le Goulven, Katell (2003) "Financing Global Public Goods: A New Frontier of Public Finance," in Inge Kaul, Pedro Conceição, Katell Le Goulven and Ronald U. Mendoza (eds) *Providing Global Public Goods. Managing Globalization*, Oxford: Oxford University Press, pp. 329–70.

Keohane, Robert O. (1996) "Analyzing the Effectiveness of International Environmental Institutions," in Robert O. Keohane and Marc A. Levy (eds) *Institutions for Environmental Aid. Pitfalls and Promise*, Cambridge, MA: MIT Press, pp. 3–27.

Lewis, Tammy L. (2003) "Environmental Aid: Driven by Recipient Need or Donor Interests?" *Social Science Quarterly*, 84: 144–61.

Lumsdaine, David Holloran (1993) *Moral Vision in International Politics: The Foreign Aid Regime, 1949–1989*, Princeton, NJ: Princeton University Press.

Maizels, Alfred and Nissanke, Machiko K. (1984) "Motivations for Aid to Developing-Countries," *World Development*, 12: 879–900.

Mascarenhas, Raechelle and Sandler, Todd (2005) "Donors' Mechanisms for Financing International and National Public Goods: Loans or Grants?" *World Economy*, 28: 1095–117.

McKinlay, Robert D. and Little, Richard (1977) "Foreign-Policy Model of United-States Bilateral Aid Allocation," *World Politics*, 30: 58–86.

—— (1978a) "Foreign-Policy Model of Distribution of British Bilateral Aid, 1960–70," *British Journal of Political Science*, 8: 313–32.

—— (1978b) "The French Aid Relationship: A Foreign Policy of the Distribution of French Bilateral Aid, 1964–70," *Development and Change*, 9: 459–78.

—— (1978c) "German Aid Relationship – Test of Recipient Need and Donor Interest Models of Distribution of German Bilateral Aid 1961–70," *European Journal of Political Research*, 6: 235–57.

Milner, Helen V. (2006) "Why Multilateralism? Foreign Aid and Domestic Principal-Agent Problems," in Darren G. Hawkins, David A. Lake, Daniel L. Nielson and Michael J. Tierney (eds) *Delegation and Agency in International Organizations*, Cambridge: Cambridge University Press, pp. 107–39.

MOFA (2003) *Japan's Official Development Assistance Charter*, Tokyo: Ministry of Foreign Affairs, Government of Japan, Economic Co-operation Bureau. Online. Available: http://www.mofa.go.jp/policy/oda/reform/revision0308.pdf (accessed 25 July 2007).

—— (2007) *Japan's Environmental ODA. Steady Progress Towards Sustainable Development*, MOFA, Government of Japan, Economic Co-operation Bureau. Online. Available: http:// www.mofa.go.jp/policy/oda/category/ environment/pamph/ 2001/oda.html (accessed 15 July 2007).

Morgenthau, Hans (1962) "A Political Theory of Foreign Aid," *American Political Science Review*, 56: 301–9.

Müller, Aike (2007) *Aid, Foreign Policy and the Environment: Explaining the Unequal Sharing of Environmental Aid Burdens*. CGG Preprint No. 5 (2007), Hamburg: Centre for Globalisation and Governance.

Müller-Rommel, Ferdinand (ed.) (2002) *Green Parties in National Governments*, London: Frank Cass.

Neumayer, Eric (2003a) "Do Human Rights Matter in Bilateral Aid Allocation? A Quantitative Analysis of 21 Donor Countries," *Social Science Quarterly*, 84: 650–66.

—— (2003b) *The Pattern of Aid Giving: The Impact of Good Governance on Development Assistance*, London: Routledge.

Noël, Alain and Thérien, Jean-Philippe (1995) "From Domestic to International Justice – the Welfare-State and Foreign-Aid," *International Organization*, 49: 523–53.

OECD (2002) "Development Co-operation 2001 Report," International Development, Organisation for Economic Co-Operation and Development, *The DAC Journal*, 3.

—— (2007a) *CRS User's Guide: What Policies Does Aid Support? Guidance for Analyses of the Policy Objectives of Aid*, Paris: OECD. Online. Available: www.oecd.org/document/21/0,2340,en_2649_34469_24661909_1_1_1_1,00.html (accessed 5 January 2008).

—— (2007b) "Social Expenditure Database (SOCX 2007)," Paris: OECD. Online. Available: http://www.oecd.org/document/9/0,3343,en_2825_503504_38141385_1_1_1_ 1,00.html (accessed 15 September 2007).

OECD/DAC (2002) *DCD/DAC(2002)21. Reporting Directives for the Creditor Reporting System*, Paris: OECD.

—— (2005a) *DCD/DAC(2002)21/ADD4, Reporting Directives for the Creditor Reporting System – Addendum 4, Annex 3*, Paris: OECD.

—— (2005b) *International Development Statistics 2005*, CD-ROM, Paris: OECD.

—— (2006) *International Development Statistics 2006*, CD-ROM, Paris: OECD.

—— (2007a) *DCD/DAC(2007)34. DAC Statistical Reporting Directives*, Paris: OECD.

—— (2007b) *International Development Statistics 2007*, CD-ROM, Paris: OECD.

OECD.Stat (2007) *CRS Online. Development Database on Aid Activities: The Creditor Reporting System (CRS) Database*, Paris: OECD, Development Co-operation Directorate (DCD-DAC). Online. Available: http:// www.oecd.org/dataoecd/50/17/ 5037721.htm (accessed 15 September 2007).

Perkins, Richard and Neumayer, Eric (2007) "Implementing Multilateral Environmental Agreements: An Analysis of EU Directives," *Global Environmental Politics*, 7, 13–41.

Porter, Gareth, Brown, Janet Welsh and Chasek, Pamela S. (2000) *Global Environmental Politics*, Boulder, CO: Westview Press.

Round, Jeffery I. and Odedokun, Matthew (2003) *Aid Efforts and its Determinants*, United Nations University (UNU)/World Institute for Development Economic Research (WIDER) Discussion Paper No. (03/2003), Helsinki: UNU/WIDER.

Samuelson, Paul A. (1954) "The Pure Theory of Public Expenditure," *Review of Economics and Statistics*, 67: 387–9.

Sandler, Todd and Arce, Daniel G. (2007) "New Face of Development Assistance: Public Goods and Changing Ethics," *Journal of International Development*, 19: 527–44.

Schraeder, Peter J., Hook, Steven W. and Tables, Bruce Taylor (1998) "Clarifying the Foreign Aid Puzzle: A Comparison of American, Japanese, French, and Swedish Aid Flows," *World Politics 50*, 294–323.

SIPRI (2007) *SIPRI Military Expenditure Database*, Stockholm: Stockholm International Peace Research Institute. Online. Available: http://www.sipri.org/contents/milap/ milex/mex_database1.html (accessed 12 July 2007).

Sjöberg, Helen (1999) *Restructuring the Global Environment Facility*. GEF Working Paper No. 13, Washington, DC: Global Environmental Facility.

te Velde, Dirk Willem, Morrissey, Oliver and Hewitt, Adrian (2002) "Aid Allocation to International Public Goods," in Marco Ferroni and Ashoka Mody (eds) *International Public Goods: Incentives, Measurements, and Financing*, Dordrecht: Kluwer Academic Publisher, 119–56.

von Stein, Jana (2008) "The International Law and Politics of Climate Change: Ratification of the United Nations Framework Convention and the Kyoto Protocol," *Journal of Conflict Resolution*, 52: 243–68.

World Bank (2007) *World Development Indicators 2007 Edition*, CD-ROM (Single User).

# 13 Environmental foreign policy

## Towards a conceptual framework

*Mihaela Papa*

During the Falklands campaign, Margaret Thatcher famously said: "It is exciting to have a real crisis on your hands when you have spent half your political life dealing with humdrum issues like the environment" (Thatcher 1982). Today environmental issues are the very source of real drama and great controversies in foreign policy. Large-scale natural disasters with high death tolls and tragic impacts on regional development, heated discussions on climate change at the United Nations Security Council, and political battles following the opening of the Northwest Passage are a few cases in point. Environmental issues are shaking up foreign policy circles, especially in the light of increasing scientific evidence of the nature of human dependence on ecosystems and of human contribution to environmental degradation and climate change.[1] On the one hand, dealing with nature is a permanent policy challenge because it operates on its own timelines and cannot be ordered to deliver environmental recovery when we need it, despite all the political will and collective action. On the other, foreign policies have a unique opportunity to transform the current system in order to mitigate environmental damage, manage it, address liability for damage, and most importantly, take special care of the least resilient socio-ecological systems.

Despite the fact that the relationship between foreign policy and the environment has been the subject of much debate both in academic and policy-making circles, conceptual issues relating to environmental foreign policy as such, irrespective of the country that makes it, have received little treatment. This chapter aims to integrate different perspectives on the intersection of foreign policy and the environment, and draw on the findings of this volume, as it defines environmental foreign policy and explores its conceptual underpinnings. Following an analysis of the environment–foreign policy nexus in theory and practice, it clarifies the concept of environmental foreign policy and then derives a conceptual framework to analyze it. Next, the framework considers a state's willingness to act on environmental concerns in foreign policy and its opportunities for action. The chapter concludes by identifying areas for further study.

## Linking environmental issues to foreign policy: theory and practice

The concept of environmental foreign policy at the most basic level encapsulates the relationship between environmental issues and foreign policy. Environmental issues have been a subject of foreign policy as long as foreign policies have existed, but their sustained presence in foreign policy-making largely emerged with the beginnings of organized international efforts to devise a global environmental agenda. The 1972 United Nations Conference on the Human Environment, held in Stockholm, was the first meeting where foreign policy-makers from different parts of the world joined to discuss the environmental future of the planet: they called upon governments and peoples to exert common efforts for the protection and the improvement of the human environment. Since then, environment as an issue area has become an integral part of the international policy-making arena. As the relationship between foreign policy and the environment strengthened, it was described in different ways and approached from various perspectives in environmental politics, international relations and foreign policy communities. Mapping out contrasting viewpoints from both theory and foreign policy practice can help us review and integrate the knowledge on the topic and can provide a background for conceptualizing environmental foreign policy. Table 13.1 comprises an illustrative list of the most common perspectives on the intersection of foreign policy and the environment.

The perspectives on the relationship between foreign policy and the environment introduced in Table 13.1 are very diverse: some are more domestically oriented (e.g. greening of foreign policy), while others are more internationally focused (environmental diplomacy); some establish a direct link between foreign policy and diplomacy in practice (Green Diplomacy Network), with others it is not fully clear how foreign policy, diplomacy, environment, sustainable development and overall "greening" are defined or interlinked. Since these terms are central to understanding environmental foreign policy, they will be further clarified.

Conceptualizing environmental foreign policy can start with clarifying the concept of foreign policy and then trying to define what makes it environmental. Foreign policy usually refers to state policy directed to matters beyond state borders, especially relations with other countries. As such, it is about the interactions between domestic and international affairs (see Chapter 1 in this volume). Contemporary policies often have consequences both inside and outside state borders, but as long as the intended primary target of a policy lies abroad, the policy can be considered foreign (Kaarbo *et al.* 2002: 3). The relationship between foreign policy and diplomacy is sometimes blurred in the literature, but foreign policy is mostly associated with the substance of a state's relations with other states and agencies and the goals it strives to achieve by those relations; diplomacy, on the other hand, is usually associated with the process of dialogue and

*Table 13.1* Perspectives on the intersection of foreign policy and the environment

| | Description and examples from theory and practice |
|---|---|
| Environmental foreign policy | Used within the Project on Environmental Change and Foreign Policy, which "seeks to understand foreign policy processes in international efforts to address adverse environmental changes at the local, regional and global levels; to analyze the actors and institutions – both domestic and international – that constrain and shape national actions on environmental issues; to show how environmental changes influence foreign policy processes; and to critically assess environmental foreign policies'' (Harris 2000, 2005, 2007). Similar use: Arquit Niederberger and Schwager (2004). |
| Environmental diplomacy or Green diplomacy | A negotiation-based approach exploring how to structure global environmental negotiations so that the pressures on national negotiators can be addressed effectively (Susskind 1994: 5; Porter *et al.* 2000); it offers first-hand insights into negotiations that led to a number of landmark agreements (Tolba 1998). The term "green diplomacy" can also be used as a synonym for environmental diplomacy (Broadhead 2002). In European Union (EU) practice, the Green Diplomacy Network was established to integrate environment into EU foreign relations as a crosscutting category through the creation of an informal network of environment experts within foreign ministries. |
| Greening of foreign policy | Describes how environmental concerns are moving domestic agencies away from their original goals towards "greener" missions and discusses opportunities and challenges of mainstreaming environmental factors into different aspects of foreign policy such as defense, trade and investment, development cooperation, diplomatic and other efforts (Anderson and Miller 2000). Integrating climate change into foreign policy was recommended as a way to improve prospects for more effective efforts to address climate change at the national and international level (Drexhage *et al.* 2007). Greening of foreign policy conceptually falls under the broader issue of environmental policy integration (Lafferty and Hovden 2003). |
| Human security approach to foreign policy, including environmental security | Concerned with the protection and empowerment of human beings around the world rather than military and strategic interests of a particular state, human security is intertwined with human rights and human development (UNDP 1994; Glasius and Kaldor 2005). In practice, foreign ministries define and promote human security perspective on international problems in different ways including foreign policy networking and establishing initiatives to place human security in the mainstream of UN activities. In environmental terms, human security is tied to protecting people from environmental stress that results from war and armed conflict, disasters other than war and the erosion of the earth's carrying capacity, but it can also cover broader issues such as ensuring sustainable livelihoods and access to natural resources (Gleditsch 2001). |
| Environmental peacemaking and disaster diplomacy | Looks at environmental cooperation as a foreign policy opportunity to achieve conflict resolution. Environmental peacemaking literature asks whether environmental cooperation can be a useful instrument of international peace by removing multiple sources of insecurity, most of which are political, economic, and social rather than narrowly ecological (Conca and Dabelko 2002). Disaster diplomacy literature asks if natural disasters induce international cooperation amongst countries that have traditionally been enemies (Kelman and Koukis 2000). In practice, international bodies conduct environmental conflict prevention programs such as The Environment and Security Initiative. |
| New diplomacy of sustainable development | Argues that traditional forms of diplomacy, based on the pursuit of narrowly defined sovereign interests have become inappropriate as societies address the ecological, economic and social dimensions of global interdependence. New issues involving energy, sustainable development, and the environment challenge sovereignty as well as territoriality and involve multiple highly diverse actors in multiple international forums (Moomaw 2005; Kjellen 2007). |

Note: * The project is briefly described in the Preface. The quote is from the project's website at http://www.ln.edu.hk/projects/ecfp/Home.htm which comprises a partial list of publications. See also Chapter 2 and Barkdull and Harris (2002).

negotiation by which states in the system conduct their relations (Watson 1982: 10). Therefore, foreign policies operate via diplomacy, which can be perceived as an institution in itself comprising three key features: communication, representation and the reproduction of international society (Jonsson and Hall 2005).

Foreign policy can be considered environmental, in its broadest sense, when it deals with environmental issues. Its "greening" refers to the process of integrating environmental protection requirements into foreign policy. Environmental protection is also conceptually nested within a larger concept of sustainable development, which recognizes that environmental, social and economic issues are interconnected in fulfilling human needs and maintaining the quality of the natural environment for future generations.[2] Environmental foreign policy, as understood here, primarily refers to state policy directed to matters beyond state borders as it aims to protect, preserve and improve the environment (see Table 13.1 for a broader definition). Since general patterns of foreign policy behavior can be identified and common explanations for such behavior exist,[3] it is possible to talk about the concept of environmental foreign policy in general, rather than exclusively state-specific, terms. This is where we now turn.

## A conceptual framework of environmental foreign policy

What elements does the concept of environmental foreign policy entail? The discussion of the theories of environmental foreign policy by Barkdull and Harris in Chapter 2 relied on a $3 \times 3$ matrix with two dimensions – level of analysis and causal variables – to help organize thinking about foreign policy towards the environment. It illustrates the complexity of environmental foreign policy and motivates us to raise two important questions for its conceptualization: (1) who are the actors conducting environmental foreign policy?; and (2) is there a way to accommodate insights from different levels of analysis when trying to understand their behavior? These questions are answered here with the mission of this Volume in mind: to step back and look again at foreign policy literature when analyzing environment as a foreign policy issue area, and to use insights from both theory and practice to understand environmental foreign policy. The resulting conceptualization is one possible (rather than the ultimate) way to think about environmental foreign policy and link its diverse elements into a basic relationship.

A useful point of departure is to define states as official decision-makers. This definition encompasses both material and ideational determinants of state behavior (Hudson 2002: 4), and anchors the conceptual framework in individual agency which is embedded in international affairs. The decision-makers can be conceived as goal-oriented. Foreign policy is simultaneously a dual challenge:[4] the challenge of meeting the imperatives of an individual state and the challenge of participating in collective action in the global arena. However, decision-makers are not alone when facing this challenge.

Contemporary policy-making comprises "policy networks" or sets of public and private actors who share an interest in environmental foreign policy, who interact and who are linked to each other through stable formal and informal relationships (Atkinson and Coleman 1992; Krahmann 2003). Therefore, states can be described as focal formal actors in an environmental foreign policy network.

The next step is to conceptualize state behavior. In order to do that, we introduce an existing theoretical approach – the willingness–opportunity framework – and apply it in the environmental realm. This approach is useful when analyzing environmental foreign policy because it avoids single explanations of outcomes and accommodates insights from different levels of analysis: whether we talk about the conventional two levels (micro and macro), three levels (as in Chapter 2 by Barkdull and Harris), four levels or more.[5] Conceptualizing environmental foreign policy behavior builds on the theoretical construct of opportunity and willingness to act as determinants of outcomes in world politics (Most and Starr 1989). Foreign policy actors are faced with many possibilities and constraints when they make foreign policy decisions. For any political event to occur, there must be willingness by the actor pursuing the action and there must be opportunity for action to occur. Willingness and opportunity are therefore causally necessary: for example, the existence of an opportunity does not mean that it will be seized – actors must be willing to seize it. Environmental foreign policy behavior can therefore be analyzed in terms of willingness to act on environmental issues in foreign policy and the ability to pursue such action. The following pages will explain the framework in more detail.

## Willingness to pursue environmental action: representing environmental concerns in foreign policy

Why do states behave the way they do when dealing with environmental matters beyond their borders? State behavior depends on foreign policy decision-makers' willingness to pursue environmental action and can be best understood by first studying how they represent the problem they see themselves as facing (Sylvan and Voss 1998).[6] Contemporary environmental concerns can fit into the concept of foreign policy via two different approaches. These approaches build on common explanations of policy-makers' goals and perceptions in foreign policy scholarship. The first approach looks at foreign policy in its pursuit of security in which environment plays an increasing role. The second approach looks at foreign policy as a portfolio of policies in pursuit of multiple goals and environment is one of them.

### *Approach to foreign policy based on human/ecological security*

According to the first approach, foreign policies pursue security, which is broadly defined and in which environment plays an increasingly important role. This approach is grounded in traditional analyses that treat security as the major foreign policy goal, in the concept of human security, and in the rapid evolution of the ecological security agenda, which has become a powerful frame in environmental protection. International relations literature, especially neorealist authors have long argued that the primary goal of foreign policy is to maintain and enhance the security of the state, and guard it against military threats. Our understanding of both security and threats has been significantly transformed in theory and practice over the last two decades. The object of security is no longer limited to the state but also includes the individual, and security threats comprise a wide range of non-military threats such as economic, social and environmental threats. Such an approach to security, often described as human security, has important consequences for foreign policy when states decide to ascribe to it: it relates its previously unrelated aspects and it is normative because states attempt to conduct an ethically responsible policy by attaching the policy to a set of pre-defined aims meant to improve human security (Debiel and Werthes 2006). Climate change is now increasingly seen as a major security challenge. States formulate a set of goals to address it, and then try to ensure that all aspects of foreign policy support these goals.

Human/ecological security has been increasingly embraced within the countries of the Organization for Security and Co-operation in Europe and discussed within the United Nations. However, its future as a universally accepted foreign policy imperative remains questionable because it has not been popular in many developing countries where the ecological security crisis will be most pronounced. Human security raises problematic connotations of humanitarian intervention (who decides to intervene and who enforces decisions and where) which illuminate inequalities in political and economic power in the international system. Framing environmental protection in human security terms raises fears that sustainable development as the central frame of the global environmental agenda is eroding. Since its key principles (additionally, polluter pays and common but differentiated responsibilities) are central to developing countries' engagement in the global environmental project (Najam 2005), the incentives for developing countries to place environment in the security frame are generally low, unless environmental change threatens their very survival. Different framing of environmental concerns, especially with regard to climate change (see Mayer and Arndt's Chapter 5 in this volume on socionatures), became obvious during the UN Security Council's first-ever debate on impact of climate change on peace and security in April 2007. While countries such as the UK and small island states saw climate change as a key to collective security in a fragile and increasingly interdependent world, representatives from China, Pakistan and G-77 downplayed the global security implications of climate change, arguing that climate change is in essence an issue of sustainable development, that needs to be responded to outside of the Security Council and by following the principle of common, but differentiated, responsibilities. This example illustrates the need for an alternative framing of environmental concerns in foreign policy that is not necessarily oriented towards its pursuit of security.

### Approach to foreign policy as a portfolio comprising environmental goals

According to the second approach to environmental concerns in foreign policy, foreign policies pursue multiple goals and environmental goals are among them. This approach is based on available theoretical foreign policy models and environmental policy integration literature. Palmer and Morgan analyze foreign policy as a portfolio of policies, i.e. they see a state constructing bundles of policies that they call portfolios which are designed to achieve foreign policy outcomes that the state wants (Palmer and Morgan 2006). Basically, states have many goals and use their foreign policies to change some things in the world they do not like and preserve the ones they like. All foreign policy actions use resources and when a state places its limited resources into a policy it faces trade-offs. Therefore, given their preferences and constraints, states select from the menu of available policies the bundle of policies that best suits their needs and goals at a particular time. Unlike the human/ecological security approach, the portfolio approach does not necessarily view environmental action as a foreign policy imperative or ethically responsible choice. Instead, depending on state-specific circumstances, environmental action may be a more or less prominent part of the foreign policy portfolio. Every state faces its own ethical trade-offs when deciding to pursue it.

The portfolio approach can conceptually illustrate the role of the environment in foreign policy and the evolution of foreign policy towards greener or more environmentally friendly missions. As a state constructs its foreign policy portfolio, environmental policy is its integral part. Non-environmental policies that belong to the foreign policy portfolio such as defense and trade can also undergo greening. Over time, we may observe whether the overall portfolio moves towards greener missions. While foreign policy portfolio approach is in line with foreign policy realities and differences in environmental norms across countries, its direct application leaves environmental goals in harsh competition with other foreign policy goals. In practice, when ad hoc environmental stress emerges or there is an ongoing environmental or resource conflict, environmental goals will surely find their place in a state's optimal foreign policy mix. However, this approach is less promising when environmental problems have not fully manifested themselves such as climate change or species extinction and once they do, there is no quick way to fix them. Thus, for this approach to work, it is necessary to discover policy designs that can effectively address long-term policy problems.

These two approaches can serve as building blocks of environmental foreign policy because they emphasize different aspects of policy-making: ecological security-oriented approach illustrates how foreign policy can produce more momentum in global environmental politics, mobilize leadership and new resources for environmental protection, while the portfolio approach enables us to understand how different elements of foreign policy are interlinked, compete for limited resources and form an optimal policy mix.

### Changing problem representations, changing willingness to act

While these two approaches are a possible way to think about state willingness to act on environmental concerns in contemporary foreign policies, the ways in which foreign policy actors represent environmental problems are not fixed. They are continuously redefined as foreign policies evolve and adapt to new situations. Chapters in this volume illustrate how environmental issues emerge and become prioritized in foreign policy decision-making both in countries where environment is already a central aspect of foreign policy and in countries where it still struggles for its place on the foreign policy agenda. Hughes and Partzsch show how the rise in water consumption and water stress becomes associated with strategic, humanitarian and environmental challenges and leads to the rapid development of water foreign policy in the United States and the European Union. Wilkening and Thrift describe the evolution of Canada's leadership role on the transboundary issue of POPs, and highlight the role of government consultations with diverse stakeholders in forming and informing state interests. Alcañiz and Gutiérrez explain how an initially small local protest in Argentina over the construction of two pulp plants on the Uruguayan side of the shared Uruguay River becomes a major foreign policy issue. They underline the importance of protesters and local civil society in framing the issue before it is taken up by the President.

State willingness to act on environmental concerns in foreign policy is pushed, shaped and sustained by policy networks, which in cases presented in the volume comprise domestically, internationally and transnationally linked actors. The structure of relations among actors within these networks is often similar across cases. Interestingly, the coalitions that form to exert pressure on top foreign policy officials cross government/civil society divisions, as lower levels of government join local civil society to exert more influence on the federal level decision-making. Government/civil society lines are also crossed, as people working for civil society organizations go to work for government and vice versa (see chapters on Argentina and Finland). The case studies illustrate the importance of studying interactions among different actors in order to explain how they affect state willingness to act and exert influence in the global arena. As Chapter 4 by Brewer on theoretical and practical aspects of government–business interactions demonstrates, such studies can advance the theoretical literature on environmental policy-making while drawing on well-established theories (here pluralistic politics and public choice) outside the foreign policy analysis field. Finally, foreign policy action in all cases studied in this volume is determined by states' ability to act and the possibilities and limitations states face in their foreign policy contexts, which is where we now turn.

## Opportunities to pursue environmental action: understanding the context of environmental foreign policy

When thinking about states' ability to act on environmental concerns in foreign policy, we can think of states engaging in world politics and facing a number of behavioral opportunities. States have a menu for choice, and what's on the menu does not determine what choice will be made but constrains what is possible and affects the probability of state behavior (Russett 1972). The menu for choice of all states has dramatically changed and expanded in the past fifty years. Some foreign policy behaviors that we observe in environmental politics today were not considered logically, technically and intellectually possible before. It would be incomprehensible for sovereign states to outsource some of their foreign policy tasks to civil society or let members of the civil society represent them at environmental conferences. One could not imagine that groups of states without experience or expertise in managing a certain natural resource could make moral claims on behalf of it and play a key role in affecting its management. The establishment of 3D online virtual embassies such as the Maldives Virtual Embassy or the Second House of Sweden, and having foreign ministers hold virtual press conferences would be technically impossible.

As the practical chapters of this volume illustrate, different strategic and structural factors interact in every state to open up a window of opportunity for state action. Every state operates within its specific political, cultural and historical context which shapes its menu for choice. Despite that, there are three questions all states face. First, are the options on state menu relevant for addressing environmental change and to what extent does state action matter in addressing environmental issues? Second, are states able to manage environmental foreign policy domestically? Finally, once foreign policy actors reach the global arena, what opportunities and challenges are waiting for them there? This part first argues that foreign policy is of great importance in preventing and addressing environmental deterioration. It discusses state ability to manage environmental foreign policy and introduces four trends in the global arena which simultaneously strengthen and undermine states' ability to act.

### Do states and their environmental foreign policies matter for environmental change?

Many authors, especially in the late 1990s, have argued that nation-states are increasingly irrelevant in an interdependent and globalizing world because the resources and threats that matter disregard governments and borders.

Furthermore they claimed that state power shifts to non-state actors, that state sovereignty is dissolving, and that the significance of states in comparison to other actors is declining (Matthews 1997). Other authors suggested that states were actually critical for tackling the world's problems and that their sovereignty was not dissolving but was disaggregated to specific state institutions which network with their counterparts abroad (Slaughter 1997). From an environmental perspective, the very concept of a state has always been artificial: whether seen from space or explored from within, the Earth is borderless. The environment comprises interdependent ecosystems that do not respect state boundaries. Also, states have appeared in dual roles: facilitating both environmental destruction and environmental protection. Thus we are not surprised that environmental scholars have been skeptical of state-centered analyses of world politics, in general, and global environmental degradation, in particular (Eckersley 2004: 5) and eager to focus on the mechanisms of collective action rather than on state behavior that makes them viable (DeGarmo 2005; 8).

In the era of global environmental change there are at least three reasons to pay attention to the state and its foreign policy. First, states are still a major means by which international politics is organized and their potential to play a positive role in environmental protection is increasing. Our knowledge of environmental threats is continuously improving, and people are more and more aware of environmental needs and eager to act upon them at every level of governance. State level emerges as a mediator between local and global governance. States engage in transgovernmental networks such as the International Network for Environmental Compliance and Enforcement, Interpol's Ecomessage and Green Customs to improve their effectiveness. The fact that states coexist with myriad other actors relevant for environmental protection enables us to assess the relevance of formal channels and explore how these actors affect the ability of states to exert influence in world politics.

Second, states have already proven that they can rise to the challenge of collective action to jointly respond to environmental threats. Some of the most notable collective foreign policy successes include massive reductions of ozone-depleting substances and securing Antarctica as a continent of peace and security. However, states have also collectively failed to provide efficient mechanisms to address other environmental threats such as climate change or biodiversity loss. A focus on foreign policies as building blocks of collective action can help us reassess the foundations of collective mechanisms available and help us understand how to improve them.

Finally, a state's foreign policy is an area of great importance because it is a key site for responsible action and for democratic accountability (Hill 2003: XVII). Foreign policy has been defined as a site for responsible action at the very start of the global environmental agenda. The Stockholm Declaration Principle 21 established that states are responsible to ensure that activities within their jurisdiction or control do not cause damage to the environment beyond their own territory. Now, states remain focal points for demands for responsible action on global environmental equity. As a key site for democratic accountability, foreign policies enable domestic audiences to formally express their distinctive interests, values, identities and concerns in the international system. The extent to which people exert influence over the content of foreign policy depends on the country but democratization is an ongoing process.

Having established that states and their foreign policies are important in addressing environmental challenges, we can now turn to the ability of relevant state actors to conduct environmental foreign policy.

### *Foreign policy actors and their ability to act on environmental matters*

The discussion of state ability to act on environmental matters in foreign policy can start with identifying who has the institutional authority to make environmental foreign policy decisions and what are the constraints states face during this process. Politicians in office, such as presidents, prime ministers and foreign ministers, are formally responsible for making foreign policy decisions. In most countries, ministries of foreign affairs provide the main input into foreign policy decisions and handle the execution of policy. Since foreign ministries operate the state's diplomatic service abroad, they need to ensure that the state's environmental agenda is well integrated into the work of the diplomatic network. Foreign ministries may try to formally coordinate environment-related activities of all government departments or the external department of the environmental ministry may take the lead on international environmental matters, directly engaging in international environmental cooperation. In democratic societies, government officials are directly accountable to political parties and the public, which can then constrain and redirect their behavior.

Differences in domestic institutional settings across countries and its effects on foreign policy formation can be illustrated in the case studies of Finland and Uganda (see the chapters by Mervio and Mutekanga respectively). The Finnish model depends on government's cooperative skills rather than strong leadership, the Ministry of Environment's coordinating role and close relationship with environmental scientists and with activists. Finland also belongs to a larger EU infrastructure, which may constrain its menu for choice. In Uganda, the situation is the opposite: leadership has had a significant influence, particularly during the military rule. The cooperation among government departments is modest and different people develop environmental and foreign policy. Foreign policy goals do not explicitly refer to environment and increased international funding available for the environment is central to addressing environmental concerns in foreign policy.

Environmental degradation stretches the capacities of all governments and puts pressure on foreign policy budgets. Foreign policy actors can count on other states' development aid for policy support, but they can also rely on a larger support system comprised of multiple stakeholders. Therefore, a state's own resources do not determine its ability to act and the limits of its environmental foreign policy reach. Thus, the opportunities of some states in the system and their menu for choice are shaped by the willingness of other actors to support them. Every year billions of dollars of official development assistance flow to the poor governments and the share of development aid directed to the environment is rising. Yet, as Müller illustrates in Chapter 12, donors share the burden of green aid unequally – the reasons for that are states' different priorities and other influential variables such as social expenditure, military expenditure, public debt and green parties in national parliaments.

This section addressed a state's ability to act during the "formative stage" of the foreign policy process which takes place before the state takes its foreign policy into the global arena (Yunus 2003: 154). It highlighted the role of institutional settings and development aid in defining the state's ability to act. The next part focuses on the "operative stage" of the foreign policy process, which takes place when foreign policy is implemented and often transformed through a continuous feedback from world politics (ibid.: 154). Once states operate in the global arena, there is a new set of possibilities and limitations they face.

### Environmental foreign policy as a collective challenge: possibilities and limitations in the global arena

Foreign policy operates within the international system, comprised of patterns of political, economic and knowledge interactions. There have never been more actors, more money and more norms and rules in this system, facilitating states' efforts to pursue environmental protection (Najam *et al.* 2006: 12). Individual states both contribute to this system, stimulate changes in it and are influenced by it. This section describes four international trends that simultaneously facilitate and undermine foreign policy on environmental matters. They include increasing institutional density and forum shopping; closer interactions with trade and human rights, adaptation to global information space, and rethinking of the international society. We explain each one of them in more detail.

First, *institutional density* can both positively and negatively affect environmental foreign policy. Through proliferation and fragmentation of global environmental governance, environmental issues have increased their presence in the international policy-making arena. States now have more opportunities to address environmental problems they find important. However, it is also easier for them to circumvent the institutions they disagree with, play overlapping institutions against each other and shop for or shift to more favorable governance arrangements to pursue their goals (Papa 2008). Such behavior can reflect opportunism of powerful or resourceful states, but it can also be a way to move an ineffective institution forward. More effective dispute resolution mechanisms within institutions can help limit negative aspects of forum shopping and contribute to the long-term viability of international institutions. Finally, institutional density necessarily changes the practice of environmental foreign policy planning. A single environmental issue can be simultaneously addressed by multiple institutions (see Chapter 7 on Argentina in this volume) and can travel across the web of global governance. It becomes an imperative to understand the potential of multiple venues for pursuing state-specific goals, strategize among them and allocate resources accordingly.

Second, environmental foreign policy is strongly affected by the evolution of *trade regulation* and is increasingly interlinked with *human rights*. As the most recent issue in global governance, environmental regulation has often conceptually and practically clashed with the trade and human rights agendas, while at the same time benefiting from them. Foreign policy actors have heavily relied on trade measures in environmental agreements. Yet, as Harashima's chapter on WTO CTE negotiations illustrates, they have also struggled to define the boundaries between environmental protection and green protectionism. Preventing environmental degradation and ensuring that those who harm or have harmed the environment are accountable for damage still remains a persistent challenge in the context of trade liberalization. Human rights can potentially contribute to addressing this challenge. Environmental claims get increasingly translated into human rights terms, and they become injected into international law through the interactive activities of intergovernmental organizations and transnational activism (Conca 2005). A case in point is conceptualizing access to water as a human right. Other opportunities include placing access to energy services within the human rights framework and using litigation as a tool to address climate change (Bradbrook and Gardam, 2006; Gupta, 2007).

Third, environmental foreign policies operate within a common *global information space*, which makes states' soft power (ability to achieve goals through attraction rather than coercion), a central instrument in global politics (Nye 2004; Chong 2007). States want to be seen as legitimate international actors supporting collective action and environmental values. They may undertake environmental commitments, but have no intention to fulfill them, and simply utilize environmental foreign policy as a symbolic tool to manage their international identities (see Chapter 3 by Cass). The nature of global environmental governance, especially its reliance on large-scale consensus building, soft law mechanisms and vibrant civil society participation, is conductive to such politics. That said, states dissenting from the mainstream or behaving inconsistently can expect anything from mild discursive responses to lynch mob-like policy pressures. Foreign policy practitioners in all circumstances, particularly dissenters, carry the intellectual burden of defending their decisions and may need to expand their skill set accordingly (Chong 2007: 197). Overall, the context of global information space provides an opportunity for states big and small to enlarge their foreign policy reach and presence. Yet, it opens more possibilities for manipulation of foreign audiences and raises fears of cultural imperialism.

Finally, climate change as one of the most serious contemporary crises in world politics, raises a question whether the *modern society of states* as we know it will continue in its current form. The impacts of climate change, especially under high emissions scenarios, suggest that the geopolitical map currently comprising 192 United Nations member states is likely to change as sea level rise threatens entire nations on low-lying islands in the Pacific and Indian Oceans with disappearance and affects millions of people living in coastal and other vulnerable areas around the world. Inhabitable lands, international migrations and changes of state boundaries due to natural and social causes can cause old states to disappear and new states to emerge. Failure to act on climate change may exacerbate the existing environmental crisis and cause a major development crisis as billions of people face shortages of food and water, increased risk of flooding as well as disrupted access to energy supplies. The problem of such a scope requires collective action at the global level and raises larger questions about the meaning of the collective and states' roles and responsibilities within it. As foreign policy actors reassess their common interests and values in addressing climate change, they test the existence of an international society of states (Bull 1977), and its role in maintaining global order.

This discussion of these four trends in the global arena, together with the previous discussion of willingness and opportunity, underscores the complexity of foreign policy decision-making in contemporary politics. Hill clearly formulated the challenge actors conducting foreign policy face:

> [They] have to consider where and how they may act, and with what effect. They have to choose between those problems in which they might make a difference and those where their involvement might prove counterproductive. And they need some reasonably coherent notion as to whom, in a chaotic world of competing claims and demands, they are responsible and to what degree.
>
> (Hill 2003: 284)

The willingness–opportunity framework enabled us to consider these issues of action, choice and responsibilities in the environmental foreign policy arena and gauge the current state of the environmental foreign policy field. Since this framework is not state-specific and needs to potentially apply to a wide variety of cases, it had to remain comprehensive in its approach. As such, it will hopefully spur further discussion of environmental foreign policy in the field, which will perfect the concept and convert it into multiple variables to be measured.

**Environmental foreign policy: taking stock and looking ahead**

This chapter discussed the environment–foreign policy nexus in theory and practice. It proposed a broad framework to think about the concept of environmental foreign policy in general, rather than state-specific terms. The framework identified states as official decision-makers, described challenges they face and networks in which they operate. Environmental foreign policy happens only when states are willing to act and have an opportunity to do so. It was proposed that states' willingness to act depends on the way decision-makers represent environmental issues in foreign policy and it was discussed how these representations change. With respect to states' opportunities, it was explained why state action matters and how it can be managed domestically. Four trends in the global arena were highlighted for their ability to both facilitate and undermine environmental foreign policy: institutional density, closer interactions with trade and human rights, adaptation to global information space and rethinking of international society.

Both this chapter and those that have preceded it encourage a broad inquiry into the role of foreign policy in addressing environmental matters. The theoretical Part I of the *Environmental Change and Foreign Policy* volume, especially the first two chapters, identified significant gaps in the scholarly research on environmental foreign policy. Other theoretical chapters approached environmental foreign policy in innovative ways by drawing on the fields of political economy, science studies and political communication. The Practice, Part II, offered studies on a large number of countries and regions tackling issues including persistent organic pollutants, water, finance, trade and biodiversity. Both parts of the book have advanced our understanding of foreign policy as a bridge between domestic and international interactions. They also illustrated that research situated on the boundaries between foreign policy analysis and global environmental politics is beneficial for both disciplines: not only can it energize existing disciplinary research and address its vulnerabilities, but it can also produce new objects for study.

Opportunities for further research, building on the findings of this volume are numerous. Some of them were directly or indirectly raised throughout the volume. The first is the need to better explain and possibly anticipate the process of environmental foreign policy change. Such an inquiry could build on efforts in the foreign policy community to derive a general theory of foreign policy change (Welch 2005) and rethink national interest as a social construction (Weldes 1999). Second, there is a need to bridge the nature–society divide in the study of foreign policy. A possible way to approach this issue is to define environmental foreign policy as a coupled human–environment system and draw on the developed scientific research agenda which studies the globalization of such systems (Young *et al.* 2006). The prominent elements of this research agenda such as measuring the effects of globalization on the resilience, vulnerability and adaptability of socio-ecological systems and understanding how and when socio-economic resilience substitutes for biophysical resilience would be particularly useful as foreign policies face environmental change. Finally, with the emerging economies as drivers of global growth and increasing focus on climate change in foreign policies of all countries, conceptualizing the foreign policy of sustainable development and studying the role of foreign policy politics, processes and institutions in efforts to promote it is a possible next step.

For now, we can conclude that environmental foreign policy has emerged as a promising area for research and an increasingly important field for policy-making. Focusing our attention on it can help us inform, evaluate and revise theories in the fields of foreign policy, international relations and environmental politics. Once academic research is combined with real foreign policy experiences and needs, it can potentially contribute to policy-making and expand prospects for effective environmental action.

## Notes

1 Examples include the 2005 Millennium Ecosystem Assessment and the 2007 Intergovernmental Panel on Climate Change Fourth Assessment Report.
2 See WCED (1987) for an elaboration of the concept of sustainable development and Munasinghe (1992) for environment, society and economy as its pillars.
3 See the rationale in Rosenau (1980) and literature on comparative environmental politics.
4 Similarly, Aron (1966: 17) sees the problem of foreign policy as the double problem of individual and collective survival and Hill (2003: 23) uses the same saying but substitutes the word development for survival. See Putnam (1988) for two-level games conceptualization.
5 For four-level analysis, see Jaffee (1990) and for multi-level, see Krahmann (2003).
6 For a broader discussion of state behavior based on rational choice explanations, see Stein (2006); for cognitive models see Berejikian (2004); for social construction of national interest, see Weldes (1999).

## References

Anderson, Terry L. and Henry I. Miller (eds) (2000) *The Greening of U.S. Foreign Policy*, Stanford, CA: Hoover Institution Press.

Aron, Raymond (1966) *Peace and War: A Theory of International Relations*, London: Weidenfeld & Nicholson.

Arquit Niederberger, Anne and Schwager, Stefan (2004) "Swiss Environmental Foreign Policy and Sustainable Development," *Swiss Political Science Review*, 10(4): 93–123.

Atkinson, Michael M. and Coleman, William D. (1992) "Policy Networks, Policy Communities and the Problems of Governance," *Governance*, 5(2): 154–80.

Barkdull, John and Harris, Paul G. (2002) "Environmental Change and Foreign Policy: A Survey of Theory," *Global Environmental Politics*, 2(2): 63–91.

Berejikian, Jeffrey D. (2004) *International Relations Under Risk: Framing State Choice*, Albany, NY: SUNY Press.

Bradbrook, Adrian J. and Gardam, Judith Gail (2006) "Placing Access to Energy Services within a Human Rights Framework," *Human Rights Quarterly*, 28(2): 389–415.

Broadhead, Lee-Anne (2002) *International Environmental Politics: The Limits of Green Diplomacy*, Boulder, CO: Lynne Reinner.

Bull, Hedley (1977) *The Anarchical Society: A Study of Order in World Politics*, London: Macmillan.

Conca, Ken (2005) "Environmental Governance After Johannesburg: From Stalled Legalization to Environmental Human Rights?" *Journal of International Law and International Relations*, 1(1–2 December): 121–38.

Conca, Ken and Dabelko, Geoffrey D. (eds) (2002) *Environmental Peacemaking*, Washington, DC: Woodrow Wilson Press.

Chong, Alan (2007) *Foreign Policy in Global Information Space: Actualizing Soft Power*, New York: Palgrave Macmillan.

Debiel, Tobias and Werthes, Sascha (eds) (2006) *Human Security on Foreign Policy Agendas: Changes, Concepts and Cases*, INEF Report (80/2006), Duisburg: Institute for Development and Peace.

DeGarmo, Denise K. (2005) *International Environmental Treaties and State Behavior: Factors Influencing Cooperation*, New York: Routledge.

Drexhage, John, Murphy, Deborah, Brown, Oli, Cosbey, Aaron, Dickey, Peter, Parry, Jo-Ellen, Van Ham, John, Tarasofsky Richard and Darkin, Beverley (2007) *Climate Change and Foreign Policy: An Exploration of Options for Greater Integration*, Winnipeg: International Institute for Sustainable Development.

Eckersley, Robyn (2004) *The Green State: Rethinking Democracy and* Sovereignty, Cambridge, MA: MIT Press.

Glasius, Marlies and Kaldor, Mary (eds) (2005) *A Human Security Doctrine for Europe*, London: Routledge.

Gleditsch, Nils Petter (2001) "Environmenal Change, Security, and Conflict," in Chester A. Crocker, Fen Osler Hampson and Pamela R. Aall (eds) *Turbulent Peace: The Challenge of Managing International Conflict*, Washington, DC: United States Institute for Peace, pp. 53–68.

Gupta, Joyeeta (2007) "Legal Steps Outside the Climate Convention: Litigation as a Tool to Address Climate Change," *Review of European Community and International Environmental Law (RECIEL)*, 16(1): 76–86(11).

Harris, Paul G. (ed.) (2000) *Climate Change and American Foreign Policy*, New York: St. Martin's Press.

—— (2005) *Confronting Environmental Change in East and Southeast Asia: Eco-Politics, Foreign Policy, and Sustainable Development*, London: Earthscan/United Nations University Press.

—— (2007) *Europe and Global Climate Change: Politics, Foreign Policy, and Regional Cooperation*. Cheltenham: Edward Elgar.

Hill, Christopher (2003) *The Changing Politics of Foreign Policy*, New York: Palgrave Macmillan.

Hudson, Valerie M. (2002) "Foreign Policy Decision-Making: A Touchstone for International Relations Theory in the Twenty-First Century," in Valerie M. Hudson, Derek H. Chollet, and James M. Goldgeier (eds) *Foreign Policy Decision Making*, New York: Palgrave Macmillan, pp. 1–21.

Jaffee, David (1990) *Levels of Socio-Economic Development Theory*, New York: Praeger.

Jonsson, Christer and Hall, Martin (2005) *Essence of Diplomacy*, New York: Palgrave Macmillan.

Kaarbo, Juliet, Lantis, Jeffrey S. and Beasley, Ryan K. (2002) "The Analysis of Foreign Policy in Comparative Perspective," in Ryan K. Beasley, Juliet Kaarbo, Jeffrey S.

Lantis, and Michael T. Snarr (eds) *Foreign Policy in Comparative Perspective: Domestic and International Influences on State Behavior*, Washington, DC: CQ Press.

Kelman, Ilan and Koukis, Theo (eds) (2000) "Disaster Diplomacy," *Cambridge Review of International Affairs*, XIV(1): 214–94.

Kjellen, Bo (2007) *New Diplomacy for Sustainable Development: The Challenge of Global Change*, New York: Routledge.

Krahmann, Elke (2003) *Multilevel Networks in European Foreign Policy*, Aldershot: Ashgate.

Lafferty, William M. and Hovden, Eivind (2003) "Environmental Policy Integration: Towards an Analytical Framework," *Environmental Politics*, 12(3).

Matthews, Jessica T. (1997) "Power Shift," *Foreign Affairs*, 76(1).

Moomaw, William (2005) "New Diplomacy for Sustainable Development," paper presented at the Annual Meeting of the International Studies Association, Hilton Hawaiian Village, Honolulu, Hawaii, March.

Most, Benjamin A. and Starr, Harvey (1989) *Inquiry, Logic and International Politics*, Columbia, SC: University of South Carolina Press.

Munasinghe, Mohan (1992) "Environmental Economics and Sustainable Development," paper presented at the UN Earth Summit, Rio de Janeiro, Environment Paper No. 3, Washington, DC: World Bank.

Najam, Adil (2005) "Developing Countries and Global Environmental Governance: From Contestation to Participation to Engagement," *International Environmental Agreements: Politics, Law and Economics*, 5(3): 303–21.

Najam, Adil, Papa, Mihaela and Taiyab, Nadaa (2006) *Global Environmental Governance: A Reform Agenda*, Winnipeg: International Institute for Sustainable Development.

Nye, Joseph S. (2004) *Soft Power: The Means to Success in World Politics*, New York: Public Affairs.

Palmer, Glenn and Morgan, T. Clifton (2006) *A Theory of Foreign Policy*, Princeton, NJ: Princeton University Press.

Papa, Mihaela (2008) "The Politics of State Dissent in International Environmental Fora: Proposing a Theory of Forum-Shopping," paper presented at the American Political Science Association Annual Meeting. Boston, MA, 28–31 August.

Porter, Gareth, Brown, Janet Welsh and Chasek, Pamela S. (2000) *Global Environmental Politics*, 3rd edn, Boulder, CO: Westview Press.

Putnam, Robert (1988) "Diplomacy and Domestic Politics: The Logic of Two-Level Games," *International Organization*, 42: 427–60.

Rosenau, James (1980) *The Study of Political Adaptation*, New York: Nichols Publishing Company.

Russett, Bruce M. (1972) "A Macroscopic View of International Politics," in James N. Rosenau, Vincent Davis, and M.A. East (eds) *The Analysis of International Politics*, New York: Free Press, pp. 109–24.

Slaughter, Anne Marie (1997) "The Real New World Order," *Foreign Affairs*, September/October.

Stein, Arthur A. (2006) "Constraints and Determinants: Structure, Purpose and Process in the Analysis of Foreign Policy," in Harvey Starr (ed.) *Approaches, Levels and Methods of Analysis in International Politics*, New York: Palgrave Macmillan, pp. 189–209.

Susskind, Lawrence (1994) *Environmental Diplomacy: Negotiating More Effective Global Agreements*, New York: Oxford University Press.

Sylvan, Donald A. and Voss, James F. (eds) (1998) *Problem Representation in Foreign Policy Decision Making*, Cambridge: Cambridge University Press.

Thatcher, Margaret (1982) Speech to Scottish Conservative Party Conference, 14 May, in *The Oxford Dictionary of Quotations*, 4th edn, 1992, ed. Angela Partington. Oxford: Oxford University Press.

Tolba, Mostafa K. (1998) *Global Environmental Diplomacy: Negotiating Environmental Agreements for the World, 1973–1992*, Cambridge, MA: MIT Press.

United Nations Development Programme (UNDP) (1994) *Human Development Report: New Dimensions of Human Security*, New York: Oxford University Press.

Watson, Adam (1982) *Diplomacy: The Dialogue between States*, London: Eyre Methuen.

Welch, David A. (2005) *Painful Choices: A Theory of Foreign Policy Change*, Princeton, NJ: Princeton University Press.

Weldes, Jutta (1999) *Constructing National Interests: The United States and the Cuban Missile Crisis*, Minneapolis: University of Minnesota Press.

World Commission on Environment and Development (WCED) (1987) *Our Common Future*, Oxford: Oxford University Press.

Young, Oran R., Berkhout, Frans, Gallopin, Gilberto C., Janssen, Marco A., Ostrom, Elinor and van der Leeuw, Sander (2006) "The Globalization of Socio-Ecological Systems: an Agenda for Scientific Research," *Global Environmental Change*, 6(3): 304–16.

Yunus, Mohammed (2003) *Foreign Policy: A Theoretical Introduction*, Karachi: Oxford University Press.

# Index

eBooks – at www.eBookstore.tandf.co.uk

# A library at your fingertips!

eBooks are electronic versions of printed books. You can store them on your PC/laptop or browse them online.

They have advantages for anyone needing rapid access to a wide variety of published, copyright information.

eBooks can help your research by enabling you to bookmark chapters, annotate text and use instant searches to find specific words or phrases. Several eBook files would fit on even a small laptop or PDA.

**NEW:** Save money by eSubscribing: cheap, online access to any eBook for as long as you need it.

## Annual subscription packages

We now offer special low-cost bulk subscriptions to packages of eBooks in certain subject areas. These are available to libraries or to individuals.

For more information please contact webmaster.ebooks@tandf.co.uk

We're continually developing the eBook concept, so keep up to date by visiting the website.

## www.eBookstore.tandf.co.uk